# GERMANY:
# 2000 YEARS

# GERMANY:
## 2000 YEARS

*Volume III*

## FROM THE NAZI ERA
## TO THE PRESENT

**Gerhart Hoffmeister**
**and**
**Frederic C. Tubach**

*THE UNGAR PUBLISHING COMPANY* · *New York*

Copyright © 1986 by The Ungar Publishing Co., Inc.

**Library of Congress Cataloging-in-Publication Data**
(Revised for vol. 3)

Reinhardt, Kurt F. (Kurt Frank), 1896–
    Germany: 2000 years

    Includes bibliographies and indexes.
    Vol. 3 by Gerhart Hoffmeister and
Frederic C. Tubach
    1. Germany—Politics and government.
2. Germany—Civilization.   I. Hoffmeister,
Gerhart.   II. Tubach, Frederic C.   III. Title.
DD89.R36   1961       943       60-53139
ISBN 0-8044-1392-4 (v. 3)
ISBN 0-8044-6273-9 (pbk.: v. 3)

Printed in the United States of America

# Contents

# Preface

This volume—a sequel to Kurt F. Reinhardt's widely acclaimed two-volume *Germany: 2000 Years*—brings up to date the political, social, economic, and cultural history of Germany between 1933 and the early 1980s—a history of traumas that reflect global contradictions between East and West to this day.

Students of German culture and civilization as well as general readers will welcome the emphasis on the heretofore sparsely covered postwar period. It corrects the overemphasis given in many books to the Weimar Republic or to the Nazi era without losing sight of the fundamental changes in Germany since 1933.

Unlike many haphazard and unintegrated mosaics, the approach is issue- and problem-oriented, while at the same time it presents the reader with enough general informational background for a comprehensive view. We stress essential features of the society, leaving technical and in-depth studies to the specialists in the various academic disciplines.

Several factors should be mentioned here:

• German history since 1933 reveals a fundamental tension between the cultural sphere on the one hand and the sociopolitical and economic sphere on the other. Literary culture at times provides the cutting edge for social change as in the case of West German writers in the early 1960s. At other times it is most influential when examining the past as in the antifascist literature of the GDR (East Germany) and of the *Gruppe 47* in the Federal Republic of Germany.

• The book looks closely at the years between 1945 and 1949. Most students of Germany view these immediate postwar years merely as a prelude to West German reconstruction. But this period of vast decentralization following the dismantling of a totalitarian regime is increasingly interesting to those who would develop models for a postindustrial society today. Most importantly, the political and social experimentation of these years pointed toward the possibility of a new unified Germany. Superpower confrontation, however, has sealed Germany's fate as a divided country for the indefinite future.

• This volume deals more extensively with features usually neglected in general treatments of modern German history, namely, German resistance to the Nazis and the expulsion of Germans from Eastern Europe.

• The book pays special attention to recent developments ranging from the political and cultural experimentation under Willy Brandt (1969–1974) to the ecological and peace issues that preoccupy West Germans in the 1980s.

• Diverse perspectives on the development of the GDR in economic, social, and cultural terms provide insights into a much neglected area of contemporary central Europe.

• In addition to the general reader and the student of German culture and civilization, the book is intended to complement college- and university-level German-language programs by providing students with historical and cultural background for their language training.

• Lastly, the discerning reader will become aware of the divergent approaches taken by the two authors. Their different yet complementary perspectives are designed to stimulate discussion and debate. The authors planned and discussed the entire volume together and contributed portions of the text as follows.

Frederic C. Tubach wrote Chapter I, "The Third Reich," except for sections 6, 8, and 9; Chapter II, "The Immediate Postwar Years (1945–1949)"; and the texts on literary culture after 1949 in Chapter III, section 4, "Culture in the Adenauer Era"; Chapter IV, section 4, "The Cultural Scene"; and Chapter V, section 2, "Society and Culture: East Germany."

Gerhart Hoffmeister wrote the introductory sections, "The Decline of the Weimar Republic"; sections 6, "World War II"; 8, "Resistance"; and 9, "Expulsion of Germans from Eastern Europe," in Chapter I; and, except for the sections written by Professor Tubach, Chapter III, "Era of Reconstruction: The Adenauer Years (1949–1966)"; Chapter IV, "The Late 1960s and Early 1970s: Era of Social and Political Experimentation"; and Chapter V, "The Early 1980s."

The bibliography is restricted to works cited and to works with a direct bearing on the information and insights provided. Italicized numbers within parentheses refer to book numbers in the bibliography; these numbers are followed by page references where warranted.

Although it is impossible to acknowledge all those who have contributed to the preparation of this book, a few of the most significant influences should be mentioned. Both authors found the works of Gordon Craig, Alfred Grosser, and Henry Pachter especially helpful, even beyond their specific citations in the text. In addition, Professor Tubach has been much influenced by discussions with students at the University of California at Berkeley (Melissa Vogelsang, Calvin Jones, and Marianne Scholl are just three of many), primarily in the postgraduate seminars on Contemporary German Culture and Society given in the summers of 1979 through 1981 and in the spring of 1982. Tubach also found Egon Schwarz's historical background of Germany most insightful. Professor Hoffmeister embarked on this joint venture inspired by the success of the undergraduate courses he taught (The Prussian Tradition, German Youth Movements, German Immigration to the United States, and The History of German Civilization). Hoffmeister also acknowledges the valuable suggestions and insightful comments of Professor Harry Steinhauer. Both authors owe a special debt of gratitude to Dr. Sally Patterson Tubach for her careful editorial work and stylistic revision of the manuscript.

Finally, both authors express their appreciation for the care that the publisher, Frederick Ungar, devoted to the manuscript and for his many valuable suggestions. The authors hope that the final result lives up to his encouragement and faith in their work. It is also the hope of everyone involved in this project that this new volume becomes a worthy supplement to Kurt F. Reinhardt's invaluable texts.

Gerhart Hoffmeister
Santa Barbara

Frederic C. Tubach
Berkeley

# Abbreviations

**APO** = Außenparlamentarische Opposition (extraparliamentary opposition)

**ASTA** = Allgemeiner Studentenausschuß (student parliamentary committee)

**BHE** = Bund der Heimatvertriebenen und Entrechteten (Association of the Displaced and Disenfranchised)

**BRD** = Bundesrepublik Deutschland (German Federal Republic)

**COMECON** = Council for Mutual Economic Help

**CDU** = Christlich-Demokratische Union (Christian Democratic Union)

**CSU** = Christlich-Soziale Union (Christian Socialist Union)

**DAF** = Deutsche Arbeitsfront (German Labor Front)

**DDP** = Deutsche Demokratische Partei (German Democratic Party)

**DDR** = Deutsche Demokratische Republik (German Democratic Republic)

**DFG** = Deutsche Forschungsgesellschaft (German Research Organization)

**DGB** = Deutscher Gewerkschaftsbund (German Trade Union Association)

**DKP** = Deutsche Kommunistische Partei (German Communist Party)

**DNVP** = Deutschnationale Volkspartei (German National People's Party)

**DVP** = Deutsche Volkspartei (German People's Party)

**ECSC** = European Community of Steel and Coal (Montan-Union)

**ECU** = European currency unit

**EDC** = European Defense Community
**EEC** = European Economic Community (Common Market)
**EMS** = European Monetary System
**EPC** = European Political Cooperation
**EPG** = European Program Group
**ESA** = European Space Agency
**FDJ** = Frei Deutsche Jugend (Free German Youth)
**FDP** = Freie Demokratische Partei (Liberal Democratic Party)
**FRG** = *see* BRD
**GDR** = *see* DDR
**HJ** = Hitlerjugend (Hitler Youth)
**KPD** = Kommunistische Partei Deutschlands (Communist Party of Germany)
**NATO** = North Atlantic Treaty Organization
**NÖS** = neues ökonomisches System (new economic system)
**NPD** = Nationaldemokratische Partei Deutschlands (National Democratic Party of Germany)
**NSDAP** = Nationalsozialistische Deutsche Arbeiterpartei (National Socialist German Workers' Party)
**OEEC** = Organization of European Economic Cooperation
**ÖVP** = Österreichische Volks-Partei (Austrian People's Party)
**RAF** = Red Army Faction
**SA** = Sturmabteilung (Storm Troopers)
**SD** = Sonderdienst (Special duties section)
**SDS** = Staatssicherheitsdienst (state security police)
**SDS** = Sozialistischer Deutscher Studentenbund (Socialist German Student Organization)
**SED** = Sozialistische Einheitspartei Deutschlands (Socialist Unity Party of Germany)
**SPD** = Sozialdemokratische Partei Deutschlands (Social Democratic Party of Germany)
**SPÖ** = Sozialdemokratische Partei Österreichs (Social Democrats [Austrian])
**SS** = Schutzstaffel (Special Security Guard)
**TAZ** = Tageszeitung (Daily paper)
**VAT** = value added tax
**VSBD** = Volkssozilistische Bewegung Deutschlands (People's Socialist Movement of Germany)
**WEU** = Western European Union

**Zentrum** = Katholische Zentrumpartei (Catholic Center Party)
**ZK** = Zentralkomittee (Central Committee)

# THE DECLINE OF THE
# WEIMAR REPUBLIC

From 1919 to 1933 the German Reich was a democratic federation of nineteen states *(Länder)* under a republican form of government with Weimar as the seat of the constitutional assembly—hence, Weimar Republic. Begun under most unfavorable auspices, the new government not only had to accept the burdens of the Treaty of Versailles of 1919, which included territorial losses, foreign occupation forces, disarmament, and enormous reparations; it also had to defeat open insurrections, such as the Spartacus League revolt (1919), the Kapp-Putsch (1920), and the Hitler-Putsch (1923); and it had to cope with disastrous inflation.

By the end of 1923, however, the republic entered a relatively stable period that lasted for about five years. A government coalition of the left (Social Democratic Party-SPD) and the center (Catholic Center Party, *Zentrum;* German People's Party, DVP) stimulated economic growth. Under the statesmanship of Gustav Stresemann (chancellor 1923; foreign minister 1923–1929), Germany was brought back into the community of nations with the Treaties of Locarno in 1925 and the League of Nations in 1926. Paul von Hindenburg, a field marshal in WWI, was elected president of the republic in 1925. It was a period in which culture flourished with much experimentation especially in literature, the cinema, the arts, and architecture. At the time of Stresemann's death in 1929, the Great Depression wrought havoc on the German economy, a fact that contributed to the undermining of parliamentary democracy.

The Weimar Constitution, drafted in 1919, provided for the division of power: parliament consisted of two houses, *Reichsrat* and *Reichstag;* there was a president, a chancellor, and a chancellor's cabinet. Elements from the French, Swiss, English, and American constitutions were combined with the German constitution of 1849 to make this republic one of the most advanced democratic states in the Western world, at least on paper. In practice the constitution suffered from several defects: on the one hand, there

1

were too many political parties in the *Reichstag,* on the other, too much power was vested in the presidency. It became increasingly evident that this constitutionally mandated system of government lacked legitimacy in the eyes of government officials, parties, and the populace. Democracy was weak from the outset because the entire social structure of the Second Reich (1871–1918) continued to exert its influence on the new system. With the economic crisis of 1929 the political situation became more and more untenable.

The Weimar Republic was a multiparty state. Although parties were not mentioned in the constitution, the republic was politically destroyed by the constant realignment of the sometimes reactionary splinter parties. It became impossible to maintain a stable parliamentary majority in the *Reichstag.* By 1930 the older parties of the Bismarckian empire, the conservative DNVP, the liberal DVP, the *Zentrum,* and the workers' Social Democratic Party (SPD), were definitely on the decline because they represented the ideals of the older generation. At the same time their parliamentary power to form majority coalitions and to shape the chancellor's political program increased. As the moderate parties lost their electorate during the Great Depression, two radical movements of the extreme right and left, the National Socialist German Workers' Party (NSDAP = Nazi) and the Communist Party of Germany (KPD), gained appeal for youthful Germans. Both were founded after WWI and were therefore more responsive to postwar political, social, and economic currents.

Because Hitler and the communists wanted to destroy Germany's democracy, on occasion the NSDAP and the KPD united in opposition to the center parties (for example, in the jointly organized Berlin transport strike of November 1932). As faith in democratic institutions eroded, it became clear that Germany's future lay either with the Nazis, the communists, or the military. By 1930 the old *Reichstag* parties, which placed party ideology above the preservation of constitutional government, showed little enthusiasm for political compromise on which the survival of the republic depended. The number of *Reichstag* sessions decreased between 1930 and 1932 from 94 to 13 meetings per year, reflecting the *Reichstag's* growing ineffectiveness.

The SPD's role in this context was especially problematical. Founded in 1875, this party had been in opposition to the Bismarck government (see the Socialist Laws, 1878 f.). It gained strength throughout the Second Reich until, in 1912, it was the most powerful party in the *Reichstag.* After WWI it turned into an antirevolutionary governing party and provided the republic with a president, a speaker of the Diet, and, between 1920 and 1923, a chancellor. Although the strongest *Reichstag* faction, it did not hold the reigns of government after 1923. In 1928 it joined a "great coalition" Cabinet supported by the *Zentrum*, the liberal German Democratic Party (DDP), and the DVP. The SPD became even more powerful because it governed Prussia, the most important constituent state of the republic with two-thirds of the German population.

In 1930 the government coalition fell apart over the vital issue of increased unemployment benefits. In this conflict the left-wing SPD represented the trade unions, and the DVP backed the entrepreneurs. Party ideology was placed above effective parliamentary governance. Documents reveal that the SPD willingly relinquished its responsibilities to govern in preference of its traditional opposition role. The SPD decided not to bring about a revolution but to wait for one. It simply lost its will to defend the republic; it left the initiative to others and fatalistically withdrew into its party organizations. In July 1930 it even collaborated with the extremist parties (KPD, NSDAP) to bring about new elections. It also tolerated the government of Heinrich Brüning, which ruled by decree on the national level, yet the SPD did not stand up for the government's policies. Further, the SPD supported von Hindenburg in the presidential election of 1932 and passively accepted Franz von Papen's illegal dismissal of the SPD government in Prussia in the same year, and thereby contributed to its own political demise. It lost votes as never before until the Nazis outlawed the SPD in 1933.

Since the onset of the economic crisis, the German working class had less cohesion than ever. In 1932 there were 7.5 million unemployed. Consequently, the loyalty of the working class to the SPD, which had traditionally represented them, and to the trade unions, which had looked after labor interests, was drastically weakened. Due to the economic slump, labor felt pushed to the wall and was willing to believe the promises the extremist parties were offering.

By 1930 German intellectuals had become increasingly radicalized; for example, the Nazi Student Organization gained a majority in the Union of German Students. Faculty and administration, with their reactionary prewar mentality, had been hostile to the Weimar Republic from its beginning. After 1918, apart from the establishment of two new universities (at Cologne and Frankfurt) and a few chairs of sociology, and despite discussions of reforms, nothing substantial changed in the conduct of university affairs.

The Nazis were successful in taking over the government in 1933 because of the widespread economic and social disintegration and Hitler's skill in exploiting the masses' dissatisfaction with Weimar politicians. Opposition to this seizure of power could have come from any of three institutions: the *Reichswehr,* the president, or the chancellor. Why all three of them failed to preserve democracy and ultimately played into the hands of Hitler is explained to a considerable degree by the lack of democratic tradition in German political life and, as a result, a lack of will to support the imperiled democratic system.

The *Reichswehr,* a professional army of 100,000 men, was supposed to be politically neutral. Its generals had taken an oath to serve the republic faithfully, but their loyalty to the president was actually greater than to the state. They were at von Hindenburg's disposal if he wanted to send federal troops anywhere in the country to maintain or restore order. The president surrounded himself with aristocratic army officers, such as General Kurt von Schleicher, who together with von Papen and von Hindenburg's son, Oskar, formed a kind of palace guard that helped accelerate the downfall of the republic through intrigue and counterintrigue.

Former Field Marshal von Hindenburg became president of the republic in 1925. A monarchist at heart and loyal to the dethroned Hohenzollern dynasty, he was legally bound to uphold the constitution, which empowered him to appoint the chancellor and the chancellor's cabinet according to democratic procedures that involved the *Reichstag.* If, however, the *Reichstag* was unable to muster a clear majority, the president had the right to appoint a chancellor and his cabinet in defiance of the *Reichstag.* He could either adjourn or suspend the *Reichstag* (Article 25 of the Weimar Constitution). Thus, he became both legislator and dictator, transforming the parliamentary democracy into governance by presidential fiat. As to the chancellor, he and his cabinet could issue emergency decrees as a way out of dealing with a variety of financial, economic, and political crises (Article 48 of the Weimar Constitution).

By repeatedly subverting the *Reichstag* and appointing his own chancellors (Brüning, von Papen, von Schleicher, and finally Hitler), von Hindenburg showed that he was hardly a staunch supporter of democracy—although he was reelected president in 1932 by the votes of the democratic SPD, DVP, and Center parties. In effect, he paved the way for the Nazi takeover through strengthening presidential government at the expense of democratic process. Moreover, he provided the Nazis with some unexpected victories. In 1932 he dissolved the *Reichstag* for the fourth time since 1928. This gave the NSDAP another opportunity to increase its parliamentary seats after an already substantial increase in the 1930 elections. Also in 1932 von Hindenburg lifted the ban on the Storm Troopers (SA) and the Special Security Guard (SS).

Von Hindenburg resorted to emergency decrees as soon as he encountered difficulties. His appointment of Brüning as chancellor was a move that virtually ended the Weimar Republic. Brüning had to contend with rampant inflation and unemployment. He needed only to turn to President von Hindenburg for support to put drastic emergency legislation into effect. Thus, Parliament had no role in shaping Brüning's tight fiscal policies against inflation and for a balanced budget. This amounted to a return to the Bismarckian system where the chancellor had been responsible only to the head of state. Nevertheless, Brüning has been considered the last chancellor to defend democracy and his cabinet as "the last bastion of democracy," which the two united right-wing parties (see the Harzburg Front, 1931), the NSDAP under Hitler and the DNVP under Alfred Hugenberg, vowed to bring down. It did not help the republic's stability that right- and left-wing radicals clashed in the streets, that too many elections kept the electorate off balance (there were four major elections in 1932 alone), and that the Allied powers vetoed the projected German-Austrian customs union proposed by the Brüning government in 1931.

Chancellor Brüning's desire to save the republic through antidemocratic means ultimately played into the Nazis' hands. He did not shy away from making conciliatory gestures toward Hitler after 1930, but he was primarily interested in restoring the monarchy in collaboration with the president and the conservative forces.

The last eight months of the Weimar Republic reinforce the impression that parliamentary democracy was steadily undercut by the government itself, not only by the parties and by economic forces. The republican system became increasingly untenable as its leaders demonstrated a lack of will to preserve the constitution and translate it into political practice.

# Chapter I

# THE THIRD REICH

## 1. Nazism: The Ascension to Power

### EVENTS AROUND 1933:
### FROM PARLIAMENTARY DEMOCRACY
### TO THE ONE-PARTY STATE

On January 30, 1933, Field Marshal Paul von Hindenburg, the venerable hero of WWI, handed over the executive power of the state to Adolf Hitler, private first class in WWI, now head of the NSDAP. They were representatives of the two generations that shaped the history of Germany during the first half of the twentieth century. Von Hindenburg, bemedaled, in military regalia, and standing erect in spite of his advanced age, symbolized the legitimacy that Hitler needed to complete his road to power. In civilian dress, Hitler bowed deeply before the field marshal in an act of deference that veiled the real significance of the event taking place: a right-wing revolution had succeeded. Never afterward was Hitler to bow his head. In his first cabinet the conservatives still held the majority. They believed they could bend him to their own political objectives. Franz von Papen, a leader of the conservatives, stated at the time: "We have engaged Hitler to serve our cause" *(104,* 3). The army, the Junkers and their agrarian political supporters, the state bureaucracy, and leaders of industry were the conservatives' political base, and they considered it powerful enough to curb the political appetites of the lower-middle-class chancellor.

Hitler at first left the cabinet alone and took on the *Reichstag.* On February 1, 1933, it was dissolved and general elections announced for March 5. With their key men in power (Hitler as chancellor, Wilhelm Frick as Reich minister of the interior, Hermann Göring as Prussian minister of the interior, and Joseph Goebbels as an effective spokesman for the party) and in control of the police, the Nazis became brazen in their acts of violence against the political parties opposing them, primarily against the socialists and the communists. The seizure of absolute power was made possible by the burning of the *Reichstag* building on February 27. The German people were understandably shocked. They saw their state and its political institutions threatened by this destructive act and clamored for extraordinary measures to preserve order. Accordingly, the cabinet decided, with the consent of President von Hindenburg, to curb political liberties in order "to protect the people and the state" (*169,* 173).

In spite of all these massive attempts at political manipulation, the Nazis did not obtain the majority of the votes in the election, but only 44 percent. However, the emergency laws passed in March played into their hands because the laws empowered the government to rule without the consent of the Parliament. The conservatives realized that they had no choice but to agree to what seemed on the surface to be nothing more than an emergency measure to ensure law and order. And the "No" to the emergency laws by the parties on the left was to no avail. Thus, the Parliament actually voted for its own demise.

In a speech before Parliament a year before Hitler's seizure of total power, von Papen had declared that an extraordinary body for governance might be necessary above and beyond the strife and chaos of parliamentary political activity. His plea for a political authority superior to the Parliament thus became a reality. And the conservatives had by their connivance paved the way for Hitler to achieve absolute power. This also concurred with their own propensity to decide political issues in a nonparliamentary, autocratic way. The ineffectiveness of the many political parties that characterized the Weimar Republic made the demise of parliamentary democracy by the determined Nazi activists all the more likely, while the population was confused by the unprecedented violence of events.

During 1933 all parliamentary parties were slowly eliminated, although their legitimacy still existed on paper if not in fact. Hitler could declare on July 6: "Political parties have finally been abolished. This is an historic event, the significance of which many have not yet understood. Now we must abolish the last remnants of democracy, especially the methods of election and the majority decision still made today in local government, in economic organisations, and works committees . . ." (*169,* 204). The most important development was the demise of the political center, particularly the Catholic Center Party. In an agreement between Hitler and Pope Pius XII, "the Catholic authorities proved willing to abandon their political party in return for a concordat guaranteeing freedom to their religious activities" (*169,* 199). The pope believed that a Hitler Germany was a bulwark against communism.

The one-party state, however, had internal rivalries that had to be eliminated. The Nazi activist groups, the SA and the SS, vied for power with the army and the party cadres. The problem of being a mass party on the one hand (from 1928 to 1932 the NSDAP had increased its membership from 108,000 to 1.5 million; *26,* 255), and an efficiently functioning elite on the other had to be solved. On June 30, 1934, a number of prominent members of the SA under Ernst Röhm (he had been accused of homosexuality) were murdered in order to eliminate the influence of a subgroup within the overall Nazi organization that had developed its own activist profile, particularly in the street brawls on Hitler's way to power. Before the Röhm purge, the "left wing" of the Nazi party under Gregor Strasser had already been liquidated. Also executed were von Schleicher and his wife, for alleged subversive activities against Hitler, and the Catholic leader Erich Klausener.

Through these "cleansing actions" the stage was set for the rise of an elite within the Nazi elite, namely, the much feared SS (*26,* 381 ff.). In due course all police functions were combined; they ranged from crime control, law enforcement, and political surveillance to execution of those deemed dangerous to the Nazi state. State and party were now merely different sides of the same coin. Orders of the leadership could be more efficiently implemented. It was the SS out of which Hitler and his right-hand man, Heinrich Himmler, later fashioned the *Sonderdienst* (Special-duties section, SD) in charge of the extermination camps. This concentration of power and the expansion of its jurisdiction insured a maximum of efficiency as well as the degree of secrecy necessary for the liquidation of people. Germany was now ready for the conquest of Europe. With violence as its main characteristic, the final phase of the Nazi revolution brought about WWII (*169,* 577 ff.; *105,* 57 ff).

Thus, the history of the Nazi party can be characterized by two distinct but mutually supportive features. It increased its membership into the millions, thereby providing the organizational and political cadres for running the state and society, and it evolved from within a highly specialized elite with unlimited power to put into effect the wishes of the party leadership.

## HISTORICAL REASONS FOR THE RISE OF NAZI POWER

Even the most careful chronicling of events that led to the Nazi assumption of power in the 1920s and 1930s leaves unexplained the underlying causes and forces that formed the background of this phenomenon. There are generally three types of explanations given for the remarkable success of the Nazis: (1) academics in Western universities place their emphases according to their fields of expertise and the analytical tools of their disciplines—economics, sociology, political science, institutional history; (2) Marxists explain Nazism largely as a symptom of late capitalism. However sophisticated and broadly applicable the Marxist explanations may be, they are in the final analysis reductionist and closed to multicausal explanations; (3) cultural historians take a more universalist stance, which tries to combine collective cultural characteristics and traumatic historical events but all too often confuses ideas with causes. All of these views and perspectives have some merit and throw light on one or the other aspect of the Nazi rise to power, but no single answer or ideological explanation is adequate.

The country never experienced a successful revolution of the lower classes, which therefore never attained any significant power in running the affairs of state and society, with one exception. In the Weimar Republic the middle class did gain a significant measure of control, but the constitution and the party structure were not adequate to the social and economic problems of post-WWI Germany. Furthermore, the German middle class, through its writers and thinkers, defined in the course of the nineteenth century cultural norms and a generally accepted value system by which the Germans developed a national identity. This contradiction between the lack of real political power and the claim to a universality of cultural and spiritual values brought forth the "nonpolitical German" as the representative of a positive cultural value that was dominant from Weimar classicism around 1800 to the Weimar Republic in the 1920s.

This nonpolitical German was considered to possess great individual virtues that had far-reaching significance. He made his appearance in German classicism with its leading cultural figures: Kant, Goethe, and Schiller. During the nineteenth century this ideal was perpetuated in the schools and in due time became a valuable coin in the cultural currency of the nation as a whole. The separation of the private from the public sphere, where inwardness was pitted against the hostile world, is traced by some historians all the way back to Martin Luther's insistence that temporal power and spiritual grace should be separate. Others trace the origin of the nonpolitical German to the profound revulsion of the German intelligentsia and middle class at the bloody excesses of the French Revolution during the Jacobin period. Many of Germany's leading writers turned the powerlessness of the middle class in the public arena into a private virtue. After the end of WWII and the collapse of Nazism, the nonpolitical German was debunked not merely as amoral but ultimately as having become an accessory to the crimes committed in the name of Germany. Heinrich Böll in *Wo warst du, Adam?* (1951; *Adam Where Art Thou?* 1955) and Carl Zuckmayer in *Des Teufels General* (1946; *The Devil's General,* 1962) portray protagonists who lose their integrity to the forces that are hellbent on destroying Germany and Europe.

In sum the nonpolitical German was an easy prey for Hitler. Furthermore, Germany's geopolitical position in the center of Europe without natural borders had a profound effect on its political culture. Twice in its history, in the Thirty Years' War (1618–1648) and the Napoleonic Wars (1796–1815), Germany's fate was drastically shaped by outside forces. Mobilization against outside forces as a way of diverting attention from internal problems is available to all governments, but in Germany such mobilization became a dominant aspect of nineteenth- and early twentieth-century political culture, and this in two important ways: (1) it served to unite Germans of all classes against a foreign enemy; (2) it rallied Germany in the name of the fatherland against liberal impulses of Western bourgeois society (see Johann Gottlieb Fichte, *Reden an die deutsche Nation,* 1807–1808). No one said it more succinctly than the German poet Ludwig Frank who claimed at the outbreak of WWI: "In the trenches the nation will be united *(172,* 68)." Mobilization and defense against the liberal West also played their role in setting the stage of Nazism. When Hitler finally came to power, however, he turned to the east for expansion in the name of race and for the sake of raw materials.

Another factor contributing to the rise of Nazism was that Germany lacked an effective opposition to conservative and reactionary trends that dominated political life from the middle of the nineteenth century on. More specifically, German labor lacked representation within the emerging parliamentary democracy. The Prussian Parliament in the nineteenth century had been dominated by the landed aristocracy, the conservative civil-service establishment *(Beamtentum),* and the leaders of industry. It contained no labor representatives. The dominant social and political elite shaped an ideology that was intolerant to political alternatives and to any opposition (see Kurt F. Reinhardt, Vol. 2, 631 ff.). In the 19th and early 20th century the Social Democrats were considered unpatriotic and unreliable to run the ship of state. Consequently, they lacked for a long time the legitimacy to hold power in the established political institutions. This ideology of a political, social, and economic elite remained a powerful current even during the heyday of open-ended experimentation with representative democracy in the Weimar Republic, and it served increasingly as an attractive reactionary alternative to the chaos of parliamentary proceedings. When the conservative Franz von Papen declared in 1932, during one of the tumultuous debates in the *Reichstag,* that Germany needed a supraparliamentary council that would operate above the din of daily political turmoil, he not only argued against political diversity from the point of view of the Prussian elite of the nineteenth century, but he also prepared the ground for Hitler, who had developed his own notion of a supraparliamentary force rising out of the ashes of the Parliament.

Another reason for the lack of political opposition had nothing to do with the rules and values guiding the political institutions but derived from the great stability that existed in Germany between labor and management. This meant in effect that nothing would emerge from labor to significantly influence politics and the direction it would take. Bismarck's extensive efforts to provide economically for the workers through social legislation (medical insurance, old-age pensions, and the like) helped to diffuse political opposition that might have emerged from the labor force. The cradle-to-grave protection provided to its loyal workers by the giant steel conglomerate run by the Krupp family restated a pattern of German economic life practiced as early as the fifteenth century by the wealthy Fuggers of Augsburg, who provided security for their workers beyond mere sustenance. The resultant loyalty to the firm reinforced feudal patterns in German political life that persisted into the twentieth century and stifled the growth of political consciousness based on class interests *(176)*.

While German labor was politically dormant, the petite bourgeoisie became deeply alienated and resentful during the course of the Second Reich. Pressured from below by labor, denied access to political power by the elite, and buffeted by economic fluctuations beyond their control, the small merchants, shopkeepers, tradesmen, low-rank civil servants, and white-collar workers became the explosive driving force of the Nazi revolution. The petite bourgeoisie, which disliked Western liberal ideas and felt threatened by industrial modernization, provided the personnel for the Nazi leadership.

The lower middle class was disenfranchised economically and politically. Its lack of any specific social context for articulating its needs made it all the more receptive to the idea of abolishing specific class interests. Thus the leap into totalitarianism was facilitated. Whereas labor and the middle class could claim—each in their own way—to be internationalist, the lower middle class was rooted in a provincial, xenophobic way of life. It was therefore particularly susceptible to demagogic bugaboo about alien powers and dark forces that allegedly had encircled Germany. The Treaty of Versailles with its spirit of revenge and its demands for excessive German reparations reinforced lower-middle-class hostility because the lower middle class was suffering the most economically.

Weimar culture with its creative pluralism, its break-throughs in the arts and sciences, its civil disorder, and its liberal life styles was another factor in the rise of totalitarianism. The spirit of the times became a veritable nightmare for the orderly burgher, whose money had become worthless and whose belief in Wilhelmian prowess had been shattered. The German of the Wilhelmian Second Reich who

had enjoyed the country's economic wealth and national prestige
was unable to cope with the disquieting instability of Weimar: a per-
plexing new architecture, a kind of music never heard before, expressionism in literature and the visual arts, and a theater of the absurd. Hitler promised a way out of all these uncertainties.

In the 1930s, while he was still consolidating his hold on power,
Hitler evoked to great effect the harshness of the Versailles Treaty,
the general economic malaise, and the rioting in the streets as symbols of the Weimar Republic. Ever since 1871, with the rise of the
Second Reich and the increase in economic power, the Germans had
associated nationhood with wealth. This was the fatal result of industrialization and nationhood coming to the fore in Germany at the
same time. WWI and the Weimar Republic had destroyed for the Wilhelmian German both economic power and national prestige. Hitler
promised the confused Germans not only a renewed pride in the nation, full employment, and a high living standard for all but also a return to law and order and an end to social experimentations.

Last but not least, the German intellectual tradition helped prepare the ground for the Nazis. It would be a mistake to call Friedrich Nietzsche and Richard Wagner precursors of Nazism, yet they
lent themselves to such an interpretation. To say that Hitler and his
political advisers, Joseph Goebbels and Alfred Rosenberg, merely
perverted Nietzsche's and Wagner's ideas, overlooks some important notions that emanated from their thought and art. The grand
manner in which Wagner fused the myth of a Germanic past with
the pretentions of his own age on a stage filled with imposing figures and great historical events was much to Hitler's personal lik-
ing, and he employed the Wagnerian style in creating his own
work of total political art in which illusion and reality were
blended to heighten the lure of momentous expectations. Wagner
had most effectively mythologized the Germanic past. This aided
the Nazi obscurantists in their claim of racial superiority. Nietzsche's works presented a profound critique of Western culture,
throwing light on what he considered the shallow optimism of
Christianity and at the same time mocking the rationalist tradition.
Neither Christian optimism nor secular rationalism comprehended
the tragic aspects of life according to Nietzsche. But he failed to see
the danger in advocating a radical transformation of values in
which Germany was to play an important role (*167,* 144). Ultimately, his insight could be translated, however faultily, into the
language of the Nazis' *Herrenmoral* (master morality: good equals
strong, bad equals weak) because it lacked all social responsibility.

Nietzsche was not the only one who envisioned great historical
moments for the Germans. The poet Stefan George painted a picture of the Third Reich in his intense vision of the grand aesthete
beyond morality (*Algabal,* 1892); but when Hitler twisted it into

swastika shape, George was aghast and fled to Switzerland, where he died in 1933.

Besides such thinkers as Wagner, Nietzsche, and George, the intellectual climate of Germany in the nineteenth century created concepts that were susceptible to Nazi interpretation. Most important of these concepts was the idea of a harmonious organic whole that could be transformed into a social reality. This idea was alive in the German classics, particularly in Goethe's perennial striving for organic wholeness. The guiding principle in the sphere of art was rooted in Greek antiquity, and it served as a central norm for literature and the arts during Weimar classicism. During the nineteenth century, however, the notion of the organic whole did not remain confined to the sphere of culture; instead it fueled the growth of social utopias in the form of folk communities. Finally, organic wholeness came to serve Nazi theories of race, which reasoned that a racially pure society could not tolerate racial diversity. This dangerous ideology was aided and abetted in anti-Semitic works from writers abroad—Joseph Arthur de Gobineau (1816–1882) in France and the British Houston Stewart Chamberlain (1855–1922), who became a German citizen in 1916.

Each factor presented here as a partial explanation for the Nazi assumption of power does not in itself suffice, nor do all the factors taken together add up to a blanket indictment of German culture as being fertile ground for Nazism. Many circumstances played an important role as did the deep paralysis of political will and the lack of foresight of the Western world. A particular constellation of factors came together in this highly industrialized nation with its weak political institutions, enfeebled by depressed economic conditions. The result was a witches' brew of various ingredients, not all of which were harmful in themselves. The danger once posed by Nazism remains with us, whether in its theocratic form, as in many parts of the world, or as an ingredient in a variety of totalitarian experiments, be they of the extreme right or the extreme left.

# 2. Ideology of Nazism and the Consolidation of Power

The ideology of Nazism did not represent a coherent system of political thought. As a blueprint for political action, however, it remained remarkably consistent and effective throughout the Nazi rise and fall. The main texts of Nazi ideology were (1) the 25-point 1920 program of the NSDAP, (2) Hitler's *Mein Kampf* (volume 1, first published in 1925; volume 2, first published in 1927), and (3) Alfred Rosenberg's *Der Mythus des 20. Jahrhunderts* (Munich, first published in 1930). All three texts are very diffuse and contradictory in their premises, developed as they were out of a sponta-neous mode of argumentation. The texts mirror the trends and the irrationality of Nazi political behavior. If anything at all, they prove that the leading Nazi ideologists were more adept at oral persua-sion than at expository writing. Indeed, written statements prior to 1933 are of limited help in illuminating the real events that oc-curred between 1933 and 1939 and during the war years. Although it is tempting to do so, it is also too simplistic to assume a neat causal connection between Nazi ideology and the horrendous events of the war and the Holocaust that followed. These events were influenced to a certain extent by ideology, but they also had their own complex dynamics, which must be understood beyond the contradictory rantings and ravings of Nazi "theorists." The ide-ology itself can best be understood by seeing its practice during the period of the consolidation of power between 1933 and 1939.

## MAIN POLITICAL STRATEGIES

The consolidation of power involved three main political strate-gies: (1) legal and political maneuvers were devised to radically transform all social, political, religious, and economic institutions into functions of the state; (2) a new "political reality" was created through theatrical mass events; (3) an all-pervasive miasma of vio-lence was applied against all who would not or could not partici-pate in the fascist revolution.

### Coordination of Institutions *(Gleichschaltung)*

*Gleichschaltung* was the term for the transformation of all politi-cal institutions away from society's varied needs and the bringing of these institutions into line with the new state, which saw itself as monocentric—one people, one empire, one leader *(ein Volk, ein Reich, ein Führer)*. The interests of individuals and classes were declared irrelevant; social institutions lost their semiautonomous status and were judged by the degree to which they could be use-fully integrated. Robert Ley, the head of the workers' wing of the Nazi party (the German Labor Front, DAF), articulated the mean-ing of *Gleichschaltung* by citing Hitler: "I no longer recognize em-ployer and employee, I only recognize deputies of work and soldiers" (*139*, 14). The division of labor implied in the terms *em-ployer* and *employee* was not eliminated but rather glossed over by the tasks given to both by the state. The radical transformation of institutional functions invalidated all elements of autonomy, what-ever their traditional legitimacy or practical purpose had been.

### Labor

The process of *Gleichschaltung* was not merely one of terminol-ogy ("TO ALL WORKING GERMANS, 27TH OF NOVEMBER, 1933: The German

Labor Front represents the organization for all working people
without reference to their economic and social position"; *169,
434*) but was backed up by the threat of violence ("GLEICH-
SCHALTUNGSAKTION, 2ND OF MAY, 1933: the SA and the SS are to seize
the property owned by the trade unions and to arrest the trade unionists"; *169, 423*).

Paralleling the destruction of labor organizations, a Nazi *Arbeitsdienst* (work-service force) was founded, a uniformed paramilitary
unit that had both symbolic and real meaning for the Nazis' relationship to labor. The uniform symbolized military obedience to
the state, whereas the work provided to these spade-carrying draft-
ees (public-work projects, above all, the building of the *Autobahn*)
lowered the unemployment rate. The *Arbeitsdienst* became a
workers' elite not in terms of the members' skills but in terms of
the legitimacy bestowed on it by the state.

The *Gleichschaltung* brought immense benefits to the Nazis. It
neutralized class interests and class differences, and it bestowed
prestige on the laborer without raising wages. Ultimately, through
central control, it allowed productivity to serve rearmament, a goal
clearly established as early as 1933, "rendering the German people
again capable of bearing arms for military service" (cabinet-
meeting minutes, February 8, 1933; *169, 380*). The first major step
toward the implementation of Hitler's *Gleichschaltung* in the economic sphere was his Four-Year Plan of 1936 under the direction
of Hermann Göring, the most prominent Nazi figure after Hitler
himself.

*Gleichschaltung* in the economic sphere represented a mobilization of all productive forces and became an indispensable part of
foreign policy on the level of ideology: "In face of the necessity of
warding off this danger [for example, Bolshevism] all other considerations must recede into the background as completely irrelevant" (*169, 402*). *Gleichschaltung* also became an indispensable
part on the level of policy as it related to the global economy. It
was clearly the intent of the Nazis to make Germany completely
self-sufficient in the economic sphere for the purpose of waging
war. The greater the emphasis was on military conquest, the more
pronounced the need became for absolute control over raw materials. This interdependence between military objectives and conquest of raw materials shaped the strategy of the general staff
during WWII. It was typical for the Nazis that, during their last
major attempt at counterattack in the Battle of the Bulge in the winter of 1944, they set the capture of fuel depots behind Allied lines
as one of their first military objectives so as to enable their tanks to
move on to further conquests. Such ad hoc objectives not only
typified the military strategy during WWII, but they were also an
essential feature of Nazi ideology in general.

The Four-Year Plan, with its emphasis on removing Germany from the context of world economy, led to pronounced conflicts inside Germany between the internationalist approach to industry advocated by Hjalmar Schacht, the financial wizard of Nazi Germany, and the nationalist point of view articulated by Hermann Göring. Göring's famous "guns versus butter" slogan referred to this controversy, in which the internationalists lost out. Schacht resigned as minister of economic affairs although he remained a loyal supporter of the Reich to the end. *Gleichschaltung* guaranteed the success of the Nazis in the economic sphere and set them on their adventurous military path abroad.

## The Churches

In dealing with the churches, *Gleichschaltung* was not necessary to the same degree as in the economic sector as long as the churches remained uninvolved in the affairs of state. Initially, the Nazis succeeded in bringing the churches into line by keeping up a Christian rhetoric, trying in this way to gain control over the church hierarchy on the highest level. They even concluded a concordat with the Papacy in 1933, a kind of friendly agreement of noninterference in each other's affairs, which had a calming effect on the German Catholic Church. The ideological thrust of Nazism, however, was all too obvious not to clash with the tenets of Christianity, and in May 1934 the Protestant Church of Germany stated that it "reject[ed] supremacy of state over Jesus Christ" (*169,* 369). Two years later, in December 1936, the Bavarian Cardinal Michael Faulhaber followed with a pastoral letter in which he stated that Nazi ideology was "developing more and more into a full-scale attack on the Christian faith and the Catholic Church" (*169*). Because the two main denominations were not specifically involved in social activism, let alone subversive actions against the state during the consolidation of Nazi power, their benign neglect worked wherever *Gleichschaltung* was not possible or not even necessary. It was left up to a few brave Christian individuals, such as Pastor Dietrich Bonhoeffer, to witness their faith and die for their beliefs near the end of the Nazi regime.

## The Press

The measures taken by the Nazis to integrate the German press into the state apparatus were swift and effective because the Nazis strongly believed that controlling the means of communication was as important as controlling the means of production. *Gleichschaltung* was achieved, to use the words of a press representative of the prestigious *Frankfurter Zeitung,* by changing "the press conference *with* the Reich government, started in 1917, to a press conference *of* the Reich government" (*169,* 334). The press simply became an institution of the state, and in due course it turned into an effective tool of Nazi propaganda in shaping opinions inside Germany and manipulating attitudes abroad. Independent journalism with its entrepreneurial spirit never had been as strong in Germany as in the United States. The German press therefore lacked a tradition to fall back on for its defense. As was to be expected, the Nazis printed their own newspapers; the most notorious was *Der Stürmer* under the editorship of Julius Streicher, one of Germany's most notorious anti-Semites and *Gauleiter* (Nazi district leader) of the province of Franconia.

## The Arts

Instructive for the *Gleichschaltung* undertaken by the Nazis in the sphere of art was the correspondence between the Minister of Propaganda Joseph Goebbels and the leading German conductor Wilhelm Furtwängler. Although sympathetic to the Nazis, Furtwängler nevertheless wanted to preserve artistic integrity and autonomy in defining standards. He stated: "But while the line of division between Jews and non-Jews is being drawn with a relentless, even a doctrinaire sharpness . . . the other line of division, extremely important, if not decisive in the long run—that between good and bad art—is being far too much neglected" (*169, 342*). Goebbels' reply stressed the supremacy of the artist integrated into objectives defined by the state: "Art must be good, but beyond this it must be responsible, professional, close to the people *(volksnah)* and aggressive" (*169*). Art based on individual liberty and the right to be different was swept away along with those artists and writers who believed it the artist's duty to be engaged in progressive social causes.

## The Universities

The institutions of higher learning were singled out for political coordination with the result that 300 university professors had left their posts by 1935. Many others, however, stayed and withdrew into their academic spheres; but a vociferous minority gave their support to the book burnings and the destruction of academe. The works of Heinrich Heine, Heinrich Mann, Sigmund Freud, and many other prominent German writers were burned in public—a symbolic act that was to demonstrate that culture must serve the state and that coercion or violence would achieve that end. The book burning was portrayed as a revolutionary act for the new Reich, although its real significance lay in cutting Germany off from its moral, cultural, and intellectual foundations. Pluralism of artistic expression, experiments of all kinds, in short, the cutting edge of historical change in the sphere of art and thought was dulled in the name of a comfortable and insipid folk art of stereotypical realism. The *Reichskulturkammer* (Office of Cultural Affairs) declared in November 15, 1933: "The revolution we have made is a total one. . . . It does not matter what means are used to achieve it" (*26,* 281). In July 1937, on the occasion of the opening of the House of German Art in Munich, which he helped design, Hitler declared that the artist "creates for the people, and we will see to it that the people in the future will be called to judge his art" (*169,* 347).

The *Gleichschaltung* in the cultural sphere set the stage for the emigration of most of the best minds of Germany. Many emigrated to the U.S.A.; others, to a much lesser extent, to England, the U.S.S.R., and to various countries. Some stayed in Germany and cooperated with the Nazis to varying degrees, as, for instance, Furtwängler, the composer Richard Strauss, the writer Gottfried Benn, and the philosopher Martin Heidegger.

## Politics as Theater

Next to the *Gleichschaltung* of all social activities, politics as spectacle and media event was an essential ingredient of Nazi theory and practice. It was not merely a matter of the clever propagandist's packaging of a political reality; rather, the staging of Nazi events in speeches, mass rallies, marches, and demonstrations was the first modern example of the medium being an essential part of the message. Goebbels stated this succinctly to Furtwängler: "Politics too is an art, perhaps the highest and most comprehensive there is, and we who shape modern German policy feel ourselves to be artists who have been given the responsible task of forming, out of the raw material of the mass, the firm, concrete structure of a people" (*169,* 343). This revealing statement by the propaganda minister explains neatly the alliance between aesthetics and power that was central to Nazi ideology.

In traditional German culture, aesthetic reflections were frequently directed toward the problem of social and individual morality. As pockets of resistance such reflections served to uphold German morality against the leveling effect of commercialization. The Nazis did not break this link between the realm of art and society, but they perverted aesthetic criteria into tools of political power.

Nowhere else was the link between aesthetics and power forged more effectively than in Leni Riefenstahl's film *Triumph des Willens (Triumph of the Will),* which recorded events of the colossal 1934 party rally in Nuremberg. Commissioned by Hitler and the Nazi party, the film introduced the "new political reality" to all the Germans in a political *Gesamtkunstwerk* (total art work). This total art combines individual fragments of daily life, individual perceptions, treasured symbols, and clichés of German culture into an overarching pattern. The slow destruction of individual entities on all levels leads toward the end of the film to a momumental affirmation of Nazism by a rigidly ordered mass of people frozen in a geometric design within the architectural frame of the Nazi rally grounds. The film, and many lesser ones like it, was produced for the masses so that the people would feel themselves to be participants in the consolidation of Nazi power. In 1934 this power was not yet as strong as the political happenings would have the onlookers believe. Visual events were supplemented by continued exposure to radio broadcasts. To this end Hitler ordered production of a mass-produced *Volksempfänger,* an inexpensive people's radio, so that his message could be heard in every town, village, and hamlet of the Reich. By 1935, 70 percent of German households had a radio, more than in any other country. Thus, Nazism also represented a revolution in communication. Readers became listeners and members of mass audiences so that the collective replaced the individual. As early as 1923, Hitler was convinced that speakers would be more important to the Nazi movement than writers (*105,* 533). The modern political happening came into being, and it helped create the political reality of the Nazi state.

## Violence and Racial Mythology

The third major factor in the Nazi consolidation of power was the threat of violence as well as its efficient use. The ideological underpinnings of Nazi violence were not as obvious as some of the explanations would have us believe. The glorification of war and heroism, set off against the complexities of everyday life in an increasingly industrialized world, provided a link between nostalgia for an age of great deeds with a brutal belief in social Darwinism, the survival of the fittest. Although nostalgia for a glorious past and brutal adherence to *Realpolitik* reinforced each other, they do not explain the most extreme forms of violence. Another ideological feature of Nazism provides deeper insight into its violent nature— the belief that nations are organic totalities in which all parts should work together in harmony for the health of the whole. Such a view interprets any strife or contradictions in the society as expressions of disease. The Nazis added the fatal racial element to this connection between nature and society, tearing it out of its traditional religious and idealistic moorings: the state "has to place race in the center of existence. The state has to care for keeping the race pure" (*105,* 446). The organic view of society called for the elimination of every person and group deemed alien to the new organism now called "Aryan," a murky term that alluded to the Indo-European origins of the German language. This ideological gibberish was offered as a rationale for violent action against all those considered non-Aryan. The disturbed society could project its problems onto an "outside force" and place blame on a "difference of race." A political continuum runs from the Nuremberg Laws for the "Protection of the German Blood and German Honor" (passed on September 15, 1935) to Himmler's plan for the mass extermination of Jews, supported by a metaphor from nature: "We have exterminated a bacterium, because ultimately we do not want to be infected by it and die of it" (October 6, 1943; *169, 533*). Thus, violence and the destruction of civilization itself became possible when accepted as an imperative of nature.

## 3.  Hitler as Mass Communicator

The impact of Nazism on Europe was so immense that the search for an explanation of the relapse into absolute barbarity still continues to the present day. The spectrum of explanations for this European catastrophe is broad and includes many mutually exclusive views. Some historians discern an authoritarian pattern throughout German history that precluded a give-and-take approach to problem-solving, whereas others emphasize the traumas of the Weimar Republic, especially the economic plight of the middle class, the harshness of the Treaty of Versailles, and the frustrations of chaotic parliamentarianism. Another cause for the rise of fascism was Hitler's personality, or, more precisely, his unique ability to create and exploit a mass psychosis to serve his ends. He was the first political figure to demonstrate that control over the means of communication is a key to political power—a fact much more significant in understanding Nazi history than the presumed psychological disturbances or evil nature of his character. Indeed, there is a danger in placing too much emphasis on a leader's charisma because it encourages the belief that historical processes are primarily irrational and therefore not controllable.

There was nothing particularly striking about Hitler's physical appearance or personal background. Born to a petite-bourgeois family in the Austrian border town of Braunau by the Inn River on April 20, 1889, he unsuccessfully attempted a career as a painter in Vienna. A private first class in WWI, he served in France, then was a political activist for right-wing causes in the beer halls of Munich. Below average in stature, sporting a narrow mustache, and cultivating the grand gesture, he had the prance of a peacock typical of the aggressive pride of the political "nouveau riche."

Prior to Hitler, poets, writers, and philosophers had honed the German language. It was a language alien to and uncomfortable in the political arena. Therefore it was all the more vulnerable to political propagandists who set out to shape it to their ends. As early as 1923 to 1925, Hitler used speech as a political weapon in his autobiography, *Mein Kampf* (*105,* 193), recognizing, as have all successful mass communicators after him, that "all propaganda has to be popular on the intellectual level and comprehensible to the most limited person of the group for which the propaganda is meant" (*105,* 197). His credo was: "The receptivity of the masses is very limited, its understanding modest, but its ability to forget is immense. Therefore all effective propaganda has to be limited to very few points" (*105,* 198). The notion of mass psychology had made its appearance in the late nineteenth century in works such as Gustave Le Bon's *Psychology of the Masses* (1895), and it reflected the emergence of mass culture in line with Jean-Jacques Rousseau's notion of a general popular will *(volonté générale)*. Inasmuch as this notion underlay the fight against the aristocracy during the French Revolution, it was used by Hitler to break down class distinctions and class consciousness, facilitating the link the Nazis made between the general popular will and their own notion of the monolithic state.

While sociologists of the 1920s and early 1930s, particularly those associated with the Frankfurt School, developed insights into the new ideas on the nature of masses and mass reaction, Hitler shaped the practical tools of mass psychology. His tools closely approximate in many ways contemporary techniques of commercial advertising. The following statement could have been made on Madison Avenue: "Every attempt at persuasion, whether in business or politics, must be made in the most simple form and also with frequent repetitions over a period of time" (*105,* 203). Thus, his speeches consisted of a series of declarative sentences that combined doubtful assertions with appeals for an unshakable faith in an inseparable whole. They were not based on logical cohesion, but on principles more closely related to music—repetitions, crescendos, accelerandos, ritardandos, rhythms, pauses—which mesmerized the listener. The organization of the speeches, the mode of their delivery, the theatricality of the event, and the rallying of huge masses had a dual purpose: the participants in such spectacles could hear their own personal fears, prejudices, and resentments expressed and justified. Yet, the rallies were organized to convince participants that they were witnessing great historical events that would shape the future of Germany and the world for a millenium.

# 4. Foreign Policy

The internal consolidation of power between 1933 and 1939 was carefully orchestrated with moves in the field of foreign policy. The approach used to bring about changes in favor of Nazi control was the same in foreign affairs as on the domestic scene. A threat of violence, carefully administered, the claim for legitimacy, suggesting reasonable goals, and the lightning-quick action that brought forth and staged a "new reality" in the balance of power— all worked together from 1933 to bring about first diplomatic and later military dominance of Nazi Germany over the rest of Europe.

Hitler had declared as early as 1923 that the primary goal of foreign policy was "securing the existence of the race" (*169, 500*). There has been speculation as to whether Hitler's primary foreign-policy objectives were racial or economic in nature, whether a race war or control over raw materials was uppermost in his mind. In fact, both issues are inseparably interconnected. Hitler's idea of *Lebensraum* (living space) for the Aryan race, as he perceived it, linked the belief in racial superiority with the dominance over raw materials. It was geopolitical thinking grafted onto social Darwinism, an alliance between biological determinism and modern diplomatic strategic thinking.

Hitler's foreign policy in the prewar years had two striking features: the Nazis believed that, on the one hand, Western democracies would disintegrate on their own accord; whereas the East, on the other hand, presented a challenge to the Nazis that justified their geographical expansion eastward. Therefore the foreign-policy goal was to divide and neutralize the West for the purpose of attacking the East. Hitler sought to achieve this by a gradualistic approach that allowed for political flexibility and extensive diplomatic maneuvering. Hitler was aided in neutralizing the West by Great Britain's perception of herself as a global power rather than as one of many European nations. This self-appointed global role led the British to continue playing the diplomatic game of checks and balances in Europe. Thus, Hitler took advantage of British continental policy. Great Britain was mistaken (just as were the conservative forces within Germany) in its assumption that it could ultimately bend the goals of the Nazis to its own end. France, on the other hand, was undergoing too many internal political conflicts to emerge as a strong counterforce to what was happening east of the Rhine River. The Stalinist purges of the 1930s and Russian xenophobia further isolated the Soviets from the West at a time when concerted efforts against the Nazis would have been effective.

Thus, the stage was set to alter the diplomatic picture of Europe and bring about Nazi hegemony. The process was gradual and painstaking, suggesting Hitler's uncanny, almost artistic, sense of timing. In 1933 Hitler declared in his "Peace Speech," "We have no use for the idea of Germanization" (*169, 510*). A year later Secretary of State of Foreign Affairs Bernhard Wilhelm von Bülow drew the practical consequence from Hitler's general guidelines: "Our only security lies in a skillful foreign policy and in avoiding all provocations". The Nazis were militarily weak at first and had not secured their internal power sufficiently for a bolder approach to foreign policy. Furthermore, the diplomatic corps was still manned by many conservative aristocrats; they served as a counterforce to the more adventuresome Nazis, who finally emerged victorious with the ascendancy of Joachim von Ribbentrop, the secretary of state of foreign affairs from 1938 onward. With these pronouncements of peaceful intentions as a cover, Hitler committed acts of provocation, each more daring than the previous one, all of them carefully calculated not to evoke a response from other European powers. In March, 1935, the Nazis introduced general conscription and started building the *Luftwaffe,* knocking out with one single internal law a major provision of the Versailles Treaty that forbade Germany to rearm. This first successful step made the next step easier for Hitler, namely, the reoccupation of the Rhineland on March 7, 1936, a region of Germany that had been demilitarized by the Treaty of Versailles.

With the completion of a successful military move within the borders of Germany, Hitler was now ready to try his hand on foreign soil. The civil war in Spain, which had started in July 1936, gave him his opportunity. He sent his "Legion Condor," the elite of his newly formed *Luftwaffe,* to aid Generalissimo Francisco Franco in his defeat of the Republican forces, who had little military support from abroad. This war was immortalized in Picasso's *Guernica,* considered to be the greatest work of the visual arts in the twentieth century to describe human suffering on a grand scale. Hitler was also greatly aided by the rise of the Fascists in Italy under Benito Mussolini. The two fascist powers united on November 1, 1936, to form the Berlin-Rome Axis. A year later, in November 1937, Japan, Germany, and Italy were united and the ground was prepared diplomatically for WWII.

Paralleling this consolidation of antidemocratic powers was a shift in the internal debate on foreign policy within Germany. In November 1937 a foreign-policy plan was concluded in private which determined that military expansion to the east should provide the German people with more *Lebensraum.* First there was the annexation of Austria in March 1938, which was to join the greater Germany *(das großdeutsche Reich);* then followed the invasion and subjugation of the rest of Czechoslovakia in March 1939 after the Sudetenland had been secured in September 1938. The carefully orchestrated gradualistic approach of Nazi expansionism abroad can best be illustrated by the annexation of Austria. It was an independent country, yet culturally and linguistically closely connected with Germany. Politically, its annexation was a more drastic move than the reoccupation of the Rhineland in 1936, a purely German territory, but it was less drastic than the takeover of Czechoslovakia, a non-German country; however, its rather large population of *Sudetendeutsche* served as an excuse for intervention on their behalf. The next logical step was an attack on a country that was not German either culturally, politically, or linguistically, a country that had no large German minority to serve as an excuse for intervention. This country was Poland. It was invaded on September 1, 1939, signaling the beginning of WWII.

The gradual escalation of demands in the field of international relations—remilitarization of the Rhineland, intervention in Spain, annexation of Austria, subjugation of Czechoslovakia, and finally, a full-fledged war against Poland—has in retrospect an inevitability to it that made Germans and non-Germans mere players on the political stage Hitler had designed. Internally, as late as 1938, the military was the only hope to stop Hitler's move toward war. His aggressive stance toward Czechoslovakia had the generals alarmed, and some of them planned to overthrow Hitler should he declare war. The famous memorandum of General Ludwig Beck makes abundantly clear the misgivings of the general staff. "I need not enlarge upon the fact that such a war would in all probability end not only in a military but also in a general catastrophe for Germany" (*169*, 301). Yet, whatever misgivings the generals may have had, there were in Germany no democratic forces, no broader political contexts within which an attempt at overthrowing Hitler could have led to a transformation of Nazi Germany. Furthermore, the Allies, particularly England, were in no position either militarily or economically to intervene effectively. The Munich Agreement of September 29, 1938, has been used by many leading American political figures from Harry Truman on as a universal example of the appeasement of totalitarianism. Viewed within the political and military dynamics of the time, however, it can be seen as a delaying tactic by the British rather than an act of diplomatic surrender. Hitler, at any rate, was not pleased with the diplomatic results at Munich, and he is said to have exclaimed, "That fellow Chamberlain has spoiled my entry into Prague" (*169*, 549). After Munich it was just a matter of time until war broke out. In a secret speech to the press corps on November 10, 1938, Hitler ordered it "to reeducate the German people psychologically and to make it clear that there are things that must be achieved by force, if peaceful means fail" (*169*, 549). Nevertheless, the German people entered WWII psychologically unprepared. There was none of the naive enthusiasm and clamor for war so evident at the outbreak of WWI. The Germans consoled themselves that it would be all over by Christmas 1939.

# 5. Nazi Culture

## IDEOLOGY

Nazism placed great emphasis on the visual arts as a propaganda tool. The Nazis considered them essential if they were to succeed in displaying their political power through carefully orchestrated mass rallies, torchlight parades, precision military parades, flag displays, and political posters and pamphlets. Visual effect suggested regularity and massiveness. In the nineteenth century, Richard Wagner had composed operas on a grand scale (for example, the *Ring* Cycle) in which he payed close attention to both aesthetic and political aspects of his musical and visual message. Hitler not only loved Wagner's music but he copied Wagner's grand visual designs as well and filled them with his own ideological content.

Although the association of the visual arts with politics was a legacy of the nineteenth century, the Nazis were the first to appreciate the importance of visual symbols and icons to modern mass culture and to exploit them systematically to promote political activism. The Nazi writer Alfred Rosenberg pointed out the conscious and unconscious associations evoked by visual symbolism: after the *Christian cross* (for Christian hope and Christ's resurrection) and after the *red flag* (for brotherhood of the dispossessed and for a proletarian utopia), there arose a new universal symbol, the *swastika,* that stood for "*Volk*-honor, living space, national freedom, racial purity and regenerative fertility" (*191, 687–8*).

The ideological focal point for defining Nazi art was race:

> Every race has its own view of life. . . . It is an example of a horrible intellectual decadence of past times that there was talk about styles without knowing the racial determinants.

> (Hitler, Speech about the Arts, September 2, 1933; *241,* 64–65)

Such views were eagerly adopted and expanded by art historians in Germany:

> The battle we are waging today again for German art is basically nothing else but the battle of the artistic tribes *(Kunststämme)* against what is un-German, foreign, not blood-related, against the Romanesque, French, Russo-Slavic, against everything that is anational, antinational, international in German art.

> (Kurt Karl Eberlein; *241,* 58)

The above racial view of art, however, did not remain unchallenged even within Germany at that time. The well-known art historian Wilhelm Pinder refuted this racist definition of the arts.

The line between (Aryan) race and Germany as a national identity was left deliberately obscure. It gave the Nazis the necessary
flexibility to use the vague term *Nordic (Aryan) race* and to define
it according to their political needs. Serious writers, such as Gottfried Benn, lent legitimacy to Nazi ideology by seeing in the new
Germany a place where new art forms would arise (*Der neue Staat
und die Intellektuellen, 241,* 78).

The Nazis stressed three essential qualities in their ideological
statements concerning the arts: (1) all artistic creativity as rooted in
"a racial collective"; (2) uniformity of style (rejection of all foreign
influence) as a positive norm; and (3) individualism and experimentation as a sign of decadence. An extensive terminology was
created to support these newly discovered aesthetic norms. Many
of the new terms had no meaning in themselves, nor were they the
result of either rational discourse or empirical observation. They
derived their impact (not their meaning) from mutually reinforcing
each other in a closed rhetorical system of self-validation that was
repeated often and everywhere: "racial biomass of a people," "pri-
mevel forces of a race," "inexhaustible depth of a nation's soul,"
"art comes from the blood," "return to Germanic roots." Related
nonracial expressions were part of the same rhetoric, for example,
"landscape and soul," "German inwardness," "the heroic," "mystic solidarity," "power and simplicity," and, above all, "blood and
soil" *(Blut und Boden),* a notion that suggested a magic link between race and habitat and thus supported Nazi geopolitical designs on a cultural level.

# VISUAL ARTS

Nazi art is best described as "national socialist realism." Set
within scenes of a heroic past or an idealized nature, everyday motifs of work and war predominate. Depictions are usually stylized
for propagandistic ends. Frozen gestures dominate over emotion
and activity. Despite ideological insistence on purity of style, techniques are eclectic and derive from realistic to romantic and neoclassical periods. Nazi art is both highly emotional and abstract.
The Nazi's attribution of a revolutionary spirit to their art stands in
striking contrast to the complete conventionality of chosen motifs
and techniques employed. Ultimately, the Nazis saw art as a way of
tying commonplace and everyday existence to the totalitarian
state. Art therefore was drained of the personal and the specific
and transformed into stereotypical forms within a new collective
consciousness. Thus, Himmler paid a compliment to the portrait
painter of SS men when he remarked about their pictures, "The
longer you look at these faces, the more familiar they seem" (*241,*
352).

In order to affirm aesthetically the positive and the naive, the Nazis launched a vigorous attack on modernity and experimentation. To expose the "degenerate" nature of modern art, they opened an exhibit on July 19, 1937, in Munich displaying the works of the most distinguished avant-garde painters and sculptors of the 1920s and 1930s: Paul Klee, Otto Dix, Wassily Kandinsky, Franz Marc, Oskar Kokoschka, and Emil Nolde. Their works were held up before the populace "in order to point to the common roots shared by political and cultural anarchy" (*241*). Traveling all over Germany, the "exhibition of degenerate art" was extremely popular. It attracted over two million visitors in four months in Munich and broke attendance records in Berlin, Frankfurt, and Düsseldorf. For some it was the last opportunity within Germany to view the bold experiments and artistic breakthroughs of the Weimar artists, who were being persecuted. The vast majority, however, concurred with the media's condemnation of the exhibit. And Nazi leadership had several reasons for attacking modern art: (1) its own integrity immunized modern art from political exploitation and especially from use as simplistic affirmative propaganda; (2) it did not depict subjects dear to the Nazis; (3) it resisted easy interpretation and simple comprehension, and therefore failed to reinforce clichés, standard perceptions, and stereotypical feelings; (4) it was highly individualistic; and (5) "degenerate art," above all, was not repetitive. It did not reinforce the commonplace assumptions that the Nazis relied on so heavily in setting their own political revolution into motion.

Alfred Rosenberg's criticism of one of the most distinguished modern painters and sculptors, Ernst Barlach, reveals the core of the Nazi value system:

> But when he [Barlach] gives shape to human beings, all is strange, completely strange: earth-bound massiveness and pleasure in the dynamics of what is heavy and massive. These are not "peasants from Mecklenburg," oh no, the peasants stride across the earth in a manner quite different from Barlach's humanity.

(*241*, 51)

The Nazis' reliance on familiar experiences and sentimental impressions in art freed them to pursue relentlessly their march toward totalitarianism in the political realm. Art under the Nazis was a "study in retrogression":

> . . . portraits of generals with uniforms studded with decorations, abbots with crosses, romantic seascapes, romantic landscapes, genre paintings of nineteenth-century life in the provinces . . . peasants in

fields . . . pictures of sunshine filtering through the leaves, peasants saying their prayers at mealtime. . . .

(*133,* 89)

Sentimental themes also prevailed in sculpture where reproduction of "harmoniously beautiful bodies of youthful male and female nudes" (*133,* 83) was emphasized.

The Mecklenburg farmer, the woman holding a sheaf of wheat, the watchful soldier with his gun at rest, the plowman in his field, the chaste nude, the blond girl with a bouquet of flowers—such visual clichés were dear to the Nazis, but they had no place in modern art that portrayed a world profoundly out of joint and given to the death instinct.

Nazi literature likewise popularized the ideological tenets of the new state. Although the role of literature during the twelve years of Nazi reign was not as important as that of the visual arts, a significant number of literary works and histories before 1933 helped prepare the cultural ground for the Nazi rise to power.

## LITERARY HISTORY

Two main schools of literary history were precursors to Nazi culture. One view asserted that history was a monument to great individual geniuses. Thus, the Germanist and cultural historian Friedrich Gundolf organized literature around great writers such as Goethe, Shakespeare, and George. The other view maintained that German literature reflected Germanic tribal and regional patterns in central Europe. Josef Nadler and his school, as the translated title of his influential four-volume work indicates—*Literary History of the German Tribes and Regions* (166)—foreshadowed the blood-and-soil literature of the Nazis and provided a cultural and philosophical justification for it. With an inspired neoromantic prose style filled with metaphors from nature and the heroic age, Nadler created the cultural equivalent of geopolitical space. In rhapsodic cadences that appeared later in Nazi speeches (Nazi Propaganda Minister Goebbels was a trained Germanist and worked on his doctorate under Gundolf in Heidelberg), Gundolf subsumed all social, formal, thematic, and individual characteristics of literature under the broad notion of the "great man." Both trends were mutually reinforcing. One ordered literature from above (according to the principle of the exceptional individual), whereas the other provided determinants from below (tribal origins), and both together formed the link between the great leader and the soul of the people *(Volksseele)* that was essential to Nazi ideology.

These schools of literary history in the 1920s had their origins in Wilhelmian Germany. At the turn of the century, Albert Soergel, a literary and cultural historian of considerable renown, preached German greatness as not heroic and nationalistic enough, concurring with a contemporary criticism of Wilhelmian literature:

> . . . All of these authors taken together lacked revolutionary substance, the norms of the heroic personality; they were too time-bound and matter-of-fact for me to attribute to them a higher significance for the upward spiritual and artistic development of our nation.
>
> *(212,* 7)

Besides Soergel, Moeller Van den Bruck preached a "revolutionary conservatism" as early as the turn of the century. Wilhelmian reactionary trends converged in his writings, which were later used by the Nazis. More than any other cultural historian, he provided a clear link between the Wilhelmian Second Reich and Hitler's Germany. Van den Bruck fervently hoped for the historical moment that would transform Germany into a great and powerful nation ready to fulfill its heroic destiny. He relied heavily on organic metaphors to describe Germany as young and vital, and he hoped for the rise of a spiritual community within its borders. Firmly convinced of the decadence of the "overcivilized" West, he saw in parliamentary democracy just another symptom of the decline of Western culture, a theme that Hitler pursued later in his writings and speeches. Van den Bruck's influential book *Das dritte Reich* (first published in 1923, republished in 1931; *The Third Reich*) served as an ideological bridge between German conservative forces from the Wilhelmian empire and the emerging Nazi movement *(193,* 349).

## LITERARY WORKS

Besides literary and cultural historians, several well-known writers pointed the way to 1933. As early as 1921, E. G. Kolbenheyer wrote a poem *(122,* 666) that prefigured the blood-and-soil mentality. He employed a turgid metaphor in which man, tree, and soil were linked in magic interaction:

> Who can force our hearts
> Who can blind our bright eyes!
> Distress teaches your pulse to sing
> Distress will turn your gaze
> Deep into yourself where the roots of your blood are alive
> And thousands of root-branches, closely intertwined,
> Are firmly pushed into heavy German soil.

The two main prose genres that flourished in the Nazi years were peasant novels and historical novels. The literary output of

Eugen Ortner, for example, glorified the sixteenth-century Fugger family of Augsburg. Merchants with extensive possessions in Venezuela, South America, the Fuggers presented a model of German colonialism that, as history showed, never came to rival the emerging British empire. Peasant novels, on the other hand, extolled the virtues of wholesome community living while portraying the evils of city life. A typical plot presented either a simple country girl seduced by a city slicker or a clean-cut peasant boy lured from the soil by a vice-ridden woman from the big city. Jews, communists, and deviants were the cause of evil, whereas the Teutonic folk symbolized goodness by striving to find living space in which to build a mystical community free of all cultural heterodoxy and class differences. Some blood-and-soil novels took place along the German border in order to pit the German peasants against alien encroachments. The setting of Otto Boris's novel *Der Grenzbauer* (1943; *The Border Farmer*) is the border between Germany and Russia.

The German version of a manifest destiny *(Drang nach dem Osten)* was extolled not only in novels but also in songs and poetry.

> To the East, to the rim of the Carpatian mountains
> fate has driven us
> there we stand plowing the wide land
> just like the ancestors in gray days passed.
> The glance turned eastward,
> the soul with a hopeful vision of
> the homeland long ago sent us to alien lands
> to build a new Germany.

> *(46, 174)*

Other writers contrast the virtue of having stable roots within the borders of Germany with the vice of cosmopolitanism without roots. Internationalism and modern technological civilization were rejected for the sake of a simple agrarian life:

> They are building the Tower of Babylon
> They ride on the ocean through the storm
> They fly over the roof of the world—
> The farmer presses his plow into the earth.

> *("Der Bauer,"* "The Farmer," *227,* 42)

Not only is the rootedness of the peasant stressed in many poems, but the role as a provider is equally praised:

> On our shoulders you all stand
> And when the loud and large city is silent

> We protect it from decay
> And feed its children.
>
> (*44*, 172)

The peasant literature glorified agriculture as a harmonious middle-class idyll in which social contradictions did not exist. Although it preached a return to nature, it had little to do with Jean-Jacques Rousseau's advocacy of the natural human being in the eighteenth century. For Rousseau, people in their natural state possessed a *perfectibilité* that provided them with the rational brain to build a civilization. The Nazi return to nature amounted to an advocacy of primitivism cloaked in sentimentality. As such it provided a convenient excuse for the escape from the complexities of civilized life.

## THE AUTHORS IN "INNER EMIGRATION"

Several well-known authors did not leave Nazi Germany but decided instead to withdraw into their own private worlds. Such an "inner emigration" was quite possible because it fitted neatly into the well-established cultural pattern of the apolitical German. Elisabeth Langgässer's *Gang durch das Ried* (1936; *Walk Through the Fields)* with its inward-looking evocation of a nature mythology is typical for the generation of writers who stayed in Germany. In his novel *Das einfache Leben* (1939; *The Simple Life*), Ernst Wiechert portrayed the life of an ex-officer who attempts to withdraw into an "inner exile" only to be brutally murdered. In the same year Wiechert wrote his *Totenwald* (1946; *The Forest of the Dead*, 1947), a work that was open in its criticism of the Nazi regime. (It was not published until after the war.) In his public speeches at the University of Munich, however, he had the courage to attack the Nazis openly (*46*, 414). He was arrested and sent to the concentration camp at Buchenwald from which he was released only through the intervention of Goebbels.

Whereas the tradition of inner emigration was used by many to camouflage political indifference or even aquiescence to political events within Germany, there were a number of writers and artists who stayed in Germany in spite of their opposition to the regime. They were able to survive only by withdrawing into their private sphere, removed from all political involvement. Two of the most prominent of these were the painter and sculptor Ernst Barlach and the novelist and cultural historian Ricarda Huch. During a 1939 writers' conference in Paris, which was attended by many German refugees, a man who hid his identity behind a mask appeared. A visitor from Nazi Germany, he extended the greetings of antifascist writers still ensconced in the Reich (*46*, 410). A fundamental distinction must be made between those writers who developed an inner emigration as a positive bourgeois ideology of intellectual and artistic autonomy and those who used inner emigration as a political strategy to create active or passive resistance to Nazi totalitarianism. In general, however, inner emigration as a political strategy of resistance remained limited. No significant antifascist literature appeared out of hidden drawers after the collapse of the Third Reich in 1945.

Most important among the authors who stayed in Germany were those who furthered the cause of the Nazis at the beginning, either explicitly (Gottfried Benn) or implicitly (Ernst Jünger), and who in time ran afoul of the regime or became disillusioned with the direction Nazism was taking toward war and genocide.

Gottfried Benn, a poet of great evocative power and formal skills and an admirer of Stefan George, belonged to those who put great faith in the formal rigors of poetry. He shunned all that was individualistic and impressionistic for the sake of artistic formalism and discipline. He placed his conception of art at the service of Nazi culture: "This era that says blood and soil will be an age of discipline, of form, of heightened spirits" (*Lebensweg eines Intellektualisten, The Life Story of an Intellectualist,* written in the form of a testament to Nazi youth, *12,* 59).

Like Stefan George, Benn believed that aesthetics and power should be brought together:

> The new youth belongs to this power. . . . May the stream of the race carry it through the years, through the homes, fields, through their meeting places and graves . . . leading to the final affirmation that the world can only be justified as an aesthetic phenomenon.

> (*12,* 64–65)

However, unlike Stefan George, who was appalled by Hitler's assumption of power, Gottfried Benn had no difficulties in expanding his definition of artistic elitism and formal discipline to include the Nazi collective folk culture as one of its manifestations: "Form: in its name everything was achieved in battle that you now see around you in the New Germany: Form and Discipline: the two symbols of the new empire" (cited by Klaus Mann, *Über Gottfried Benn,* p. 187). Along with advocating formal disciplines, Benn also longed for a more primitive, primeval existence: "Oh, if only we were our distant ancestors,/A clump of slime in a warm swamp" (*"Oh, daß wir unsere Ururahnen wären,/Ein Klümpchen Schleim in einem warmen Moor"*). Klaus Mann, in a letter to Benn from exile in Le Lavandou, France, on May 9, 1933, passionately attacked Benn's advocacy of this irrational primitivism: "Today it almost seems like an inescapable law that too strong a sympathy for the ir-

rational leads inevitably to political reaction if you don't pay hell-
ishly close attention."

Benn's plea for the complete autonomy of art for the sake of
form and discipline is akin to the Nazi's belief in a complete autonomy of the state for the sake of control and power. The Nazi's
search for legitimacy in a folk soul and racial substratum bears re-
semblance to Benn's search for a precivilized primal existence.
Thus, it was not so much that Benn succumbed to Nazi politics but,
rather, that the norms of his artistic creed in the early 1930s resembled Nazi ideas of the totalitarian state. This explains Benn's early
praise of Nazism.

Ernst Jünger's personal experience as a lieutenant fighting
against France in WWI is the subject matter of his early work *In
Stahlgewittern* (1920). In memory of the heroes of that "great
war," Jünger erected a visual monument in his own imagination:

> A picture: the highest alpine peak, hewn in the shape of a face under-
> neath a massive steel helmet that calmly and somberly surveys the land
> down the German Rhine River out into the open sea. . . . One day the
> time will come. . . .

> *(118, 7)*

Jünger inveighed against civilization and advanced the case for the
"heroic core of life": "Compassion is not appropriate in a tragic
world, on the stage of a struggling soul." He carried this Nietz-
schean elitist position a step further and used it to justify martial
conquest: "A conquered province is a great binding symbol"
*(118,)*. By 1939, however, Jünger had undergone a radical change
of mind. His *Auf den Marmorklippen* (1920; *By the Marble Cliffs*;
1947) portrays the life of two brothers who had been part of a rov-
ing band in their youth but had withdrawn from strife to study languages and plant life. Their research led them to discover a
peaceful principle inherent in physical matter: "And joyously we
are overcome by the knowledge that destruction has no place inside the elements . . ." *(117, 77)*. Jünger no longer saw war as a vir-
tuous and uplifting event: "In our weak hours destruction appears
to us as a terrible apparition" *(117, 78)*.

Benn and Jünger are representatives of the conservative cultural
tradition in Germany. The ease with which the views of these
writers could be incorporated into the new collective framework
of totalitarian culture compromised them deeply as it did their conservative contemporaries in politics.

In spite of their insistence on the "Germanness" of their literature, the Nazis could utilize the cultural figures of the German past
only in a very limited way. The Nazis' advocacy of this past tended
to focus on the mythological element of a pre-Christian Germanic

paganism or on a medieval world of fictional knights in armor. In secondary schools and universities, the traditional curriculum based on the established literary canon of the *Bildungsbürger* was not greatly changed in spite of the Nazis' changing emphases. This speaks for the relative autonomy and the relative lack of social relevance of the institutions that upheld the cultural norms and literary canons since the early nineteenth century. The Nazis had their own literary models; however, they did not or could not alter radically the established curriculum of the schools and universities. Goethe's Faust was upheld as a builder of dams and a man of action. Faust's penchant for strife was attributed to his Germanic soul. Friedrich von Schiller was praised for his rebelling in *Die Räuber* (1781) against the brittle authority of a dying order, but the Nazis treated his later works with caution because of Schiller's advocacy of freedom of thought and the deeply moral character of his writings. Heinrich Heine could no longer be read, but the Nazis were particularly attracted to the medieval mystic Meister Eckhart, in whose "joyous message of German mysticism" (*191,* 218) they saw an affirmation of the German racial soul. They radically separated Eckhart's "I am the cause of myself" (*191,* 223) from its theological meaning—he was trying to redefine humanity's closeness to God—and attempted to portray this speculative genius as the prototype of a Nazi leader.

## ARCHITECTURE

Architecture was the ideal manifestation of the Nazi ideology of culture and politics. Many of the Nazi leaders saw their own political work in architectural terms; when they spoke about building a nation and designing a new community, architectural metaphors abounded. Some of them had been trained as architects, for instance, their leading spokesman Alfred Rosenberg. Also Hitler stated in *Mein Kampf* that he had intended to become an architect (*105,* 20). More than merely employing architecture as a convenient metaphor for building a nation, however, the architectural structures were a way of staging the Nazis' new political reality in visual terms. For instance, the colossal party-rally grounds at Nuremberg, with a massive frontal colonnade behind a prominent speaker's platform and a sweeping concrete edifice that framed the actual parade grounds, were not just designed for conveniently holding people. These structures had a specific ideological purpose. Indeed, as Leni Riefenstahl's film *Triumph des Willens* shows, people were removed from their individual settings and molded into large blocks, and these large blocks in turn appeared as a huge organized mass that was as much a part of the architectural frame as the architectural frame was completed by the structured masses it contained: "In these buildings the *Führer* gives shape to the image of the noblest characteristics of the German community" (*31*, 124). The *Bauwille* ("will to build") did not end with the design of buildings and rallying grounds. It was ultimately directed toward redesigning entire cities and shaping landscapes to fit the Nazis' notion of self-preservation. Whether completed or on the drawing boards, architecture embodied the Nazi's vision of the perfect state.

Berlin was to be the architectural center of this structured political universe; it was to be another Mecca or Rome, symbolizing the power center of the movement. In January 1937 Hitler appointed the brilliant Albert Speer as the chief architect of the city of Berlin. He was given considerable freedom and was responsible directly to Hitler. Speer's plan was to design Berlin along the line of two intersecting monumental avenues supported by four concentric ring roads. Collosal buildings attesting to Nazi power were to make the city into a political monument. Likewise, the countryside was to be given structure in this comprehensive architectural vision. Monuments at visible and strategic places, castles serving as educational institutions for the young Nazi elite, temples for art exhibits, sport stadiums, military barracks and exercise grounds, as well as centrally located squares and plazas for parades and rallies, were designed to represent the Reich. The *Autobahnen* crisscrossing the country are visible reminders of Nazi ingenuity and devotion to the pragmatic needs of the people and the military as well as to the aesthetics of a structured landscape. Yet there were limits to these architectural visions. Although Nuremberg, for example, became associated with the Nazi presence (Leni Riefenstahl filmed the huge party rallies that were held there), the city was architecturally quite the opposite of the Nazi ideal of symmetric grandeur poured in light-colored concrete. With its gabled houses, medieval walls, narrow streets, small shops and inns, it was the city of the guilds and tradesmen. It attests to the power of Nazi symbol making that Nuremberg could be visually appropriated in the minds of the people even though parade grounds had to be built at a considerable distance from the city center. Basically, Hitler rejected the medieval city, which incorporated in its architecture the many functions of the merchant and guild culture and the value of artisan individualism. He simply made it part of his architectural propaganda. He also rejected the modern correspondent of the medieval city, namely, the industrial town with its "department stores, bazaars, hotels and skyscrapers" (Hitler, *133*, 108). Needless to say, all modernism in architecture as practiced by famous architects such as Le Corbusier and Walter Gropius were anathema.

Yet Nazi architecture represented not as radical a break from European architectural developments as some ideological statements may seem to indicate. The concept of the "City Crown," a democratic community center (*133*, 108) that would fulfill the individual and collective needs of the inhabitants, was adopted from the Weimar Republic. In matters of design, this architecture was primarily an extension of the neoclassical tradition that had emerged in Europe at the beginning of the twentieth century as a reaction against the "overladen historicism of the late nineteenth century . . ." (*221*, 71). Greco-Roman buildings served as historical models. Particularly the Pantheon in Rome with its massive dome (built in 27 B.C.) was held up as an ideal structure.

A comparison of the Olympic stadiums in Berlin and Munich highlights the ideological posture of Nazi culture in contrast to that of postwar Germany. Framed by a colonnaded façade that intensifies the impression of total Nazi power, the Berlin stadium of 1936 stresses large inner spaces to heighten the "feeling of community" (*221*, 32)—a geopolitical statement in architectural terms. By contrast, the Munich stadium of 1972 articulates an optimistic outlook on the German experiment with parliamentary democracy: the principles of construction are an integral part of the architectural statement. The process of creating the Munich stadium (with the nuts, bolts, support braces and the over-all construction design visible) took precedent over the finished product and the façade.

## FILM

The impressive contribution made by the German expressionist film to Western culture during the Weimar Republic was brought to an abrupt end in 1933. Yet even during the Third Reich, filmmakers and movie stars enjoyed considerable prestige as well as some freedoms and privileges not available to others. That Göring took a personal interest in Gustaf Gründgens, one of the leading German actors of the time, is well known (see Klaus Mann's documentary novel, *Mephisto*, written in 1936, but not published in the FRG until 1981). Before agreeing to film the Berlin Olympic Games, Leni Riefenstahl extracted from the Nazi leadership the promise that there would be no party control over the making of the film and that Hitler would never ask her to make another film (*110*, 74). However, despite the modicum of artistic freedom granted, the finished product, *Olympiad (Olympia)*, did nothing but flatter the Nazi cause.

Throughout the war, the population was provided with many sentimental escapist films that had stereotypical plots and characters. The films illustrate to what degree the consumption of mass culture can be divorced from current events. More important than the entertainment films were a few very skillfully made propaganda films with an anti-Semitic orientation. *Jud Süß* (1940; *Power*) based on a novel by Lion Feuchtwanger, portrays a character who is part Jewish and part German. His dual background is used to depict a battle between good and evil in one man. Another film, *Ohm Krüger* (1941), which portrays the Boer War in South Africa, is stridently anti-British. The older generation of Germans preferred the sentimental escapist movies, but the younger generation tended to flock to the films that had contemporary political import. The effect of these propaganda films on the younger generation was devastating (*110, 169*). All film showings were accompanied by the *Deutsche Wochenschau* (weekly newsreel), which played an ever more important role in rallying support for the increasingly difficult war effort. Prior to the age of television, it was the only visual means the Germans had to form an opinion of the war. Consequently, the Nazis, particularly under the tutelage of Propaganda Minister Goebbels, took great pains in preparing war stories and events for general consumption. The newsreels were stylized to reflect German prowess in victory and heroism in defeat. The subject matter was changed frequently and rapidly so as to minimize the viewers' time for reflection. Musical accompaniment and a strident commentary underscored the propagandistic objectives.

## RADIO

The broadcasting of political events and the semiliterary *Hörspiel* (radio play) played an important role in the Nazi state. Already before Hitler's assumption of power, the importance of the radio for literature and mass communication had been recognized. Goebbels captured its importance for consolidating totalitarian power in his evocation of an entire nation listening to orders:

> . . . Around midnight, in the north and south, east and west, in the large cities and small towns, on lonely coastal islands and in forlorn Black Forest villages, the young and the old, the mighty and the humble, the poor and the rich crowded around the radio and a whole nation was stirred by the magic wing beat of a great historical hour. At that moment, the radio had become political for the first time.

> (*46, 368*)

Before 1933 the impact of the radio play had been a subject of analysis and debate. Whereas some maintained its importance for collective culture, others stressed the individual emotions stirred by the medium (*46, 370*). Both effects fitted neatly into the Nazis' effort to link subjective sentimentality with general totalitarian objectives. Broadcasts and radio plays had the function of reproducing in sound the total experience of a political happening for those who could not participate directly. Speeches were carefully orchestrated with chants, marching boots, applause, and background musical accompaniment.

All forms of expression in the spheres of the arts and literature were without exception integrated into the totalitarian state. Artists and writers succumbed to various degrees to this new culture or embraced it enthusiastically. Those who felt deeply alienated took to inner emigration. Many writers and artists left Germany, taking with them into exile what was precious in German culture.

Significant about the emergence of totalitarian culture was the Nazis' ability to use directly or to translate with little effort the many elements of traditional conservative German cultural values into their own revolutionary context. This was due to the fact that conservative beliefs in Germany tended to focus on a collective system of values. In contrast, the American conservative tradition in the twentieth century has a close affinity with the individualistic, even the anarchic, if we disregard its contemporary theocratic variant.

## NAZI LANGUAGE

The Nazis preferred the spoken to the written word. Hitler's autobiographical work *Mein Kampf* (105) is nothing more than a collection of speeches and declarations. By definition, speaking and listening needs a public and consequently encourages collective behavior. Reading, on the other hand, generally takes place in private and involves only one person with a text. As Christa Wolf noted, reading is more conducive to individualism (240). The Nazis' preference for speaking over writing was determined by necessity. Speech was the most effective way of integrating individuals into a collective framework.

The reduction of language to a propagandistic tool characterized Nazi culture and continued to distort the German language even after the end of the Third Reich in 1945. When one of the leading postwar writers, Heinrich Böll, declared, "It was extremely difficult after 1945 to write half a page of prose" (22), he was referring to the profound abuse the language had suffered through propaganda. A typical deformation involved natural metaphors. Political maneuvers were described as flowing from "natural laws." Interracial marriages became "decompositions of the blood," and interplay between different cultures was synonymous with "poisoning of the folk soul." Social, economic, and political facts were not described directly but were instead translated into metaphors that were left unexplained. Thus, metaphors could be freely chosen and applied with great flexibility to any propagandistic purpose. The use of language as a descriptive tool was undermined in this way for the sake of a language of magic evocation.

Exaggeration was another characteristic distortion of the Nazis' use of German. "Changing one's mind," for example, was called a "profound transformation of consciousness." The founding of the Nazi state was not reckoned in years or centuries but as the beginning of a millennium *(das tausendjährige Reich)*. Paralleling this monumentalization was the employment of extreme diminutives, particularly from the biological world. Enemies, for instance, were referred to as "maggots," "bugs," or "bacilli." Such grand verbal gestures, which alternated between the sublime and the disgusting in sweeping hyperbolic leaps, had a profound effect on the enthralled masses. But this lack of rhetorical proportion also revealed the extent to which the Nazis were incapable of perceiving the world around them in a rational way *(143)*.

Nazi discourse also relied heavily on dualistic patterns: evil/ good, Aryan/non-Aryan, pure/mixed, creative/parasitical, honest/ deceiving. All of these patterns were mere restatements of a basic ideological belief in the Nazis' own superiority. Speakers were free to move from one dualistic pattern to the next. On the surface this gave the listeners the impression that they were following an unfolding thought process, whereas in reality one dualistic pattern merely replaced another in a static and ritualistic evocation of the Nazi world view.

The frequent use of rhetorical questions was also designed to lull the listener into considering Nazi speeches as open-ended, earnestly searching for answers, although in fact the a priori given was evoked over and over.

Key ideological terms were derived from biology, sport, religion, mythology, and warfare. Positive or negative connotations were often transformed into their opposites. For example, the pejorative term *fanatical* was taken to mean "deeply committed." *Culture,* on the other hand, could be changed to mean "effete aestheticism." Goebbels was moved to say, "If I hear the word 'culture' once more, I am going to reach for my pistol." Likewise, the eighteenth-century enlightenment concept of *objectivity* lost its traditionally positive meaning and became debased by a set of irrational and magic notions. Thus, *objectivity* became "soul-less," *cosmopolitanism* became "treason" and *intellectuality* was seen as a "destructive force." Such shifts in meaning were never questioned; justified on the basis of Nazi dogma, they needed no further validation.

A favorite Nazi propaganda phrase was to "tear the mask off things." But in actuality, far from tearing the mask off things, Nazi language disguised its underlying motives to dominate and murder its opponents by attributing these intentions to them. Neither the Nazi language nor the Nazi state allowed for any third terms by which contradictions might be understood. Nazism and its language formed a self-validating system that permitted no changes but offered instead only an endless ritualistic evocation of the same. Thus, the Nazis' "immutable laws of history" were nothing but a projection of their own rigid and static dogma.

In sum, the Nazis perfected language as a propagandistic tool by giving it a dual role: on the one hand, they called forth great historical events and "immutable laws of nature." On the other hand, they appealed to the most primitive instincts of dominance and hatred in the individual listener. The individual was made to feel part of great historical events, whereas these events were given substance and force by the people now willing to believe in them. Such mutual reinforcement also functioned between speaker and listener. The orator became the spokesman of his people while at the same time posing as their faithful servant. The crucial point of this magic use of language was that it allowed neither speaker nor listener to postulate a point of reference outside the totalitarian structure. The result was the ultimate perversion of the Christian *logos*.

# 6.  World War II: Main Events

In the early morning hours of September 1, 1939, Hitler's army crossed the border into Poland. This open aggression against a neighboring country unleashed WWII, which rapidly spread from Europe to engulf more than fifty countries. During the war, the lives of at least fifty million servicemen and civilians were lost; as a result of the war, the largest forced migration of people in history took place.

The main causes of WWII can be found in the fascist response to the unsolved problems of WWI, the ill-conceived Treaty of Versailles, the severe economic depression, and the inability of weak democratic European governments to cope with these crises and to prevent right-wing takeovers. As a result, the driving forces of Europe's political life in the 1930s became Adolf Hitler in Germany, Benito Mussolini in Italy, and Francisco Franco in Spain. With Hitler, however, rests the responsibility for beginning a war that was neither foreseen nor desired by the German people and opposed by his own general staff.

Nazi demands for more territory revived German imperialism from the Wilhelmian era. They also were a backlash against the Treaty of Versailles, which took away all of Germany's colonies as well as one-sixth of its land. The Treaty forbade a union with Austria in spite of the Austrian Parliament's vote in favor of such a union; it led to the occupation of the left bank of the Rhineland and to the internationalization of German rivers; it demanded huge war reparations and decreed the dismantling of factories and the forced delivery of coal, livestock, and parts of the German merchant fleet to the victorious powers. Although a revision of the Treaty was under way before Hitler's rise to power, these harsh conditions contributed to the failure of the Weimar Republic and to the rise of totalitarianism.

The war was the final step in Hitler's attempt to rescind the results of the Treaty of Versailles and to give Germany the victory that had eluded the Kaiser in WWI. Hitler promised to devour his enemies one by one and avoid the stalemate of trench warfare. Instead he would employ Karl von Clausewitz's ingenious blitzkrieg method to crush six countries in three months (1940).

Hitler's immediate pretext for starting war was the unresolved problem of the Free City of Danzig and the Polish corridor to East Prussia. He demanded a revision of the eastern frontiers as decreed at Versailles and the return of Danzig to Germany. This gave him the excuse to invade Poland. Stalinist Russia, which had signed a nonaggression treaty with Hitler's Germany in August 1939, had sanctioned a partitioned Poland in accordance to which it would annex East Poland after the German conquest. Immediately the battle lines were drawn. As in WWI, Great Britain and France confronted the Axis (*Dreimächtepakt* formed by Germany, Italy, and Japan in September 1940), which did not close the door to a possible alliance with the Soviet Union. In spite of his arrogant promises not to repeat the WWI mistake of battles on several fronts, Hitler did just that and worse: his troops overran the neutral countries of Denmark, Norway, Belgium, and the Netherlands. After the defeat of France within five weeks (the armistice of June 22, 1940, was signed in the same railway coach at Compiègne forest as in 1918), a turning point came in the war when the British Royal Air Force defeated the German *Luftwaffe* in the Battle of Britain between September 1940 and May 1941.

A year after France's fall and on the anniversary of Napoleon's attack 129 years earlier, Hitler invaded Russia, anticipating another blitzkrieg victory over an "inferior race." Three million German soldiers, ill prepared for winter warfare, were sent across the border. They were spread along a 2,000-mile front line to "save the entire world from the dangers of Bolshevism." This slogan was used to cover up the fiendish design of liquidating the Slavic race in Russia's western regions in order to make room for German settlers and to gain access to Russia's raw materials. The attempt to simultaneously subdue three bastions of Soviet power—Leningrad, Moscow, and Stalingrad—led to Hitler's military undoing in Russia.

As the German troops bogged down during the first Russian winter, Hitler, repeating the mistake of WWI, declared war on the United States in December 1941, shortly after his ally Japan attacked Pearl Harbor on December 7. Thus the stage was set for a global war in which German soldiers held the line at four fronts. At its height in September 1942, the Axis empire extended from Norway to Greece and North Africa, and from France to Stalingrad. Domestically, Hitler crushed all resistance within Germany and committed genocide according to his racist theories.

Several towns that line the path of WWII have become symbols of memorable historical events. Munich became a synonym for appeasement. Dunkirk came to signify the retreat and evacuation of British, French, and Belgian troops in May 1940. The bombing of cities became symbolic of the terror exerted by each side: the destroying of Rotterdam, one hour after the Netherlands had already surrendered in May 1940 and then the destruction of Coventry and its cathedral in November 1940. These attacks were answered by Allied bombings of military and civilian targets, culminating in the firebombing of refugee-filled Dresden in February 1945, an air raid in which an estimated 135,000 persons perished. As in the case of many other German cities and towns before and after, Dresden was put to the torch in an effort to intimidate the population. The terrible irony was that the government continued to increase its hold over a suppressed populace that was continually traumatized by bombings and strafings. Finally, Auschwitz and all the other concentration camps came to symbolize the extremes of racial brutality and the use of a war machine for genocide.

If the Axis enjoyed the apogee of its power during the late summer of 1942, the beginning of the end already loomed when the Germans lost the air battle over Britain in May 1941, and definitely by December of 1941, when the Russians counterattacked for the first time in the Battle of Moscow, and, finally, when the United States joined the war after the Japanese bombing of Pearl Harbor. German scholars prefer to take the defeat at Stalingrad in February 1943 as the turning point of the war, because this debacle was quickly followed by surrender in North Africa in May 1943, the Allies' landing in Sicily in July 1943, and D-Day in Normandy on June 6, 1944. At Stalingrad the Russians beat the Germans at their own game, namely, the *Kesselschlacht,* encircling battle. The Russians destroyed an entire army caught partially in their trap by Hitler's order not to retreat from the exposed forward position. The overextension of the front line (by now about 3,000 miles long) made the supply routes vulnerable to partisan attacks during the harsh Russian winter. Goebbels' propaganda machine tried to exploit these decisive defeats to push the German people into a total-war effort *(232).*

The early period of staggering German successes prior to the downturn in 1942 took everyone by surprise and rallied even the German skeptics around the *Führer,* whose military victories seemed to restore for many the superiority and glory of the German nation. But catastrophes followed, climaxing in the collapse of the Third Reich in April of 1945.

Why had so many countries besides Japan and Italy joined Germany in its war efforts, namely, Bulgaria, Finland, Hungary, and Romania, not to mention the divisions of volunteers from Slovakia, Spain, and Vichy-France sent to fight the Soviet Union? As neighboring countries they had little choice, crushed as they were under the Nazi heel. Moreover, they were impressed by the initial German victories, and many were attracted to the racial policies. Collaborators, such as Vidkun Quisling in Norway, were in agreement with Nazi ideology, and Marshal Henri-Philippe Pétain of southern France (1940–1944) was not unsympathetic to Nazi aims either.

The German people, threatened by the Allies' demands for unconditional surrender since January 1943 and at the same time spurred on to a total-war effort, were in an untenable position. They had lived under a totalitarian regime since 1933. The historian Golo Mann explains the surprising bond between the dictator and the people by citing the following motives: "patriotism, habit of obedience, fear, cynicism" *(152,* 971). In the end, however, this cohesion did not prevent a rapid collapse of the Third Reich. Within a year of the last German offensive on the eastern front in July 1943, the Russians had recaptured their lost territory, defeated the four Axis satellites (Romania, Bulgaria, Finland, and Hungary), and taken Vienna as well as Warsaw. As Russian armies rolled toward Berlin, the Allies raced toward the heart of Germany from the west to meet the Soviets at the Elbe River in Torgau. By the time part of Berlin was reduced to rubble under the final onslaught of the Red Army, all German cities and middle-sized towns had been laid waste by Allied bombing. Hitler committed suicide in Berlin in April 1945. The destruction of civilian life and property had reached incalculable proportions because of Allied attacks, Hitler's measures against the "enemies of the people" within Germany, and the systematic extermination of the Jews accelerated during the last months of the war.

Despite the horrors, heroic deeds were performed in the resistance movement both outside of Germany, where the guerrilla movement in the Balkan States, the U.S.S.R., Italy, and France led to success, and inside the Reich where it failed but, according to Churchill, provided the only light in the overall darkness.

# 7. Holocaust

The systematic liquidation of European Jews stands out as the most brutal legacy of the Third Reich. The path led from the gradual exclusion of Jews from German society in the 1930s to the "final solution" (Nazi euphemism for genocide) toward the end of the war. Beginning in 1933 the Nazis tried to homogenize German society by eliminating all distinctions based on class, religion, economics, and institutional loyalty. For the populace, this meant either falling in line with the Nazis' totalitarian dictates, flight into exile, or, for those unfortunate enough to be marked as "unintegratable," physical removal and elimination. The Nazis' racial mythology postulated an Aryan superiority as a justification for violence against those deemed inferior. The more the Nazis succeeded in branding the Jews a foreign race, the better were the chances of convincing the Germans of their own uniqueness. After 1933, however, the underlying aim of propaganda was more the self-definition of a totalitarian state than the scapegoating of Jews for all the German ills since the Treaty of Versailles.

During the early stages of Nazi rule, two laws were introduced that drastically curtailed the civil liberties of the Jews. In April, 1933, the "Aryan Paragraph" decreed that Jews could not hold civil-service positions. On September 15, 1935, the "Nuremberg Laws for the Protection of German Blood and Honor" forbade marriages between Jews and Germans, and stripped the Jews of their German citizenship. Initially these state-sponsored anti-Semitic laws reduced random acts of violence against the Jews. During their first years in power, it was not in the interest of the Nazis to cause major social disruptions at a time when economic conditions were unstable. They also felt it prudent to keep a low profile before the rest of the world and to profit coincidentally from the legitimacy that Italian fascism had achieved under Mussolini since 1922 in the eyes of significant segments of Western society. Yet the gradual stripping of civil rights followed well-planned steps. The Jews were slowly excluded from significant professions: they were no longer allowed to be lawyers (July 22, 1934), professors (December 13, 1934), writers (April 12, 1935), engineers (January 20, 1938), and real-estate agents (July 6, 1938). Students were expelled from universities (July 7, 1935) and children from public schools (November 15, 1938). Paralleling this gradual exclusion were the limits set on their freedom to participate in social activities. Jews were excluded from public baths (July 28, 1935) and hunting (February 1937); they were prohibited from changing their names (January 5, 1938); and restrictions on movement were introduced in local as well as nationwide laws. In this erosion of rights between

1933 and 1938 the Nazis did not press the attack on Jewish civil liberties to the point where public reaction, either nationally or internationally, might have been triggered. A general lack of sensitivity among the German populace gave the Nazis a free hand in pursuing their repressive policies against individuals and groups. Furthermore, those Germans who might have wanted to object had no means of expressing their displeasure without great personal risk.

In 1938 there was radical change in the treatment of Jews. The signal for that change was a seemingly spontaneous uprising of the German people against the Jews. But the "uprising" actually consisted of a series of carefully planned acts of violence perpetrated by Nazi thugs all over Germany during the *Kristallnacht* (Night of Shattered Glass) on November 9. The German public in general did not approve of the events of the *Kristallnacht,* partially out of sympathy with the Jews and partially because an attack on persons and property constituted a general disturbance of the peace. Even Göring complained that the wanton destruction of Jewish property damaged the economic well-being of Germany (*169,* 477).

The *Kristallnacht* initiated the second phase of persecution after the systematic exclusion of Jews from social, economic, and cultural life. It marked the beginning of their physical liquidation. A basic shift in methods of violence ensued—from open, random actions on the streets, which were seen and heard by everyone, to the hidden application of an efficient apparatus for organizing, transporting, and killing millions of human beings. The Holocaust became a triumph of technical perfection in the name of the abstract principle of racial superiority. A Nazi elite perfected the machinery for the reduction of human beings to a disposable mass just as ten years earlier Goebbels had talked of transforming the inchoate mass of Germans into an instrument of the state.

From a psychological point of view, the world witnessed a coming together of superego and the instinctual without any third instance to mediate between them. This fatal harmony between order and instinct characterized Nazi mentality on a personal and on a collective level: a smoothly running bureaucratic machine functioned as an instrument of a totalitarian state and, therefore, as an expression of mass will, bestowing legitimacy on the most base instincts of sadism and violence of its ruling elite. Under Nazism, public morality was exterminated along with the victims.

Shortly after the invasion of Poland, the beginning of WWII, Hitler announced on October 6, 1939, that "resettlement plans" for the Polish Jews had been drawn up. Six days later the first deportations of Jews from occupied Czechoslovakia to Poland took place. As of November 23, all Jews in Poland and Germany were required to wear a visible emblem (a yellow star) in order to distinguish them from the rest of the population. On July 31, 1941, a few weeks after

the Nazi invasion of the Soviet Union, Göring gave Reinhard
Heydrich, chief of the Gestapo, orders to carry out the "final solution." To help him in the task, Heydrich mustered up the bureaucratic talents of the regime. Adolf Eichmann, one of the leading
transportation experts, was selected to set the extermination machinery into motion. He had made a name for himself with his organizational talents in resettling Austrian Jews after the annexation
of Austria to the Reich (*136,* 107). By December 1941 the annihilation of the Jews in the East had become a matter of official state
policy (*136,* 293). Large extermination camps were constructed—
Bergen-Belsen, Buchenwald, and Auschwitz among others. By the
summer of 1942, more than 150,000 exhausted slave laborers had
been murdered. In Auschwitz alone 4 crematoriums with 46
ovens, able to dispose of 12,000 bodies daily, were operating at
full capacity. The Warsaw Ghetto with its almost half a million
Jews fought back against impossible odds. Estimates as to the number of Jews killed in the Holocaust vary, but it is generally estimated that 6 million European Jews perished at the hands of the
Nazis.

The following breakdown is generally considered to be the most
accurate statistical account of Nazi brutality against the European
Jews (*10,* 335).

## TOTAL JEWISH LOSSES IN THE HOLOCAUST

| | |
|---|---|
| Polish-Soviet area | 4,565,000 |
| Germany | 125,000 |
| Austria | 65,000 |
| Czechoslovakia | 277,000 |
| Hungary | 402,000* |
| France | 83,000* |
| Belgium and Luxemburg | 24,700 |
| Holland | 106,000 |
| Italy | 7,500* |
| Norway | 760 |
| Romania (excluding Bessarabia, northern Bukovina and northern Transylvania) | 40,000 |
| Yugoslavia | 60,000* |
| Greece | 65,000 |
| | 5,820,960 |

*Number may be underestimated.

These 5.8 million Jews were 34 percent of the entire Jewish population of Europe. In addition, there were more than 2 million other
victims: political undesirables, the mentally retarded, homosex-
uals, Russian prisoners of war, gypsies.

However, cold statistics, rational discourse about causes, narrative accounts of murderous events, fictionalized representations in
film—none of these efforts at communication come to terms with
the Holocaust as an experience of individual human beings. The
mere word *extermination* has an abstract ring to it that covers up
rather than reveals the particular brutality of Nazi mass murder. Extermination was carried out by working malnourished victims to
death in slave-labor camps, by physical torture individually administered, or as a result of sadistic medical experiments (for example,
bones of living human beings were amputated to be used for trans-
planting, high pressure- and low-temperature chambers were built
to test the physical limits of the human body). Eventually gassing
became the most frequent means of extermination when mass
shootings were determined inefficient.

It is not just the limit of language but also the statistical figure of
5.8 million itself that hides the unspeakable suffering of one individual human being in the Nazi inferno. The voice of one of the
survivors from the Polish concentration camp at Treblinka speaks
for the suffering of all:

> . . . When we carried, or more correctly, dragged, the bodies away,
> we were made to run, and were beaten for the least delay. The dead
> had been lying there for a long time. They had already begun to de-
> compose. There was a stench of death and decomposition in the air.
> Worms crawled on the wretched bodies. When we reached the huts in
> the evening each one of us began to search for people he had known
> the day before—in vain—they were not to be found, they were no
> longer among the living. . . .

(4, 355)

Even when seen through the eyes of one of the victimizers, an en-
gineer in charge of the technical machinery, the eerie truth becomes tangible, specific, and indelibly edged into the collective
conscience of twentieth-century humanity:

> Then they climb up a little staircase and see the truth. Nursing mothers
> with an infant at the breast, naked; many children of all ages, naked.
> They hesitate, but they enter the death chambers, most of them silent,
> forced on by those behind them, who are driven by the whiplashes of
> the SS men. A Jewish woman of about 40, with flaming eyes, calls
> down [revenge] for the blood of her children on the head of the mur-

derers. Police Captain Wirth in person strikes her in the face 5 times with his whip, and she disappears into the gas chamber. . . .

(*4*, 350)

Meanwhile Himmler, the man in charge of concentration camps, stated before an assembly of SS officers meeting in Poznan, Poland, on October 4, 1943:

All in all, however, we can say that we have carried out this most difficult of tasks in a spirit of love for our people. And we have suffered no harm to our inner being, our soul, our character . . .

(*4*, 345)

Where were the Allies? Why did they not act?

The first detailed account of mass murder reached the West in May-June 1942. The report, prepared by the Bund leadership in Poland, said that the Germans had "embarked on the physical extermination of the Jewish population on Polish soil." The number of victims was estimated at 700,000. In June and July, the gist of the report was broadcast over the BBC and published in the press, first in Britain and then in the United States.

(*10*, 300)

Nothing was done.

Indeed, there is much evidence of Allied culpability in denying help to the European Jews fleeing from Nazi violence and extermination: In the U.S., "from July 1, 1932 to July 1 1938, only 26% of the available German quota visas were issued, and of those, 31% were not given to Jews," thus preventing persecuted Jews from entering the country (Congressional Record, Vol. 130, Nr. 92, June 29, 1984). Great Britain and Canada proved even less willing to accept Jews.

The most tragic case of Allied indifference involved the voyage of the *SS St. Louis*, which carried 907 primarily German Jews across the Atlantic. In violation of previous agreements, the ship was denied entrance to Cuba. Subsequent attempts to help these hapless victims of the Third Reich land on U.S. shores failed. Eventually the *SS St. Louis* had no choice but to return to Europe, where most of its passengers met their deaths in concentration camps (Congressional Record, Vol. 130).

The Holocaust remains with us not only as a central fact of modern European history but also as a warning for the future:

It is essential to realize that we live in an era in which Holocausts are possible, though not inevitable. The Holocaust was produced by factors that still exist in the world, factors such as deep hatreds, bureaucracies capable and willing to do the bidding of their superiors, modern technology devoid of moral directions, brutal dictatorships, and wars. If this is so, who can say which peoples could be the future victims, who the perpetrators. Who might the Jews be next time?

(*10,* 336)

# 8. Resistance

The German resistance—who were the participants? Why did they fail? Did they make a difference? Historians have raised these questions since WWII and have assessed them from a variety of viewpoints. But only recently have documents become available that facilitate a relatively objective assessment of the facts. During WWII the question of survival and accomodation was paramount among the German people. After 1945 nobody wanted to be reminded of the past. People were busy rebuilding their shattered lives. There was little interest abroad in acknowledging the existence of a German resistance movement during the war, when Allied propaganda equated Germans with Hitler, and then during the cold-war period, when interest in the anticommunist posture of Nazism revived. A noteworthy exception to this neglect was Winston Churchill's statement to the British House of Commons on July 20, 1946:

> In Germany an opposition lived, which was progressively weakened in its numbers through its sacrifices and through enervating international politics but which belongs to the noblest and greatest things ever produced in the history of all peoples.

Although the German resistance was not a unified movement, it was active from 1933 until 1945. At first it did not include the middle class, which had been neutralized by the promise of jobs, national glory, and revenge for the defeat of 1918. Instead resistance was limited to the workers and organizers in the Social Democratic and Communist parties who had opposed the Nazis before 1933 and who continued with their illegal underground activities. As early as 1933 about half a million dissenters, mainly leftists, were imprisoned (*236,* 132). Between 1935 and 1936 the Gestapo crushed most of the remaining organizations.

The second phase of resistance started in 1934 with the establishment of the totalitarian system through *Gleichschaltung* and by increased terror after most of the liberal or leftist opposition had been muzzled or liquidated. This phase lasted until 1942 and involved many groups. The final period began in the fall of 1942 when German defeat on the battlefield already loomed large. By that time even the successful removal of Hitler probably would have come too late to influence the outcome of the war. Several attempts on his life preceded the well-known abortive attempt of July 20, 1944.

Today it is clear that resistance existed not only in the form of systematic opposition by political groups and the military but also in a passive form by the general public. This kind of opposition was also found in Austria and German-occupied territories where it was often transformed into partisan activities. It extended far beyond German borders if the antifascist efforts of German exile writers are taken into consideration. Resistance took many forms, including the dissemination of hostile jokes and "unofficial" news, the refusal to say "Heil Hitler," sloppy workmanship, slowdowns and strikes, sabotage, radio transmissions and distribution of leaflets, even the planning of assassinations, and guerrilla warfare (236, 21).

Of particular interest is the diplomatic and the civil-service opposition, which used established government channels to work for a quick end to the war. These resisters were found in the lowest governmental echelons as well as the counterintelligence branch (for example, Hans von Dohnanyi) and also in the Foreign Ministry (for example, State Secretary Ernst von Weizsäcker). Many individuals opposed to the system turned to inner emigration and continued their pursuits as academics, physicians, lawyers, or artists without agreeing to the party line (236, 203 f.). Those opposing the regime publicly lost their livelihood (1,300 in 1933 alone; 236, 216) and were either imprisoned or killed (236, 205).

Members from four major sectors of the population resisted the Nazis actively: the churches, the political parties and workers, the middle-class youth and its leaders, and the military (236). By the outbreak of WWII, approximately a million Germans had been sent to concentration camps for primarily political reasons.

Rural Catholic communities with their cultural infrastructure and the Protestant Bekennende Kirche (Confessional Church), headed by Martin Niemöller, protested against the Nazi-dominated Deutsche Christen, the persecution of Jews, and the suppression of human rights. Niemöller, in 1937, was among the first of many pastors who were sent to concentration camps. Among Catholics, Clemens August von Galen, bishop of Münster, gained equal stature as an outspoken opponent of forced euthanasia. Dietrich Bonhoeffer, a towering figure from the Bekennende Kirche, strove for Christian unity in opposition to Hitler, the "Antichrist." For Bonhoeffer, who maintained contacts with George Bell, Anglican bishop of Chichester, and with leading German politicians of the resistance, freedom was not to be found in lofty ideas but only in deeds. Like

most of his collaborators, he was caught and hanged shortly before
the end of the war. Yet his writings *Widerstand und Ergebung,
Briefe und Aufzeichnungen aus der Haft,* 1951 (*Letters and Papers from Prison,* 1951); *Gemeinsames Leben,* 1939 (*Life Together,* 1954) remain a monument to this great moral man.

After the opposition parties, particularly the SPD and KPD, had
been crushed and their members in the *Reichstag* murdered, only
small cells continued their work. One of the most important resistance groups, whose members came from all walks of life and political convictions, was the *Rote Kapelle* (Red Band). This group
sympathized and established radio contact with the Soviet Union
and also provided Moscow with military information (*236,* 188–
203).

Resistance also emanated from certain university and youth organizations that traced their roots back to romantic idealism and
opposition to the conventionality of Wilhelmian Germany. These
groups were banned and their leaders persecuted. Many of them
were killed in prison or concentration camps. The *Hitlerjugend*
(Hitler Youth, HJ) took on the outward appearance and the organizational patterns of these earlier youth groups but perverted their
goals and methods (*236,* 79f.). Hans Scholl and his sister Sophie,
members of the resistance group *Weiße Rose* (White Rose), organized a number of underground cells in Munich and other big
cities; but they and five of their friends as well as their mentor, philosophy professor Kurt Huber, were arrested for distributing leaflets at the Munich University and executed in 1943. Hans Scholl's
motto in prison was: "Hold out in defiance to despotism."

Motives among military resisters ranged from fear of defeat in
war and loss of career to genuine moral outrage and disrespect for
Hitler among aristocratic Prussian officers. Approximately 25,000
death sentences were passed in military courts between 1939 and
1945. There can be no doubt that among them a considerable
number of common soldiers died because of their courage to disobey, mutiny, or to commit treason by aiding the enemy. Of particular interest, however, are the generals and officers, who were the
only hope for a successful opposition to Hitler. After Ludwig Beck,
chief of the army general staff, had resigned during the summer of
1938 in protest of the imminent invasion of Czechoslovakia, military resistance was coordinated by the *Große Organisation,* a cell
led by Hans Oster and Hans von Dohnanyi in the security branch
of the army under the protection of Admiral Wilhelm Canaris from
1941 until its discovery in 1943. This circle of conspirators maintained contacts with the army (Beck, Field Marshal Erwin von
Witzleben, Friedrich Olbricht, Henning von Tresckow), the
churches (Bonhoeffer, Clemens August von Galen), labor (Jakob
Kaiser, Wilhelm Leuschner, Julius Leber), the civilian opposition

(Carl Friedrich Goerdeler, former major of Leipzig), and the Vatican. Goerdeler had formed a shadow cabinet and used his practical experience as a local politician to unite the noncommunist civilian opposition with the disaffected military. After the liquidation of the *Große Organisation,* the Kreisauer Circle, under the direction of Helmuth James von Moltke in Silesia, became the center of resistance. It provided new energy to the movement by linking the aristocratic military caste with a civilian underground composed of workers and the middle class. Its long-range goal was to build a Germany based on Christian socialism, but the accelerating war prodded this group to risk a coup d'état (*91,* 253).

Claus von Stauffenberg, chief of the general staff of the reserve army, had links to the *Große Organisation,* Goerdeler, and von Moltke. He acted on behalf of a considerable number of top generals, their staffs, and of commanders in the field, who in one way or other were all privy to the culminating plot of July 20, 1944, to kill Hitler. Von Stauffenberg was not willing to shoot Hitler on the spot because he had a second job to do—namely, to direct the coup in Berlin. Von Stauffenberg placed a bomb under an oak table in a barrack in Hitler's *Wolfsschanze* (Wolf's Lair, East Prussia) where a meeting was to take place. But Hitler survived the blast. This abortive attempt did not dissuade the rebel troops from marching on Berlin in an attempt to secure key offices of the Reich government. But they were halted by the SS and guard batallions after news of Hitler's escape had spread. Von Stauffenberg was executed that night in Berlin, and about the same time the leaders of the resistance (von Moltke, Leber, von Tresckow, Oster, Beck, Goerdeler) were arrested. Nearly all were executed before the end of the war, including the most celebrated German hero of WWII, Field Marshal Erwin Rommel, who was forced to take poison. Among the most active resisters (for example, Gerhard von Schwerin, captain in the general staff, and Fabian von Schlabrendorff, *196*), there was a definite "preponderance of Prussian names" (*187,* 169). Perhaps as many as 5,000 conspirators (among them 2,000 officers) were sentenced to death, tortured, and executed. The system waded in the blood of its opponents, who were the best from all classes, creeds, and regions.

One question remains unanswered. Why was this elite unsuccessful in its many attempts to remove Hitler and his clique? Perhaps, most importantly, because the tradition of subordination and obedience permeated not only the Nazi system of the leader's absolute power but also the German mentality in general; it erected a powerful barrier to surmount. Beyond this, Allied policies compounded rather than relieved the problems confronting the German internal opposition. First of all, Allied appeasement policy before 1939 hampered the resistance. "The Munich appeasement

[1938] had been a catastrophe for the German resistance" (David Astor, *Die Zeit,* July 22, 1969, p. 3). The Allies were not helpful in providing contacts or arms to the underground. Secondly, the Allied demand for an unconditional German surrender in January 1943 deprived army commanders of an important incentive to rebel openly. Contacts of the Goerdeler-Beck group with England and America via the Vatican, the bishop of Chichester, and Swedish bankers until 1944 did not lead anywhere. Thus the conspirators were finally thrown back on their own resources and consciences (*91,* 254 f.).

Why was the European resistance movement so successful outside but not inside the Reich? The examples of Napoleon in France and Stalin in Russia show that resistance against a dictatorship in one's own country has always been much more difficult and dangerous than against foreign occupation troops. This was especially so, when fighting the best-trained terror machine the world had ever seen: a most efficient system consisting of police, Gestapo, the SS, the SD, and special squads, all of them dominated by brutal diehards who could rely on countless sympathizers to denounce all manifestations of antifascist activity. The physical logistics of reaching Hitler, particularly after February 1943, when he was constantly hiding from the public, compounded the difficulties. Hitler seemed to have had a foreboding whenever an attempt on his life was planned. Moreover, military personnel had an especially hard time justifying disobedience before their own consciences and their people. They had sworn the Fahneneid (oath of loyalty) to the *Führer* and had become the means by which he achieved his early *Blitzkrieg* (lightning war) successes. Also, they could not expect the populace to support their conspiracy.

And yet, the documents reveal that the resistance did not fail for want of commitment. As early as July 1938 Beck wrote to Manfred von Brauchitsch: "There are limits to your obedience—when your knowledge, your conscience, and your sense of responsibility prevent you from carrying out an order." Many shared this view and were to pay for it with their lives. Major General von Tresckow maintained, "The moral worth of a man begins at the point where he is ready to sacrifice his life for his convictions" (*187,* 161). He believed, in 1944, a coup attempt should be made at all costs, even if it failed: "For it is no longer a question of practicality but solely of the German resistance movement having dared to strike the decisive blow" (*196,* 138). Like the Christian leader Bonhoeffer, German army generals were willing to accept the defeat of their nation and to sacrifice their lives so that Germany, Europe, and Christian civilization might survive. In the best tradition of the Prussian ideal, to be bound to duty alone, they listened to their consciences and acted accordingly. Their actions became especially remarkable because no tradition of resistance to authority had existed in German history. Rebellion was viewed as the devil's work and later on as undermining the supreme authority of the state.

Many pondered the question of how one could oppose Hitler, thereby risking the lives of German soldiers at the front, and at the same time remain loyal to Germany. Willy Brandt, for example, was long considered a traitor because of his participation in the Scandinavian underground. But it was precisely his actions and the sacrifices of others like him that contest the notion of a collective guilt of the German people. Their courageous resistance, although unsuccessful, constitutes the only honorable chapter in the otherwise dark first half of twentieth-century German political history. It was men and women like these who helped rebuild democracy after 1945 and who "shaped the outlines of postwar cultural renewal" and inspired the "basic guidelines for West European integration" (237, 111), in particular Kurt Schumacher, Konrad Adenauer, Gustav Heinemann, Eugen Gerstenmaier, Jakob Kaiser, Willy Brandt and Hans Speidel.

# 9.  Expulsion of Germans from Eastern Europe

The turning point in the history of Slavic-German relations came in 1945 when descendants of the medieval German settlers were expelled. The expulsion of Germans east of the Oder River was not the consequence of a long latent Slavic desire for revenge harking back to the Middle Ages, but of Hitler's ferocious *Drang nach Osten* (drive to the East) to secure additional *Lebensraum* (living space) for the German people by subjugating the Slavs. Heinrich Himmler and his SS were put in charge of extermination and slave labor to fulfill Hitler's goal to destroy the *Lebenssubstanz* (life sustenance) of Poland. Himmler echoed Hitler's sentiment in stating he was concerned with other peoples only "in so far as they are usable as slave laborers to support our culture."

After the brutal subjugation of Czechoslovakia in 1938 and Poland in 1939, Russia was taken by surprise in 1941 by the attacking German army. Here too extermination and enslavement followed with the aim of replacing the "inferior" Slavs by Nordic stock. Himmler proclaimed that Slavic children did not need more than four years of schooling. They should be able to sign their names, count to fifty, serve their masters obediently, praise God for allowing them to be ruled by the German superrace. Under district administrator Erich Koch, this genocidal policy reached its peak in the Ukraine, where the SS and special squads behaved like the

Mongols after the battle of Liegnitz in 1241, raping, torturing, and murdering the populace. All in all, Nazi forces killed 35 million Slavs and Jews—on the battlefield, in concentration camps, through mass executions, and starvation. Seven million foreign workers were conscripted for slave labor in German factories. The SS-planned genocide of the Slavic race was carried out quite often with the complicity of the German army.

The twentieth-century invasion of four million German soldiers across the eastern front contrasts sharply with the colonizing efforts in the thirteenth and fourteenth centuries. The latter also had their dark moments but by and large led to the peaceful coexistence of Slavic and German farmers. The murderous advance following 1938, however, could only arouse resistance and hatred in the oppressed peoples. It was Nazi hubris that unleashed the wrath of the victors and led to the expulsion of the German population, largely farmers.

Until recently, the expulsion and dispossession of Germans from eastern territories has not been adequately documented. A sixty-page West German government document dealing with this subject, completed in 1969, was never published because of anticipated political repercussions. More recently several books on this topic have appeared *(20; 51; 199)*.

The Potsdam Conference in 1945 was the final step in a series of international conferences that began in Casablanca where in 1943 the formula for Germany's "unconditional surrender" was determined. The Big Three—Churchill, Roosevelt, and Stalin—conferred at Tehran in November to December of 1943 and decided: (1) to expand Poland's German borders to the Oder-Neisse rivers in compensation for the loss of eastern Poland to the Russians up to the Curzon Line; (2) Russia would receive northern East Prussia and Königsberg (now Kaliningrad); and (3) Germany would be divided according to a map drawn up for the Roosevelt-Churchill Conference of Quebec (London Protocol, September 1944). Poland and Germany were also topics of the Yalta Conference in February 1945 when the plans previously discussed at Tehran were agreed upon in principle.

The redrawing of the map of eastern Europe, particularly as it affected the transfer of German territories to Poland and the Soviet Union, set the stage for the mass exodus of Germans from the east. Their great westward movement had already begun during WWII: *Volksdeutsche* (ethnic Germans) were brought back to the Reich from the Baltic states and Bessarabia (the lower Danube) as a result of population-transfer treaties negotiated by Hitler in 1939 and 1941 and the military evacuation organized by the retreating German army after 1943. This involved 350,000 Russian Germans mainly from around the Black Sea. However, major phases of the refugee migration were the result of a disorganized flight from the Russian army toward the end of the war and of state-decreed expulsions immediately after the war. The peoples of eastern Europe took revenge and mistreated many of the millions of fleeing Germans. Russian soldiers verified the harsh treatment meted out to the East Prussian population. Among others, Lev Kopelev, who showed mercy toward German women and children, was sentenced after the war to ten years' imprisonment because of "sympathy with the German enemy" *(125)*. Field Marshal Bernard Law Montgomery reported the raping and murdering of German civilians by the "barbarous Asiatics." The American military command, on orders from the State Department, shares some responsibility for the forceful expulsion of over a million *Volksdeutsche,* especially young people from the Sudetenland of Czechoslovakia and the Siebenbürgen region of Romania, as well as Russian Germans from the Volga (45,000 were handed over officially). Hundreds of thousands of prisoners of war and refugees who had reached the British and American lines held by Eisenhower's troops were herded back at gunpoint into train convoys of the Russian army during the so-called Operation Keelhaul between 1945 and 1946. Only half of the 3.8 million German war prisoners returned; the others disappeared in the Siberian labor camps *(15).*

The German navy rescued two to three million civilians and soldiers by taking them from Pillau (now Baltysk) along the Pomeranian coast to the west or across the Baltic to Sweden and Denmark. But some ships were sunk by Soviet torpedoes, famous among them the *Wilhelm Gustloff* and the *Goya,* and up to 25,000 evacuees drowned.

Germans awaiting expulsion were often put into internment camps and slowly starved to death. This was the case in the former concentration camp Theresienstadt in Czechoslovakia. A Jewish inmate described the lot of the newcomers:

> Many among them had undoubtedly become guilty during the years of occupation, but the majority were children and juveniles who had only been locked up because they were Germans. Only because they were Germans . . . ? This sentence sounds frighteningly familiar; only the word "Jews" had been changed to "Germans." The rags with which the Germans were clothed were smeared with swastikas. The people were abominably fed and maltreated, and they were no better off than one was used to from German concentration camps. . . .

(*51,* 125)

Similar excesses occurred in Polish camps, such as Lamsdorf in Upper Silesia where only 1,500 internees out of 8,000 survived. Indiscriminate expulsions began on February 5, 1945, when Poland took control of the Reich's territory east of the Oder-Neisse. This was followed by the Czech uprising on May 5, which led to mass excesses against the Germans and the murder of at least 130,000. In the lands beyond the Oder, an estimated 400,000 were killed. All told, two million Germans did not survive the exodus because of starvation, exposure, and murder.

Bertrand Russell was one of those who protested strongly against the desperate condition of these people on their arrival in West Germany and Berlin. He wrote in *The New York Times* on October 19, 1945:

> . . . an apparently deliberate attempt is being made to exterminate many millions of Germans, not by gas, but [by] depriving them of their homes and of food, of leaving them to die by slow and agonizing starvation. This is not done as an act of war but as part of a deliberate policy of "peace."

Two questions are pertinent: (1) What was the role of the Western Allies in preparing the expulsion of the eastern Germans? (2) What did the Allies do to prevent or minimize the effects of the expulsion? It is well known that the Allies were the first to approve the concept of transferring the Sudeten Germans as early as 1942. The Tehran Conference led to a formal agreement of the Reich's enemies to compensate Poland for the Soviet taking of Polish land in the East by moving its borders westward. Churchill figured prominently in laying the groundwork for the eventual transfer. In spite of the Atlantic Charter of 1941 in which he and Roosevelt affirmed the "right of all people to choose the form of government under which they will live" and expressed the "hope to see established a place which will afford to all nations the means of dwelling in safety within their own boundaries," it appears that neither Churchill nor the American presidents ever subscribed to the policy of *total* expulsion of the Germans. On the contrary, at the conferences of Yalta and Potsdam in 1945, England and the United States favored a selective gradual transfer. Churchill, "the early champion of the principle of population transfers" (*51,* 89), eventually turned away from his previous conviction:

> The Soviet-dominated Polish government has been encouraged to make enormous and wrongful inroads upon Germany, and mass expulsions of millions of Germans on a scale grievous and undreamed-of are now taking place.

> (March 5, 1946; *51,* 89)

By 1946 it became clear that the figure of nine million transfers, agreed upon at the Potsdam Conference, was a gross underestimate. In the end, nearly fourteen million Germans were forcefully expelled. Faced with Stalin's intransigence and successes in the east, the only thing the Western Allies could do after Potsdam, short of military action, was to try to see that the transfers were "effected in an orderly and humane manner" (Article 13 of the Potsdam agreement). After the spring of 1946 this attempt succeeded partially by stopping some convoys, providing medical teams at departure stations (as in Stettin), or by finding out in advance how many expellees to expect and when.

The nightmare continued, however, for the expellees and refugees who reached the western occupation zones as they were confronted with a battle for survival in an overpopulated, war-torn country. Private relief efforts were blocked until March 1946 in the U.S. Zone in spite of the severe winter that had caused a large death toll from exposure and starvation, especially among the unsettled refugees. When the first CARE packages arrived, they saved many lives.

Despite the abuse and deprivations heaped upon them, the German expellees renounced in a charter of August 1950 "all thought of revenge and retaliation . . . in memory of the infinite suffering brought upon mankind, particularly during the past decade." (51) Since that year, excluding the refugees from the GDR (*Deutsche Demokratische Republik,* German Democratic Republic), more than a million ethnic Germans arrived in West Germany, most of them (600,000) from Poland. Many opted not to remain in the FRG (*Bundesrepublik Deutschland,* Federal Republic of Germany), but rather emigrated to the New World. Among them were about 200,000 *Schwaben* (Swabians) from the agricultural lowlands of the Danube basin (also called *Schwäbische Türkei*), an area shared by Hungary, Romania, Bulgaria, and Yugoslavia. A large number of their communities had been massacred at the end of the war. With the help of U.S. senators, such as Paul H. Douglas and Everett M. Dirksen, the emigrants settled in the United States in metropolitan areas including Detroit, Chicago, Cleveland, New York, Philadelphia, St. Louis, Cincinnati, and Los Angeles. Many became teachers, doctors, lawyers, and businessmen.

In the course of Willy Brandt's *Ostpolitik* in the early 1970s, the existing boundary line between Poland and East Germany at the western Neisse was affirmed as inviolable by the FRG (although still without the official sanction of an international peace treaty). A bad chapter in German-Slavic relations thus came to a close.

# 10. Exile Literature and Culture

The Nazi assumption of power in 1933 caused the mass exodus from Germany of most of the leading cultural figures—writers, artists, scientists, theologians, and musicians. They feared persecution because of race and political beliefs, or they simply were convinced that independent creative work would not be possible in a totalitarian system. The German intellectuals who left were of such reputation that we may rightfully speak of the emigration of German culture from Germany. Although the emigrants spread all over the world, by far the largest group settled in the United States, whereas others chose primarily to live in the Soviet Union, Mexico, and England. Despite their differing political and social backgrounds, all were profoundly antifascist and deeply committed to preserving the values of their native culture. The cultural historian Prince Hubertus zu Löwenstein, a conservative who chose exile in the United States, articulated a mission for the emigrants: "We believe that our present duty is to cultivate a German territory of the spirit" (56, 154). This view was also shared by the author Johannes Becher, a communist, who fled to the Soviet Union to preserve his native culture abroad—"the ever-present treasures of our people" (56, 363).

The fate of the exiles from Nazi Germany is a

. . . story of a generation that had to suffer the cataclysms of two world wars, that had to live in a time when our world regressed a thousand years in a moral sense, while that very same mankind rose to unheard-of heights in technology and scientific research.

(Stefan Zweig, *Die Welt von Gestern: Erinnerungen eines Europäers*, 1941; *The World of Yesterday: An Autobiography*, 1943).

Whereas the fate of the exiles was specifically linked to the historical trauma of the Nazi years, these writers and artists became in a larger sense representatives of modern culture in its increasing isolation from the social and technological forces of the twentieth century.

Most of the refugees from Germany survived the war in foreign lands. Some, however, could not accept what Stefan Zweig considered the end of European culture. For him "the meaning of an entire life ha[d] turned into an absurdity" (247, 492) and he committed suicide in 1942 in Brazil.

At the time of the emigrants' arrival in the United States, the country had an isolationist policy. A *Fortune* magazine poll in 1939 reflected the general antipathy toward immigrants: 83 percent of those polled advocated closing the borders; only 8.7 percent were against this idea, and the rest (8.3 percent) had no opinion. There was, however, a more receptive mood toward the immigrants within American institutions of higher learning, so that many of the refugees found places where they could continue their work.

The influx of German exiles to the United States increased the population by only .2 percent (56, 148). Nevertheless, they not only left their mark on American educational and cultural institutions, but they also represented a side of Germany that was antifascist, culturally conservative, and supportive of American democratic institutions. After the war, they provided a cultural complement to the increasing economic and social cooperation between Central Europe and the United States.

Writers Heinrich and Thomas Mann, Alfred Döblin, Bertolt Brecht, Carl Zuckmayer, Lion Feuchtwanger, Franz Werfel, Ernst Toller, Klaus Mann, and Erich Maria Remarque, filmmakers Fritz Lang, Billy Wilder, and Josef von Sternberg, scientists and mathematicians Albert Einstein and Johannes von Neumann, the existential theologian Paul Tillich, political and economic thinkers Hans Morgenthau and Hannah Arendt, the art historian Erwin Panofsky, the legal genius Hans Kelsen, and the conductor Bruno Walter are among the best known of their generation. Many more became part of the American intellectual life, teaching at the Institute of Advanced Studies at Princeton, the University of Chicago, the University of California at Berkeley, and other institutions across the country. Of the writers attracted to the Soviet Union, Theodor Plivier and Johannes Becher are among the most distinguished. (Heinrich Mann, Bertolt Brecht, and Anna Seghers went to East Germany after the war.) Unlike their western counterparts, they were integrated into the political life of the Soviet Union and were supported by the government as long as they remained *linientreu,* that is, faithful to the party line. One of their notable journals, *Das Wort (The Word, 56, 166),* included not only socialist writers but also antifascist bourgeois authors such as Thomas Mann. Because of their institutional, organizational, and political integration many of the German socialist writers provided cultural support in the transformation of the Soviet-occupied zone of Germany into a state within socialist eastern Europe.

The two most important cultural figures of the emigrant generation are Thomas Mann and Bertolt Brecht. Although both were antifascists, they nevertheless represented two divergent cultural traditions rooted in opposite world views.

During his immigrant years, Brecht wrote his *Furcht und Elend des Dritten Reichs* (1935–1936; *The Private Life of the Master Race,* 1944) in which he documented in 24 scenes the effect of Nazism on simple people as they were caught in an inextricable web of suppression in their everyday lives. In 1938 he completed the first version of his famous play *Galileo.* Here he portrayed a genius whose scientific insights were ahead of his time, but who was nevertheless forced by circumstances and his own weaknesses to recant what he had discovered to be true. This probing play was followed in 1941 by *Arturo Ui,* a brilliant exposé of the leading Nazi figures and the historical circumstances surrounding their rise to power. The play for which Brecht became best known, written in 1939 shortly before the outbreak of World War II, is *Mutter Courage und ihre Kinder* (*Mother Courage and Her Children,* 1941). Caught up in the Thirty Years' War (1618–1648), the protagonist struggles for survival in a war from which she nevertheless profits. It is the complexity of the main character—she is a good mother but also a greedy profiteer—that transcends the political message the play intends to convey.

In his lyrics Brecht confronted the problem of the émigré on a personal level:

> Don't drive a nail into the wall,
> Throw your coat on a chair!
> Why bother about four days?
> Tomorrow you'll go back. . . .

("Thoughts Concerning the Duration of the Exile")

And a few years later:

> The city of my fathers, how can I find it?
> Following the swarms of bombers
> I come home.
> Where does it lie? Yonder where huge
> Mountains of smoke arise.
> There in the flames
> It stands. . . .

("The Return")

In the considerable critical and creative armory of Brecht, there is one element that must be considered the most relevant to the time of the Nazis: it is the view, often expressed in his essays and embodied in all of his plays (if we exclude his Stalinist phase in the early thirties), that "truth is tangible." With this insistence on what can be rationally understood and verified, he was in direct opposition to the Nazis who allied the abstract with the emotional to bring about a union between a self-validating transcendence and unreflected instincts. After the war, such issues as his epic theater, alienation effects, and his views on the function of art and literature in society became more and more important not only in the West but also as part of political debates in the East. At the outbreak of WWII, however, Brecht's work had an immediate antifascist role to play in its particular insistence on the tangible and the rational in a working definition of truth.

When Thomas Mann went into exile in Switzerland shortly after the Nazis came to power, he still felt himself to be a cultural elitist, reluctant to take a direct political stand. Nevertheless, he made no secret of his dislike of the Nazis, and their increasing excesses caused him to become increasingly outspoken in his support of democracy. In his reply in 1936 to a letter from the dean of the University of Bonn revoking his honorary doctorate, Mann pointed to the guilt of the German universities in the spread of Nazism; and in 1938, when he came to America for what turned out to be a 14-year stay, his essays, speeches, and radio broadcasts strongly urged Hitler's defeat.

"Where I am, is Germany," he said, showing he still felt himself to be a representative of German culture, a culture in which he could feel both pride and guilt. He did not believe any part of German culture could be exonerated from responsibility: all of Germany, past and present, had played a part in the march toward Nazism, even he himself:

> From Fichte's romantic idealism, to the Teutonism of the Father of Gymnastics Jahn, Hegel's glorification of the state, via Richard Wagner . . . the British renegade, Houston Stuart Chamberlain, via the court historiographer and lackey of Prussianism, Heinrich von Treitschke and Heinrich von Sybel, the line goes down with increasing barbarism and malignancy towards Oswald Spengler, the clever ape of Nietzsche . . . to Alfred Rosenberg's *Myth of the Twentieth Century,* without anyone being able to say where the "good" Germany stopped and the "bad" Germany began. Where is the watershed?
>
> (*154,* 126)

Thomas Mann's main work during the Nazi years, the 2,000-page *Joseph* tetralogy (*Joseph und seine Brüder,* 1933–1942; *Joseph and His Brothers,* 1947–1948) and the difficult *Doktor Faustus* (1947; *Doctor Faustus,* 1948), written after the war, represent contrasting possibilities inherent in the cherished cultural ideals that Mann received from, among others, Goethe, Schopenhauer, Wagner, and Nietzsche.

The *Joseph* novels show the optimistic possibility. In them a proud, narcissistic young man, Joseph, highly intelligent and with obvious imaginative gifts, is gradually brought to maturity and a high position of leadership. Mann playfully develops the Old Testament story in which nature, mythological events, and the fates of generations are subtly intertwined. The nature imagery of growth, fullness, and human fulfillment suffuse the entire work. Mann's broad humor and gentle, humanistic treatment of myth stand in strong contrast to the deadly serious brutishness of Nazi mythology. Thomas Mann, the genius of irony, used the Nazis' own weapons against them in the most optimistic of his works.

In *Doktor Faustus,* however, Mann acknowledged the dangerous side of these cultural ideals. He used the old Faust book of

1587 as a starting point, finding its terrible warning and doom
much more appropriate than the optimism of Goethe's *Faust*. Furthermore, he changed the hero from a professor to a musician because Mann felt that music was central to the German soul. The
novel tells the story of the composer Adrian Leverkühn who, as a
proud and cynical genius, seeks demonic help to break through to
a new form of music. Mann put much of himself into Leverkühn
and into the humanistic narrator of the novel, Serenus Zeitblom,
who is also deceived by the demonic forces, believing falsely that
they can be controlled and used for the benefit of society. But
Mann-Leverkühn and Mann-Zeitblom are not the only ones moved
by the devil; all of Germany is as well. Zeitblom tells the story during WWII, and this lends the book an apocalyptic tone as it evokes
the fate of Germany in the first half of the twentieth century. Leverkühn's search for a breakthrough in music, where the final result
will be absolute order, is paralleled by the Nazi attempt at a totalitarian political-military breakthrough following the collapse of
bourgeois society, which had cherished its individual freedoms. In
the end all seems lost as both Leverkühn and Germany fall into the
pit, but a small hope of redemption is symbolized by the note that
lingers on at the end of Leverkühn's *Apocalypsis cum figuris,* suggesting that something may be salvaged from the chaos. Mann's
final thought, however, is one of contrition: Zeitblom ends the
novel with the words, "May God have mercy on your poor soul,
my friend, my fatherland."

In his exile, then, Thomas Mann was able to maintain an aesthetic balance while deeply committed to his struggle against Hitler. He courageously acknowledged the general German guilt
while at the same time stressing the greatness of Germany's cultural past.

Many writers of less renown than Mann and Brecht wrote novels
and plays in exile that attempted to come to grips with the trauma
of the Nazi dictatorship. In most of their works, shaped by the urgency of the moment, immediacy and directness were more prevalent than symbolic density and reflection. A good example of this
genre, which combined documentary and fictional elements, was
Klaus Mann's *Mephisto.* It tells the story of the famous German ac-
tor Gustaf Gründgens and his accommodation with the Nazi leadership, particularly with Field Marshal Göring. Another notable
example of this antifascist exile literature is Lion Feuchtwanger's
novel *Exil* (begun in 1935 and completed in August 1939, one
month before the outbreak of WWII) in which a composer, Traut-
wein, struggles to free a friend from Nazi imprisonment. Three
years earlier, in his historical fable *Der falsche Nero* (1936; *The Pre-
tender,* 1937), Feuchtwanger had presented a biting satire of the
rise of Hitler, Göring, and Goebbels.

The most notable among these antifascist writers was Heinrich Mann, whose works played a significant role in the GDR in the postwar period. Particularly his comprehensive autobiographical work *Ein Zeitalter wird besichtigt* (1945; *Reviewing an Epoch,* 1945) is an example of an emerging socialist consciousness. *Lidice* (1943) was Heinrich Mann's personal and artistic reaction to the SS massacre of a Czech village in retaliation for the assassination of Heydrich, one of Himmler's most notorious henchmen.

Another writer of the emigrant generation was Alfred Döblin, known today for his pre-WWII novel *Berlin Alexanderplatz* (1929; *Alexanderplatz, Berlin,* 1931) in which he portrayed individuals trapped in the web of a bewildering urban life during the later days of the Weimar Republic. From 1939 to 1950 Döblin devoted most of his artistic energies to the trilogy *November 1918.* The first two novels draw a picture of the political and social conflicts after the collapse of Wilhelmian Germany at the end of WWI. The third volume, written while he was an exile in the United States, reflects his turn to religion (he had converted to Catholicism). Social and political conflicts are now metamorphosed by Döblin into a conflict between heaven and hell.

The novelist and essayist Johannes Becher, who had fled to the Soviet Union, played an active role in organizing socialist writers under the aegis of the Soviet Union from the late twenties onward. Just as important as his writings are his speeches outlining the function of literature in a socialist state. In 1935, before the international Congress of Writers in Defense of Culture, he advocated the nurturing of proletarian literature as well as the study of the great works of the German cultural past. This is important in light of postwar efforts in the GDR to align the German cultural past with socialist aspirations.

It is remarkable that in the German postwar efforts to come to terms with the *unbewältigte Vergangenheit* (unintegrated past) of the Nazi period, the exiled writers have had little influence on the cultural developments of the FRG. In the GDR, on the other hand, writers in exile, particularly because of their antifascist orientation, were much more influential and widely read.

# THE THIRD REICH

Political Poster 1932: Our Last Hope: Hitler.

Political Poster 1932: The Worker in the Realm of the Swastika! Therefore Vote Row 1 Social Democratic.

Political Poster 1938: Step by Step Hitler Tore Up the Treaty of Versailles:

1933: Germany leaves the League of Nations;

1934: Army, Navy, and Air Force are being rebuilt;

1935: The Saar comes home. Currency value is reestablished;

1936: Total Liberation of the Rheinland;

1937: War debts are cancelled;

1938: Austria is annexed to the Reich; *Grossdeutschland* becomes a reality.

Therefore all of Germany Votes for Her Liberator Adolf Hitler on April 10. All Say: "Yes!"

POLITICAL AND MILITARY ASPECTS

Hitler standing with Goering, Himmler and others at Nuremberg rally. (Reproduction from the Collections of the Library of Congress)

Hitler saluting a torchlight rally, ca. 1933. (Reproduction from the Collections of the Library of Congress)

Hitler's triumphal entry into the Sudeten territories.

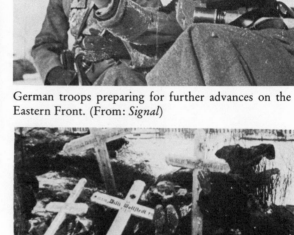

German troops preparing for further advances on the Eastern Front. (From: *Signal*)

Graves of German troops abandoned during the retreat from the Eastern Front. (From: Imperial War Museum)

Map of Hitler's gains before October 1939 and the Second World War.

Gottfried Benn, 1886-1956.
(Courtesy of the German
Information Center)

Ricarda Huch, 1864-1947. (Bildarchiv Herder)

Elisabeth Langgässer, 1899-1950.
(Bildarchiv Herder)

INNER
IMMIGRANTS

Ernst Jünger, 1895-
(Bildarchiv Herder)

Albert Einstein, 1879-1955. (Courtesy of the German Information Center)

EXILE LITERATURE
AND CULTURE

Bruno Walter, 1876-1962. (Courtesy of the German Information Center)

Paul Tillich, 1886-1965. (Courtesy of the German Information Center)

Heinrich Mann, 1871-1950.
(Ullstein Verlag)

Thomas Mann, 1875-1955.
(Bildarchiv Herder)

Walter Gropius, 1883-1969.
(Courtesy of the German Information Center)

Anna Seghers, 1900-1983. (Courtesy of the German Information Center)

Bertold Brecht, 1898-1956. (Courtesy of the German Information Center)

Burning synagogue in Frankfurt. (Courtesy of the Leo Baeck Institute)

## ASPECTS OF THE FINAL SOLUTION

Title page of a children's book: The Poisonous Mushroom: A Stürmer Book for Young and Old. Stories by Ernst Zimmer. Pictures by Fips. A Stürmer Publication—Nürnberg. (Courtesy of the Leo Baeck Institute)

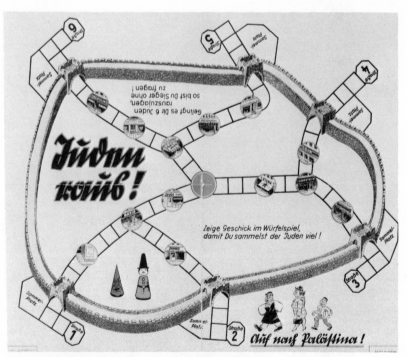

Board game: Jews Out! Throw the dice in just the right way and you'll round up lots of Jews today. If you can chase 6 Jews out, you're a winner, there's no doubt. Off to Palestine! (Courtesy of the Leo Baeck Institute)

Assembling Jews for transport to the East. (Courtesy of the Leo Baeck Institute)

30,000 Jews were trapped in the ramparts in Theresienstadt. Norbert Troller, artist and inmate. (Courtesy of the Leo Baeck Institute)

Men's living quarters in former barracks in Theresienstadt. In the foreground, a young woman mourns her husband. Henry Behr, artist and inmate. (Courtesy of the Leo Baeck Institute)

Corpses of Jews (Poland). (Courtesy of the Leo Baeck Institute)

Carl von Ossietzky: Writer and pacifist; awarded Nobel Peace Prize in 1935; charged of being an enemy of the state; died in prison. (Courtesy of the German Information Center)

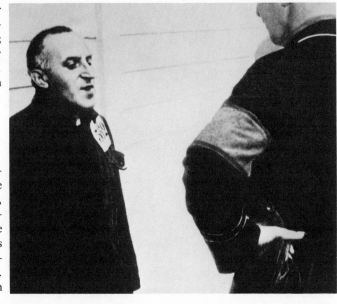

Eight postage stamps dedicated to German resistance fighters who on July 20, 1944, made an abortive attempt on Hitler's life. The leading resistance fighters were executed and thousands were imprisoned. (Courtesy of the German Information Center)

# RESISTANCE

Execution site of many of the political resistance fighters in 1944. (Courtesy of the German Information Center)

# Chapter II

# THE IMMEDIATE POSTWAR YEARS (1945-1949)

## 1. State of Destruction

Before his suicide on April 30, 1945, Hitler deputized Admiral Karl Dönitz as the official head of Nazi Germany. The admiral capitulated to the Allies on May 8, 1945. The Third Reich had come to a fiery end. The collapse involved all aspects of society: the population was decimated, cities lay in ruins, communication systems ground to a halt, the economy was destroyed, social institutions ceased to exist, families were torn apart, and millions had to flee their homelands. One of the most economically and technologically advanced countries had become destitute, its standard of living reduced below the level of an underdeveloped country. As with the Holocaust, statistics are eloquent in expressing the extent of the upheaval and destruction WWII wrought on Europe and Germany *(32)*.

Of the nearly 55 million people killed in WWII, Germany lost 4 million soldiers on the battlefields. In addition, 10 million German soldiers were prisoners of war at the conclusion of hostilities. Although more than half a million civilians died in the cities, primarily as a result of Allied air raids *(16, 55, 113)*, these bombings probably did little to hasten the end of the war. The 61 cities with a population of more than 100,000 in 1939, which contained 32 percent of the entire German population and 45 percent of its industrial work force, were more than 50 percent destroyed.

Berlin was 19.5 percent destroyed and suffered 78,000 war dead, 49,600 of them through Allied bombing. The city had 4.3 million inhabitants before the war, and at the end of it only 2.6 million were left. Many had fled the city to live in rural areas or small towns less likely to be bombed. Cologne was 72 percent demolished and 45 percent of Munich lay in ruins. In July 1943, during 9 days of bombing, half of the city of Hamburg was razed. Particularly devastating were the firestorms that resulted from incendiary bombs. The fatality figure for the 9 days was 55,000. Almost a million people fled the city after those raids. But none of the German cities suffered the destruction of Dresden. The bombing of Dresden during the night of February 13–14, 1945 was the most devastating of the entire war in Germany; it stands next to the bombings of Hiroshima and Nagasaki as the most destructive Allied act against civilian populations of the Axis enemy. In 1939 the population of Dresden was 630,000 inhabitants. This figure had swelled to well over a million by the night of the raid because half a million refugees had crowded into the city from the east. In two days 135,000 lives were claimed.

The destroyed cities left 7.5 million homeless. The entire population faced severe food shortages. Roughly 13 million Germans were uprooted at the end of the war, primarily from the Eastern Provinces and Eastern Europe. Homeless, and in some cases fleeing the Soviet Army, a huge migration started westward. Many sought lost relatives, scavenged for food, or searched for former homes in the bombed-out cities. Survivors of the migration crowded into the western area of Germany. During the final months of the war, the German navy transported 2 million civilians across the Baltic Sea and deposited them on western shores.

The industrial base had also collapsed. Output of basic raw materials, such as coal and iron, was drastically reduced; the production of consumer goods had virtually ended. Because of the loss of fertile lands to Poland, agriculture was not broad enough to sustain the entire population. Allied demands for reparations further aggravated the economic situation. The Soviet Union insisted on dismantling many factories in its occupation zone. It asked for reparations from the zones controlled by the Western Allies for the loss of 20 million Russian lives.

# 2. General Politics: The Division of Germany and the Allied Conferences

Poor Germany, occupied by four powers, there under the banner of hammer and sickle, here in the middle of bourgeois restoration.

—a French reaction to postwar Germany

It would have been better if a successful revolution and not lost wars had been at the beginning of our democratic developments.

—Theodor Heuss, the first president of the Federal Republic of Germany, 1948 (50, 280)

Two political systems, parliamentary democracy and state socialism—neither of which had strong roots in the political culture of the defeated country—were introduced to Germany at the barrel of a gun. The division of the country into French, British, American, and Russian occupation zones was intended as a temporary measure, but in the course of the next four postwar years it became the permanent outline of the political, social, and economic map of central Europe. The future of an occupied Germany—but not the division of Germany into two separate states—was decided at two Allied conferences during the war (Tehran, November 28 to December 1, 1943, and Yalta, February 3 to 11, 1945, and particularly at a major conference after the war in (Potsdam, July 17 to August 2, 1945). Whereas the Tehran Conference stressed the reeducation of the German people and the deindustrialization of the country, the Yalta Conference was more precise in determining the features of postwar Germany. At the Tehran Conference it was decreed that the eastern German provinces of Silesia, Pomerania, and part of East Prussia would go to Poland; the rest of East Prussia would be given to the Soviet Union. Also determined was the division of Germany into various states. The Yalta Conference decided where to draw the demarcation line that would take effect after the war between the Western Allies, which were moving toward the center of Germany from the Rhine, and the Soviet army, which was advancing across Poland toward Berlin. The line was meant to constitute a temporary border, but it later became permanent between the two German states. Critics reproached Franklin D. Roosevelt for having made too many concessions to the Russians at Yalta; however, at the time the demarcation line was drawn up, the Allied armies were bogged down on the western front while the Russians were advancing rapidly. Thus the line agreed upon at Yalta proved to represent a reasonable guess as to the final advance of the armies. Because the German western front collapsed during the last months of the war, the Western Allies were able to move farther east into Germany than they had anticipated. Consequently, American forces, which had occupied the uranium-rich provinces of Saxony and Thuringia, relinquished them to the Soviets after the war, whereas the Soviets permitted the Allies to enter the city of Berlin as agreed.

Germany was divided into four zones. The Soviet Union took control of the eastern area—namely, Saxony, Thuringia, Mecklenburg, and the lands around Berlin to the Baltic Sea. Great Britain assumed power in the northwestern part of Germany—the provinces of Lower Saxony, North Rhine-Westphalia, and Schleswig-Holstein. The United States held southern and west-central Germany—Hesse, Bavaria, and part of Baden-Württemberg. The French commanded the southwest corner of the old Reich—part of

Baden-Württemberg and the Saarland west of the Rhine River. Berlin was divided among the Allies, and an agreement was reached concerning western Allied access to the former capital situated within the Soviet zone. An Allied control council had the final authority over all of Germany, but each of the four supreme military commanders had executive power for his zone of occupation.

The Potsdam Conference was overwhelmed by the amount of unresolved problems. The unexpectedly fast military collapse of the Nazi regime in 1945 caught the Allies by surprise. Although they had clear ideas concerning demilitarization and denazification, a vacuum existed in terms of political and economic goals. Inasmuch as the Potsdam Conference abandoned the division of Germany into independent and small *Länder* and treated Germany as an economic whole, the four zones at once fell under the influence of the different occupying powers. Almost immediately the Soviet Union started to structure its zone politically in accordance with socialist values, whereas the United States gave a different shape to the western part of Germany, particularly in the economic and cultural spheres. Thus a lack of agreement among the four occupying powers as to Germany's political and economic future prepared the ground for the ultimate division of Germany.

In the *political sphere* the Soviets imported an elite cadre of Moscow-trained German immigrants who were quickly placed into the center of the emerging political life. In the western zones the Allies did little initially to encourage political activities on more than a local or regional level. Their primary interest was to stimulate and control local community governments rather than supra-regional political party activity. At the same time the United States showed a clear preference for conservative or right-of-center German political figures, ignoring or discouraging social democrats and those progressives who were pleading for a radical change in the economic sphere. In fact, this Allied military policy against left-of-center politicians is reflected in an AFL Executive Committee Report of January 21, 1947, in which Allied occupation authorities were blamed for supporting upper-middle-class "conservative elements in industry rather than the rank of workers and the employed (172)."

In the *economic sphere* the early divergence between the eastern and western zones was even more striking. Aside from the wholesale dismantling of industrial plants in the industry-rich provinces of Thuringia and Saxony, the Soviets introduced a radical land reform: they confiscated the large landholdings of the Prussian Junker caste of 14,000 and distributed the land among more than 500,000 peasants. American economic policy stressed recovery rather than radical reform to develop the western zones under its economic sphere of influence.

In the treatment of *social institutions*—schools, legal systems, civil service—and their personnel, the differences between the West and East were also pronounced. Consistent with their political beliefs, the Soviets introduced a radical reform of the school system, shifting emphasis away from the children of the middle class and focusing on working-class offspring. Admission to advanced schools was blocked for the middle class. These changes fundamentally restructured society and forced the middle class to consider emigration to the western zones. Later on, after the borders were sealed, only flight across closed borders remained. Furthermore, the Soviets were consistently antifascist and dismissed members of the Nazi party from their posts. By contrast, no general and permanent dismissal of Nazi administrative personnel took place in the western zones. Thus the management of society on various levels did not really change hands. Only the most prominent Nazis were removed from their positions. Some of them were punished with fines and short prison terms, but many of them worked their way up into the institutional hierarchy of West Germany after a few years.

In *cultural terms* the divergence between East and West was also great. American civilization with its well-defined mass culture made its presence felt in West Germany soon after the war. Coca-Cola, Benny Goodman, Camel cigarettes, and nylons were the signs of the New World, eagerly absorbed by the German population, particularly the youth. The Soviet Union had no mass culture to import that might have put a distinct mark on its occupation zone. However, in terms of their cultural and ethnic diversity, the Soviets had a supportive view of other cultures despite their doctrinaire politics. As a result, traditional German cultural values and norms were nourished much more in the eastern zone than in the western part. Cultural divergence, characterized by "Americanization" in the West and "conservative" attitudes toward culture in the East, remain distinguishing features of the two German states to the present day.

In West Germany economic recovery determined the postwar years. However, immediately after the war, the first task for the average German, including the refugees from the East, was to find food and shelter. The extent of the shelter problem becomes obvious when we realize that, for instance, Frankfurt on the Main, which had 178,000 residential homes and apartments before the war, had only 44,000 usable units left afterward. A generation of able-bodied men had either died in the war or was imprisoned. Thus the search for food and shelter fell upon the women, the so-called *Trümmerfrauen* ("women of the ruins"), who had to find ways and means for their families to survive amidst the physical ruins of the cities and the moral ruins of the country.

# DECENTRALIZATION AND ITS HISTORICAL IMPACT

The most important historical change during the immediate postwar years was the vast decentralization of a modern industrial state. This decentralization occurred not only because of Allied policy in the economic and political spheres; it was also a natural result of the collapse of all national social and institutional structures. Individual initiative was aroused. Self-help groups within the extended family and ad hoc organizations in villages, on city blocks, and in local regions sprang into existence everywhere. After the Nazis' grandiloquent cant of nationalistic and super-European visions and historical expectations, the Germans experienced the simple fact that for individual and small-group survival butchers, bakers, and carpenters were more essential than generals, ministers of propaganda, and even *Führers*. These years of decentralization, small-group reliance, and organized self-help set a significant trend for postwar political development in West Germany to the present day. Whereas the *Wählerinitiativen* (voters' initiatives, first promulgated by the author Günter Grass to help the SPD develop grass-roots, action-oriented support in the mid-sixties) may have lacked the local, single-issue focus of the postwar survival efforts, the *Bürgerinitiativen* (citizens' initiatives, developed in the seventies), hark back in their single-issue orientation to the self-help groups that sprang up after WWII. As a matter of fact, the powerful ecological movement that characterizes political culture in the eighties shows an affinity with immediate postwar survival and grass-roots activism.

In general terms the years from 1945 to the founding in 1949 of the two German states, FRG and GDR, may be seen from two different perspectives: (1) the groundwork was laid for economic recovery, the *Wirtschaftswunder* (economic miracle) of West Germany; (2) opportunities were lost for a neutral and united Germany with a political system combining features of both East and West. The outline of such a system was evident as early as 1946, and it might have brought a democratic socialism to an undivided Germany. But the emphasis on economic recovery in the West and the rigid structuring of political life in the East prevented the development of this alternative form of governance.

# 3. Economic Recovery of West Germany

Immediately after the war economic recovery was hampered in all occupied zones of Germany by several factors aside from the destruction of cities and industrial plants. The coal-rich province of Silesia, which produced approximately 20 percent of German coal before the war, became part of Poland. Silesia also had been one of the few agriculturally productive areas in Germany. The industrial Saarland was annexed by France (until 1955) as reparation. Furthermore, the Allies had agreed at the Potsdam Conference to curtail German industry severely and dismantle some of it outright: "Production of metals, chemicals, machinery, and other items directly necessary to the war economy [were to] be rigidly controlled and restricted" (*218*, 179). The breakup of the huge cartels that had fed the war machines of the Kaiser and Hitler, particularly the steel conglomerates and the chemical combine of I.G. Farben, led to further economic weakening. The industries earmarked for dismantling were precisely those essential to rebuilding the war-ravaged country: tools, tractors, oil, and rubber. Severe production restrictions imposed on raw materials as well as finished products (steel, cars, industrial machinery) further hampered recovery. Initially, economic difficulties were greatest in the American zone of Germany. It was the most densely populated region of the old Reich and it lacked an adequate industrial base as well as agriculturally productive land. A common comment after the war was that the United States "got the scenery." Changes in the economic policy of the Allies toward West Germany, however, came quickly. Germany was potentially too productive a country to leave out of the western economic sphere. In addition, the emerging cold-war confrontation between the Soviets and the Allies made West Germany crucial to geopolitics. Economic integration into the West and the related Truman doctrine of communist containment both stimulated the recovery of the western zones. At the same time, however, these developments undercut any chances that existed after the war for a unified neutral Germany.

## ECONOMIC STIMULATION BY THE WESTERN ALLIES

The Potsdam Conference of 1945 constituted a big step away from the 1944 Morgenthau Plan, which had envisioned the complete deindustrialization of Germany. The Western Allies' post-Potsdam decisions moved away even further from the earlier deindustrialization plans. Lucius Clay, the U.S. deputy military governor of Germany, noted, "The destruction of Germany was much more extensive than the Allies realized," and, he concluded, "we must have freedom here to bring industries back into production" (*84,* 5–6). Aside from their geopolitical concerns, the Allies were also genuinely interested in helping Germany maintain a minimal industrial base to assure survival of its people. The burden of an unproductive Germany would have been a liability for the Western Allies: "Particularly U.S. and British taxpayers would have to carry the tax burden of preventing starvation in Germany" (*218,* 199).

Economic reconstruction took the form of an economic *Abgrenzung* (demarcation), that is, a separation of the western zones from the Soviet zone of Germany. U.S. Secretary of State James F. Byrnes's speech on September 16, 1946, in Stuttgart represented the first move toward a permanent separation of the two parts of Germany. Byrnes proposed a bizonal American and British commission that would coordinate economic efforts in agriculture, industry, transportation, finance, and communication. The Economic Administrative Council that went into operation on January 1, 1947, effectively canceled key reparation agreements made with the Soviets at Potsdam. This signaled a fundamental shift in U.S. policy from inter-Allied cooperation (with an emphasis on economic decentralization) toward a reconstruction policy aimed at German self-sufficiency and integration into the West.

## The Marshall Plan

One of the largest barriers to a swift economic recovery was the complete collapse of the financial structure. Germany had lost all its foreign assets and gold reserves. The value of its currency had been drastically reduced through wartime inflation. No foreign loans were available, yet monetary foreign exchange was necessary to stimulate foreign trade. It is within this context that the Marshall Plan for western Europe (and the western zones of Germany) came into existence. On June 5, 1947, Secretary of State George C. Marshall outlined in a speech at Harvard University an approach to European economic recovery based on monetary support for the Europeans: "The truth of the matter is that Europe's requirements for the next three or four years are so much greater than her present ability to pay, that she must have substantial additional help or face economic, social, and political deterioration of a very grave character . . ." (*181,* 26 passim). The economic crisis was above all fed by low productivity, inflation, and a lack of money to stimulate international trade. The plan for European recovery focused on four objectives: (1) to increase productivity of the continent; (2) to create an internationally sound financial structure; (3) to develop economic cooperation between the various nations; and (4) to reduce the dollar deficit by stimulating exports (*181,* 37). Under the auspices of the European Marshall fund, western zones of Germany received 1.5 billion dollars (*218,* 238). These funds were distributed to stimulate production of essential goods, raw materials and basic machinery being the top priorities. Repayments were postponed to allow the buildup of capital for further investment. Low-interest loans were extended, particularly in such crucial areas as iron, steel, and housing. Besides essential foodstuff, Marshall-fund money was used to obtain a great variety of consumer goods.

In March 1948 the OEEC (Organization of European Economic Cooperation) was founded for the purpose of stimulating trade among Europeans and coordinating their efforts for economic recovery. By the middle of 1949 trade restrictions between the various nations had been reduced by 50 percent.

## Currency Reform

As late as 1948 the western zones of Germany still had not been able to deal with one important stumbling block to economic recovery. Germany's currency was wildly inflated because of the war economy and Hitler's fiscal policies during the thirties. There was a surplus of nearly valueless money and no goods to buy. A black market developed in which American cigarettes became the prime currency and coffee, tea, and chocolate a secondary currency. Many rare items not available on the regular market were exchanged as the black market flourished. The reichsmark had little purchasing power on the black market. Three to five marks, representing three hours of labor, only bought one U.S. cigarette.

In order to put the German currency on a sound footing, a radical *Währungsreform* (currency reform) was introduced by the postwar director of the Bi-Zonal Economic Administration, Ludwig Erhard, a professor of economics (he became chancellor of the FRG in the sixties):

> The currency reform will affect far-reaching changes both in the structure of our industry and in the state of the labour market, which, in view of the prevailing material and social conditions, must be brought into some kind of new and organic equilibrium as soon as possible. A successful currency reform . . . will close all the easy escape routes, leaving openings only for work and effort that are of value to the nation's economy. This is a difficult road but it is the only one that will lead to recovery.
>
> (*63,* 32–33)

With the backing of the Western Allies the entire banking system was reorganized and modernized. The central point of the currency reform, however, was the drastic devaluation of the old reichsmark. On June 20, 1948, each inhabitant of the three western zones was given 40 new deutsche marks (DM) in exchange for 40 old reichsmarks. Even more important than the sudden introduction of a new currency was the fact that all cash and bank deposits were subjected to an exchange rate of 100 old reichsmarks for 6.5 new deutsche marks. Overnight bank deposits were reduced by over 93 percent. This had an immediate effect. Money had become valuable, and it was once again profitable to produce and sell goods. Suddenly all the stores were full of much-needed consumer items and the black market disappeared quickly. Along with these drastic financial measures, Erhard kept only the most basic and still scarce food supplies and raw materials under price control and exposed most other consumer goods to the fluctuation of the free market's laws of supply and demand. During the second half of 1948, industrial production in West Germany increased 50 percent. Thus the basis was laid for the "economic miracle" to take place in the 1950s under Konrad Adenauer.

These far-reaching economic decisions were all the more effective because the Allies did not have to consider normal market forces, such as outdated management practices, competition, and a labor movement. Indeed, the effectiveness of the economic measures lay precisely in the Allies' almost absolute control over the West German economy. This mixture of strong central executive power, on the one hand, and the laissez-faire entrepreneurial spirit, on the other, proved to be the ideal stimulants for postwar economic recovery. High profits for private industry and massive accumulation of taxes by the state insured the success of what was to be called the *soziale Marktwirtschaft* (social market economy, a term coined in the thirties). This social market economy was built on a compromise between governmental and economic spheres (*218,* 234):

> As things are today, the state must provide the economy with the principles and broad outlines of a policy and with objectives designed to guide and regulate its functioning. In this respect, the state . . . should have the initiative. But to go further and reduce the independent businessman to the status of a mere puppet or servant of the authority's will would be to destroy all the values derived from personality and to rob the economy of its most precious source of inspiration and strength.

> (*63,* 10)

Abundant tax revenues enabled the government to continue the tradition of supporting the population with the social benefits of old-age, disability, and health insurance.

## INTERNAL REASONS FOR RECOVERY

External economic stimulation fell on fertile ground in Germany. Erhard's radical *Währungsreform* was only possible in a country with a tradition of mobilizing its resources and manpower —this time not against imagined or actual external military threats but against real internal economic disaster. The Allied military control was authoritarian and effective. Furthermore, traditional German discipline aided economic recuperation with the collective sense of purpose necessary to assure success. For instance, the housing-and-shelter crisis was solved on an emergency basis with a minimum of friction. Each person was permitted a small amount of living space. Additional space beyond the minimum was assigned to refugees from the eastern provinces and the bombed-out cities. Renters and owners had to share their living quarters with strangers. The names of residents assigned to a living unit were posted on front doors so that the German authorities under Allied supervision could check on compliance with the emergency measures.

In addition to a spirit of mobilization and collective discipline, the traditional German work ethic was still very much alive. The English translation "profession" or "job" is not adequate for *Beruf,* which connotes a person's particular "calling" and thus a measure of his or her worth. Unlike the Protestant work ethic of the United States, which relates work to private conscience and inner worth, the German work ethic, derived from the medieval craftsmen and guilds, emphasizes the result of work, the well-fashioned product, as a public act and a symbol of the worker's pride. This traditional public pride in the product still finds expression in contemporary Germany and, to a greater extent, in Japan in the workers' personal identification with the firm. Thus, on one level, modern corporations benefit from feudal ideas of social estates in both countries. Worker identification with the work place and the vocation has played an important role in twentieth-century Germany. Hitler exploited the trait to help create his war machine. And in the postwar period the laborer's continued willingness to produce much more than was required became a crucial factor in the economic recovery.

As the lower- and middle-rank civil-service personnel's Nazi-party affiliation was no cause for dismissal in the western zones, the traditional civil-service apparatus remained in place and also played a role in the economic recovery. Most business executives likewise retained their posts except for the most prominent who had war-crime records, such as Krupp von Bohlen und Halbach. He sat among the accused at the Nuremberg war-crimes trials in 1946. The majority was kept on the principle that "After all, those top industrialists were not Nazis, they were just good businessmen" *(172)*. In spite of widespread Nazi affiliation the Western Allies declined to carry out a concerted antifascist housecleaning that would have disrupted the apparatus of governance. Although maintaining the old civil service was morally questionable, it was economically efficient. Judges retained their benches, teachers their classrooms, transportation experts their desks, and bureaucrats their government offices. This wholesale continuity of Nazi personnel is a remarkable feature of postwar recovery and represents a chapter of West Germany's repressed history that was opened only decades later when the economic boom toward the end of the Adenauer era had run its course and political activism raised moral issues about the Nazi past. Postwar Allied policy in this regard became a target when the examination of the Nazi past finally was undertaken. No case is more striking than that of Hans Karl Filbinger, former minister president of Baden-Württemberg. As a wartime judge of the *Wehrmacht* he had been particularly zealous in condemning deserters to death, in one case even after the Nazi Reich had officially capitulated.

Whereas there was remarkable stability in the civil-service apparatus, a new middle-management entrepreneurial group appeared in the economic sector that was culturally cosmopolitan, economically pragmatic, and politically disinterested, with its personal perceptions sharpened by the need for survival. This younger materialistic generation of Germans, survivors of the war, became one of the organizational driving forces for postwar recovery and also contributed heavily to the apolitical atmosphere of the Adenauer era.

Even Allied bombing during the war may be cited as one factor for the remarkable economic resurgence. Industrial machinery and plants had to be replaced because they had been destroyed or severely damaged in the bombing raids. New replacements were technologically up to date. Thus Allied bombing helped solve the problem of obsolescence and provided the emerging German industry with a competitive edge over the industrial plants of nations less ravaged by the war.

Perhaps no factor, external or internal, was more important to the recovery than the emphasis placed on the production of socially and economically essential goods and services. German postwar society between 1945 and 1949 was not consumer-oriented. Productivity emphasized such basics as food, shelter, and clothing. This focus on essentials created a rational and effective economic base for decades to come. West Germany's reemerging industrial society was for years its own best market. After the war it was a vast underdeveloped area with a great economic potential.

In sum, economic productivity and the fulfillment of basic needs were closely related. A central Allied executive authority, not hampered by precedents or counterbalancing interest groups, provided the inital investment capital to stimulate growth. The population was socially disciplined and devoted to a productive work ethic yet in great need of a higher material standard of living after years of suffering and deprivation. All of these factors interacted between 1945 and 1949, setting the stage for the remarkable recovery of West Germany out of the ashes of the Nazi Reich.

## THE SOVIET ZONE

The process of economic recovery was much slower in East Germany for several reasons. First, unlike the United States, the Soviet Union had sustained major damages during the war. Most of the industrialized areas of the Soviet Union (European Russia) had been occupied by the Nazis and most of it lay in ruins. Consequently, the Soviets made a massive effort to dismantle the industrial plants of their zone to rebuild their own war-ravaged economy. They were in no position to duplicate the Western Allies' economic moves, such as the Marshall Plan, with concerted reconstruction efforts. The deportation or forced hiring of German industrial specialists for reconstruction in the Soviet Union deprived East Germany of key personnel such as engineers, foremen, and plant managers. Not only were its industries dismantled but the Soviet zone of Germany was also cut off from the primary industrial centers of the former Reich, particularly the Ruhr, Saar, and Middle Rhine regions as well as from Silesia, which now belonged to Poland. Secondly, the Soviets imposed a radical reorganization on East German society: major land reforms, dismissal of personnel with a Nazi past, and particularly the disenfranchisement of the middle class. These changes caused major social upheavals that hampered economic reconstruction. A third reason for the slow recovery of the eastern part of Germany was that the centralized Soviet-style economy was not flexible enough to rise to the unique economic challenges of an industrial society in ruins, which had, however, an enormous economic potential for recovery.

## THE COLD WAR AND ITS IMPACT

The quick economic recovery in the western zones was closely related to the emerging cold-war confrontation of the United States and its Allies with the Soviet Union. No country was more dramatically affected by this global confrontation than Germany. Foremost, the cold war brought about the eventual division of Germany into two separate states, dividing families, villages, and regions, and artificaly hampering communication on personal and social levels. In the years immediately following WWII, there was only one superpower, namely, the United States. It possessed three-quarters of the world's invested capital and two-thirds of the world's industrial capacity. It had military bases all around the globe, and the atom bomb. By comparison, the Soviet Union, a huge country now entrenched in the middle of Europe, was militarily and economically weak. Consequently, in the immediate postwar years, the fate of Europe and Germany was to a large degree in the hands of the United States. Aggressive economic policy brought Germany's western zones completely into the American sphere of control. Although Truman's doctrine of communist containment had a global perspective, Germany was one of the main areas of confrontation between the United States and the Soviet Union.

One of the first major points of disagreement involved reparations. In order to compensate for the lack of an industrial base in its zone comparable to the Ruhr region in the West, the Soviet Union was to receive from the western zones 25 percent of the industrial equipment that had survived destruction there. In return the Soviets were to provide a set amount of food products from their occupation zone, which was predominantly agricultural. Disagreements surfaced, and the four-power Allied Control Council was unable to deal with them. The Allied Control Council finally collapsed on March 28, 1949, when the commander of the Soviet zone, Marshal Vassili Sokolowski, left the council in protest over not being informed about an important political decision concerning the future of the western zones of Germany. This decision involved nothing less than the creation of an independent German state out of the western zones. In effect, the unilateral political move of the Western Allies complemented their earlier steps toward integrating the western part of Germany economically into the American sphere of influence. As a result of these unilateral decisions, the joint four-power government of Germany came to an end (*213,* 19). The four-power status of Berlin, however, remained unchanged. When the Western Allies introduced Erhard's new German currency into West Berlin—a provocative economic move considering the four-power jurisdictional status of the city—the Soviets reacted militarily by blockading the land routes from the western zones to West Berlin. The Western Allies responded with a massive *Luftbrücke* (airlift) that kept vital supplies flowing into the city. The citizens of West Berlin did not cave in under the economic hardships caused by the land blockade of the city. Apart from the Cuban missile crisis in 1962, the Berlin blockade in 1948 was the closest the East and West came to a full-fledged war. The crisis came to an end when the Soviets lifted their blockade in return for the Western Allies' promise to hold a foreign-minister conference prior to founding an independent West German state.

At this conference in the spring of 1949, the Soviets made one of their last attempts to maintain a united Germany under four-power control. They advocated the formation of a German government that was to become effective one year after the departure of the Allies. The Soviets' policy was to hold on to the Potsdam agreement of 1945 with their emphasis on reparations and a Germany that was one economic entity. What complicated matters was that France, one of the four Allied powers, had not been a signatory to the Potsdam agreement. Therefore France did not feel bound by its provisions, particularly the one that affirmed Germany as an entity. The key factor, however, of the immediate postwar developments in Central Europe was the relative weakness of the Soviet Union vis-à-vis the United States. This explained the defensive nature of Soviet foreign-policy moves, which did not contemplate a permanent division of Germany during the first few years after WWII. Therefore regarding "the historically interesting question as to whether the West or the East had a greater share in bringing about the division of Germany, the Soviet Union and the East German side appear to have the better documentary evidence in their favour [that the West was primarily responsible]" (*213,* 2). The Soviets, of course, had their own reasons for leaving Germany economically intact. Their political sphere of influence would have been greater in a united Germany, and they would have reaped some of the benefits of the more rapid economic recovery in the western zones.

The issue of a united Germany is not solved to the present day because no formal peace treaty with Germany exists. The constitution of the Federal Republic of Germany still contains a clause concerning unification. Willy Brandt's *Ostpolitik* in the late sixties attempted to stabilize the de facto division of Germany by proposing the constitutionally acceptable formula of "two states and one nation." In the late seventies and early eighties the powerful peace movement in West Germany, with its plea for a nuclear free zone in Central Europe, has rekindled the idea of a unified and neutral Germany. The question of a German identity continues to occupy German writers on both sides of the divide to the present day.

For the two German states, the global issues of cold-war confrontation versus détente are not just matters of foreign policy. The cold war brought about the division of the country, which resulted in personal hardships, particularly for the East Germans. Détente, on the other hand, makes daily life easier on both sides of the border and in a modest way keeps alive the idea of an eventual reunification.

## MISSED POLITICAL OPPORTUNITIES

To see the crucial years between the end of WWII and the founding of the two German states only in terms of economic recovery, followed by the establishment of parliamentary democracy, overlooks some historically significant missed opportunities, namely, those to restructure West German society politically and culturally. Both political systems, Marxist-Leninism and parliamentary democracy, were imposed on the Germans as a result of the war. Even the Germans living in the western zones were not eager to simply accept the American political system without some essential modifications. The first steps toward creating an indigenous German postwar political culture were remarkable in several respects. There existed an openness to socialist ideas as well as to the free-enterprise system. The writer Alfred Andersch states this unambiguously:

> We are threatened by two-fold education—for planning in the East, for freedom in the West . . . by absorbing eastern socialism and western democracy [Germany] can unite the two on a higher level and develop a synthesis that might serve the entire world as a model.

*(172, 288)*

Casting aside the missionary goal of the statement, it is nevertheless characteristic of the widely held view after the war that neither imported capitalism nor socialism held the political key for Germany. This desire to combine socialism with western free enterprise is easy to understand. The Germans' first political impulse was to accomodate the victors of both East and West. After all, they had seen the embrace of Americans and Soviets at the conclusion of the war, and one of the first German publications, the *Süddeutsche Mitteilungen (South German News),* headlined on June 16, 1945: "Complete Unity in Peace: Marshal Zhukov in Frankfurt to give victory medal to Eisenhower and Montgomery." In addition, there was a widespread belief that the large monopolies that had supported Hitler would be permanently broken up and that a restructuring of the economic system was imminent. It was generally expected that an antifascist transformation in West German society would take place. But the much-acclaimed United States reeducation of West Germany with its denazification program had no major impact. Every German citizen had to fill out an elaborate questionnaire; if the answers indicated Nazi-party affiliation, the person underwent an interview. On the basis of such a general assessment of past political behavior, Germans were classified into five groups ranging from criminal to innocent. These categories determined the amounts of fines and in a few cases the length of a prison term, usually short. Although the attempt was laudable, it was doomed to fail because of its overemphasis on the psychological aspect. The American reeducation policy stressed such elements as inculcating Germans with the political habits prevalent in parliamentary democracy: "The deeper significance of majority and minority positions would be taught, as well as the principle of harmonious interrelationship between them" ("Germany after the War," Columbia Univeristy conference in 1944 by the Joint Committee on Post-War Planning, *82,* 415). Whatever its effects, the reeducation program did not amount to an antifascist restructuring of the society; rather, the rapid economic recovery on the basis of the free-enterprise system determined the direction of West Germany's political culture. It led to political restoration that was to last until challenged in the waning days of the Adenauer era.

## Early *Länder* Constitutions (East and West)

Beside writers and cultural critics in favor of combining both features of the political and economic systems, the provisional constitutions of the various *Länder* prior to the formation of the two German states provided similar general outlines for a new political order. For instance, in the Constitution of the State of Hesse enacted October 29, 1946, by the constitutional assembly of that state and adopted by the voters in a referendum held on December 1, 1946, Article 38 declares:

> The economy of the *Land* has the function of serving the welfare of the entire population and satisfying their requirements. For this purpose, legislation must provide the measures necessary to guide manufacture, production and distribution in an appropriate manner, to insure everyone a just share in the economic results of all labor, and to protect everyone against exploitation.

The framers of this and other state constitutions were particularly sensitive to the problem of economic abuse: "Property, the nature of which is conducive to the misuse of economic freedom in this manner, must be transferred to public ownership in accordance with legislative provisions" (Article 39). In more practical terms there were several constitutional provisions that outlined public ownership of coal, iron, steel, banking, and the insurance business. Likewise, major land reforms were planned because, "Large landed estates, which history has shown to contain the risk of political misuses or to favor militarist tendencies, must be expropriated within the framework of special laws on land reform" (Article 42). These constitutional *Länder* outlines were finally amended when the federal constitution was drawn up for the FRG in 1949. Several plebiscites and the majority of the emerging political parties supported the *Länder* constitutions. In general these constitutions encouraged the democratization of the political decision-making process to allow grass-roots activism to give direction to the parties. The trend toward grass-roots party activity runs through the political culture of the FRG to the present day. *Länder* constitutions also emphasized control of monopolies. This was true even in the more conservative *Länder* of Bavaria and Baden-Württemberg. Furthermore, the removal of elected officials through direct plebiscite was encouraged to insure accountability and to prevent political power from being held without easy recall. Lastly, all constitutions insisted that important posts go to reliable democrats, that is, to people without Nazi pasts.

Key constitutional provisions for *Länder* in the Soviet zone envisioned a freedom for the citizenry that never came to pass: the Mecklenburg Constitution, enacted by the *Landtag* of that state on January 15, 1947, declared: "All citizens, without distinction, are admitted to public office in accordance with their qualifications . . ." (Article 7). Article 9 affirmed: "Every citizen has the right to reside in a place of his own choice in the *Land*. He has the right to immigrate." This promise remains unfulfilled. In education the Mecklenburg Constitution decreed that, "The schools shall provide everyone with a comprehensive education, commensurate with his abilities and talents, irrespective of the social position of the parents and of religious denomination" (Article 97). These articles of the Constitution were later modified or not carried out at all. When it became official policy in the GDR to encourage children of the labor class, but not of the middle class, free access to educational opportunities effectively ended. Thus socialization of industry in the western zones of Germany and political freedoms in the Soviet zone fell victims to the diverging policies of the wartime Allies and emerging cold-war confrontation.

An eclectic approach to both imported political systems was also evident in the manifestoes of the various democratic parties that had reconstituted themselves after the war. In the Soviet zone political activities started soon after the war with the avowed aim of creating a popular front of the left with the Leninist-Stalinist party at the head. The Western Allies were much more reluctant to encourage political party activity beyond the communal and regional level. Although no Allied wartime decision determined the outcome, it was quite clear that the Western Allies emphasized an economic and the Soviets a political approach to their occupation zones.

# 4. Political Parties

The SPD (*Sozialdemokratische Partei Deutschlands,* Social Democratic Party of Germany) represented the main party to the left of center. As early as 1944, when the Nazis were still in power, a number of Social Democrats worked toward a "Union of the Left." In their Buchenwald platform, drawn up in May 1944 while still in the concentration camp, they agreed on a political manifesto to unite Social Democrats, Communists, and Catholics in an antifascist front. As concentration-camp interns they felt a common bond, but it did not last beyond the end of the war. Yet in the early postwar years the Social Democrats continued to rely on antifascist sentiments as a political rallying point. The party was led by the political firebrand and deeply moral politician, Kurt Schumacher, SPD deputy in the Reichstag before 1933 and a concentration-camp victim for ten years. He was fervently socialist as well as resolutely against the KPD (*Kommunistische Partei Deutschlands,* Communist Party of Germany) because of its pro-Soviet orientation. This attitude of the Social Democrats embodied in their principle spokesman pointed toward an early split in the ranks of the political left. As could be expected, in the Soviet zone the idea of a unified *Volksfront* (left) was supported, particularly as it meant eventual victory for the KPD because of its better internal organization and its backing by the Soviets. Furthermore, the returning SPD exile groups from England did not support the *Volksfront* idea adhered to by the communists who had returned to Germany with the Soviet army. By October 1945 the Social Democrats in the West decided that they would not be responsible for the party in the Soviet zone, and by May 1946 the party program was in place: although the SPD opposed a unification with Soviet-led communists, it advocated the general socialization of all means of production and declared itself the "party of all working people who live from the result of their own labor" (*214,* 540). The SPD came down hard on monopolies and uncontrolled free enterprises, and it supported a unified Germany that would remain neutral and unable to rearm. The SPD advocacy of socializing the economy had broad support not only in the party itself but also in the population at large. Even the conservative CDU (*Christlich-Demokratische Union,* Christian Democratic Party) initially wanted the abolition of monopolies and briefly considered socializing the means of production. Both major parties, which were to shape postwar German political culture (the SPD and the CDU), started out with similar economic platforms that differed only in degree:

Owing to the power given to it by the masses, the democratic state must be moved into an ever more clearly defined opposition to a capitalist economy, which is ruled ever more exclusively by a group of capitalists motivated by profit. The socialization of industry, finance, and the breakup of the big landed estates are necessary in order to place a socialist stamp onto the economic order of the state. (*69*, III, 9 9 ff.)

—SPD, Schumacher, 1945

The predominance of big capital, of private monopolies and cartels will be ended. . . . Public ownership should be increased, as necessary for the common good. The postal service, the railroads, coal industry, and production in general should as a matter of principle be central to the public concern. Banking and insurance should be subjected to state control. (*69*, II, 34 ff.)

—CDU, *Kölner Leitsätze* (Cologne Principles), 1945

But this common focus soon disappeared. The discussion held in March 1946 between Schumacher and Konrad Adenauer, head of the CDU (later West Germany's first chancellor and thus overseer of its economic recovery), has historical importance for postwar politics:

But then Schumacher said: "Under these circumstances I would be willing to cooperate with you. However, under one condition: You and your young party, Mr. Adenauer, must accept the preeminence of the SPD. This does not seem to me to be an unfair request. Because every objective observer must admit that the SPD is and will remain the largest and most promising party."

Adenauer replied icily: "I am personally of a different opinion. I do not believe that the SPD will be the largest party. This decision should be left up to the coming election."

(*168,* 56)

History proved Adenauer and his conservative party correct, and Schumacher and the Social Democrats in error. Why? The SPD was in terms of the age of its members an old party. Most of its 1946 membership was made up of pre-Hitler faithfuls. It still considered itself exclusively a workers' party, and the middle class, faced with a political choice after the war, did not overlook the fact that the SPD was bound to Marxism ideologically, no matter how anti-Soviet it was in practical politics. This Marxist orientation limited the SPD's attractiveness for many voters. But even more important, its insistence on socialization ran counter to the Allied-led economic recovery based on an aggressive free-enterprise approach. It is an irony of history that the SPD, which based its ideology on an economic theory, failed to understand the dynamics of the postwar recovery and its influence on political culture.

A further reason for the limited political success of the SPD can be found in the German labor movement. In terms of its ideology and actual voter base, the SPD drew its strength from German labor. The labor movement, like the rest of the country, was confronted with a choice between a radical transformation of the economic system on the one hand, and continuing collaboration with management on the other. In view of the political history of German labor, it is not surprising that the German labor movement opted for cooperation with management. It had been given a stake in running German industry under the unique principle of *Mitbestimmung* (codetermination). Under this law the German laborer had a measure of legally established influence in the management of many key industries. His representatives sat on supervisory and management boards. Codetermination, combined with cradle-to-grave social legislation (put into effect by Bismarck in the nineteenth century), insured a continuing stability of a labor-management relationship unknown in other Western democracies. Such extensive cooperation between industry and labor after the war, fueled by the general spirit of mobilization against material want, helped the economic recovery of West Germany and hindered the radical change of society along socialist principles envisioned by the Social Democrats. Under these circumstances the SPD had to yield preeminence to the conservative party in the immediate postwar years. Its antifascist thrust was not enough to bring the SPD to power.

The CDU was much better suited to provide the political impetus for the economic boom. Unlike the SPD, the CDU did not build on the party structure or on the members who were active before 1933. It was a centrist or right-of-center party that started out with an open-ended social program that combined a Christian, pan-European ideology with economic liberalism. The left-wing features of the early party manifestoes that emphasized a "Christian socialism" were discarded, although the platform of the CDU (the so-called Ahlen program), ratified in February 1947, still contained socialist elements.

The early socialist features in the CDU party program were balanced by a vague support of the "strengthening of the economic power and the freedom of the individual," which eventually became the cornerstone of post-war economic and political recovery. The CDU decision to socialize large industry was intended to disassociate the new conservative party from big industry and from the old conservative parties that had helped Hitler to power in the waning days of the Weimar Republic. The socialist elements in the CDU program had less to do with economics than with the need to establish legitimacy. On the other hand, support for free enterprise was in tune with the freewheeling economic reality the Allies introduced. Adding to the conservative party's strength was its avowed belief in pan-European Christian culture. This Christian European cosmopolitan attitude appealed to Germany in its need to become part of a new Europe based on old principles. It was symbolized by the two dominant political figures of France and Germany, Konrad Adenauer and Charles de Gaulle, as they knelt side by side in the Cathedral of Reims. The pan-European Christian attitude provided the moral base upon which to build a conservative political party after Hitler. Its openness toward regional interests also strengthened the CDU. The party's insistence that it was no longer bound to a particular denomination increased its appeal beyond the Catholic vote, which traditionally had backed the Christian conservative parties during the Weimar Republic. Nevertheless, the party's main strength remained in the Catholic regions of Germany (Rhineland-Westphalia, Baden-Württemberg, and Bavaria). Because of the postwar division, the predominantly Protestant areas of Germany were either under Soviet occupation or had been given to Poland. Only northwest Germany (Lower Saxony and Schleswig-Holstein) was Protestant. The religious geography of the FRG contributed to the strength of the CDU and its sister party, the CSU (*Christlich-Soziale Union,* Christian Socialist Union), a Bavarian variant of German conservatism. Today the CSU with its pronounced regional flavor, under the controversial but brilliant leadership of Franz Joseph Strauss, represents the right wing of the parliamentary parties. Because of its regional focus, its national base remains limited, impeding the emergence of a strong united right wing party.

There were various smaller parties. The old FDP (*Freie Demokratische Partei,* Free Democratic Party) was also reconstituted after the war. Despite its distinguished history, it was not a prominent political force in the immediate postwar years. The only other party worthy of note was the BHE (*Bund der Heimatvertriebenen und Entrechteten,* Association of the Displaced and Disenfranchised). This loose organization attracted the German refugees from the east. Politically a volatile group with a primary goal of regaining lost German territories, it could have become a potent force if it had not been for the remarkable feat of postwar economic recovery. But the refugees were integrated into the political and economic life of West Germany, and consequently the BHE lost its appeal as a rallying point for undoing the results of WWII. The role of the KPD in the western zones was of minimal importance. Once the SPD had decided not to link up with the KPD in an *Einheitsfront* (united front of the left), the influence of the KPD was limited to the Soviet zone where as early as July 14, 1945, the Soviet military government had encouraged the establishment of a "united front of all antifascist parties."

In sum, the political culture of the western part of Germany during 1945 to 1949 may be characterized as open to experimentation with a new political model that was described by the conservative CDU as "a Christian socialism" and by the SPD on the left as a "third way" in which socialism and the free enterprise system would be combined. As economic integration became a reality in the West and political integration proceeded apace in the East, the political culture changed rapidly toward a two-party parliamentary democracy (SPD and CDU) in West Germany, and a one-party organization (SED) in East Germany.

# 5. Culture

The important works of the bourgeois tradition resurfaced. At the same time the new literary stirrings departed radically from the German cultural past as they attempted to come to grips with the problems of survival. The writers of the eastern zone tended to link up with the antifascist writings of German authors in exile.

The last productive years of Thomas Mann coincided with the postwar years. During this period he wrote *Doktor Faustus,* several short stories and essays, and his novella *Die Betrogene* (1953; *The Black Swan,* 1954). But in postwar West Germany the influence of writers such as Mann was limited mainly to a representative role in bourgeois society that still continued to define cultural norms for a diminishing class of German *Bildungsbürger* (educated middle-class cultural elite). In contemporary mass culture the works of Thomas Mann and Hermann Hesse survive as quality leisure commodities.

The first stirrings of postwar literature dealt with the overwhelming traumas of war and the chaos of postwar life. Prior to the founding of the *Gruppe 47,* a group of young German writers, the so-called *Kahlschlag-Lyrik* (the writing of lyric poetry as a clearing-out activity) was exemplary of the new attitude and aesthetic style. Günther Eich's *"Inventur"* ("Inventory") is an example:

> This is my cap
> this is my coat
> here is my shaving kit
> in a linen bag
>
> A tin can:
> my plate, my cup

Into the white tin
I carved my name . . .

Carved here with this
precious nail
which I hide from greedy eyes . . .

The lead pencil
I like best
During the day I write the verses
That I thought up at night . . .

(1945; *231*, I, 10)

All the metaphors and symbols of traditional lyric poetry were gone. What remained was the need to point and name, a first act of creation following total destruction, a resurrection in language of the things that help people survive. The mundane objects of daily life provided writers with a first hint of their identity as survivors.

# THE FOUNDING OF *GRUPPE 47*

After the initial literary reactions of the chaotic experiences of the immediate postwar years, German literature developed new contours with the founding in 1947 of a loosely knit group of young writers and critics *(134)*. This *Gruppe 47* became the central focus for literary activities during the Adenauer years. It provided a cultural counterweight to the all-inclusive concentration on economic growth in the emerging consumer society. The origin of this group of writers and critics goes back to the POW camps in the United States. The German authors and critics Alfred Andersch and Hans Werner Richter, U.S. prisoners of war, founded a prison journal, *Der Ruf (The Call),* in which they outlined their political-cultural creed *(235)*. They advocated a democratic socialism that would combine the best features of Western democracy with socialist elements. This syncretic approach played a significant role in defining German postwar political consciousness. However, American authorities forbade the publication of the journal after a short time for being too "nihilistic." After release from an American prison, Andersch and Richter joined up with a group of young writers who were to become prominent figures in postwar German literature. Eventually most of the best-known writers belonged to the *Gruppe 47:* Heinrich Böll, Günter Grass, Hans-Magnus Enzensberger, Martin Walser, Günther Eich, and Ilse Aichinger. Initially they had the modest goal of meeting once or twice a year to read their own works to each other in the experimental and open-ended atmosphere of the *Gruppe, die keine*

*Gruppe ist* "the group that is no group" *(135,* 31). In spite of its understandable resistance to a collective identity so shortly after the fall of the Reich, the *Gruppe 47* nevertheless became a powerful cultural influence during the Adenauer era.

All the participants believed in the primacy of the individual. More specifically, these writers advocated a "new literary-artistic subjectivity" (Richter, 1947; *189,* 8) as an inalienable article of faith. Hans Werner Richter articulated this belief prior to the founding of this remarkable cultural circle over which he was to preside: *"Das Individuum wird zum ruhenden Pol eines neuen gesellschaftlichen Seins"* ("The individual will become the stable center of a new social existence"; *189,* passim). The group established a radical individualism against the ideals that had led to the collective disaster of Nazi Germany, moreover, against all ideologies that professed to explain the world by giving it a rigid order. Consequently, *Ideologielosigkeit* (being devoid of ideological positions) became the new norm that set the stage for later depoliticalization. (Political concerns had been paramount to Richter and Andersch in their prison journal a few years before). By inference the radical individualism of the *Gruppe 47* was also directed against any kind of organization, political or otherwise. This explains their often repeated claim of not being a group at all. In the long run, however, the writers underestimated their impact on postwar German literature.

Their trademark was a pluralism of writing styles that defied manifestoes and theoretical straightjackets: "The direction? The mode? The Ism? That is not important for the Group 47. What is important is that an artistic writer writes for us and that he writes well according to his own style" (Walser, 1952; *135,* 2). Their individualism was directed against *Innerlichkeit,* the inwardness and withdrawal into a sentimentalized private sphere that had offered neither refuge nor resistance when totalitarianism was in full swing.

Despite its artistic subjectivism and rejection of traditional cultural norms, the *Gruppe 47* exhibited characteristics deeply rooted in German culture. First of all, the writers envisioned a literature with redemptive features and a religiously intense appeal to the moral core of the individual. They considered literature an elitist activity with a great potential for bringing about major social changes, even a "renewal of Germany." Secondly, the group's initial belief in a classless context and its resistance to a political or ideological profile is due to the general disorder of the immediate postwar years and to the suppression of class consciousness during the preceding Nazi years. This presumption of classlessness determined the writers' notions of "American individualism," which they considered free of all ideological boundaries. Thus they overlooked the fact that individualism on this side of the Atlantic is firmly embedded in a social contract of limits and opportunities (*172*, passim). Finally, small-group efforts on behalf of particular needs and aspirations had been an important part of German culture since the eighteenth-century Pietists.

Next to its belief in radical individualism, the group was keenly interested in the problem of language. It was not like the concern of some *fin-de-siècle* Austrians (Hofmannsthal), whose *Sprachnot* (the inability to express things adequately) reflected the psychological ennui of the upper middle class. The language problem of the *Gruppe 47* was social and political. The task was how to rid the German language of the damage it had suffered during 12 years of Nazi misuse. Heinrich Böll, speaking of the postwar situation, stated the problem succinctly: "It was extremely difficult shortly after 1945 to write even one half page of prose" (*135*, 334). Also the writers whose antifascism was clear and whose understanding of the function of language was sophisticated could not escape the deleterious effect of Nazism in their own use of language. When Andersch sent out his clarion call for democracy, for example, he blustered: *"Die Jugend Europas wird einen fanatischen Kampf gegen die Feinde der Freiheit führen"* ("The youth of Europe will fight a fanatical battle against the enemies of freedom"). It is quite apparent that regardless of its genuine freedom-loving content, this proclamation still had the tone and cadence of Nazi speech (*135*, 331).

Yet the overall effect of the group was to bring into the German language a simple directness that removed the distinction between journalism and literature. The group discarded the bourgeois tradition of writing that had characterized German literature from Goethe to Thomas Mann in terms of subject matter, diction, and artistic personality. Bypassing bourgeois literature, the writers and the more progressive among the reading public showed an intense need to become acquainted with the literary, philosophical, and artistic experiments from which they were excluded since 1933. Existentialism (Sartre), psychoanalysis (Freud, in particular), and avant-garde art (expressionism) were avidly absorbed. Plays and novels of the English-speaking world were seen and read for the first time—the works of Ernest Hemingway, Eugene O'Neill, James Joyce—as well as the German authors suppressed by the Nazis, especially Franz Kafka (who wrote in German although he lived in Prague). Cultural impulses from abroad were a welcome release from repression not only for the trend-setting writers of the *Gruppe 47* but also for the educated populace at large. The new "cultural sphere" full of individualism and anarchic overtones reflected the general decentralization of society, ad hoc experimentations, and self-help actions so characteristic of the immediate postwar years on all levels. This sphere of culture, in which writers, critics, and editors could communicate with one another, became a legitimate vantage point of social and literary life through which the consumer society of the Adenauer years could be understood and criticized in the decades to come.

During its early years, 1947 to 1950, the group did not bring forth literary works of major importance. The cultural theoretician Theodor Adorno had declared that after the extermination camps it would no longer be possible to write poetry. But this was not the main cause for the early silence. More important than the moral collapse of German society was the overwhelming personal trauma of totalitarian repression and wartime destructiveness—a subject difficult to translate into literary fiction. Even years later, after the *Gruppe 47* was producing works of great literary merit, a central theme remained the inability to integrate the traumatic events of 1933 to 1945 into the lives of protagonists and, by inference, to bring the Nazi past within the artistic grasp of authors. The themes, attitudes, and styles that characterized the bourgeois traditions of writing since the nineteenth century could not be readily adapted to deal with the traumas of Nazism. Only very few writers, among them Thomas Mann, Bertolt Brecht, and Anna Seghers, were able to articulate in fiction what had happened in Germany since 1933—Thomas Mann through his ability to abstract and symbolize events; Brecht and other socialist writers out of the moral convictions derived from their socialist loyalties. Furthermore, right after the war there was no established public sphere where these young writers could have advanced their literary endeavors. The reading public, such as it was, tended to show its allegiance to the traditional bourgeois writers that now could be read again, particularly Mann and Hesse.

Expressionism, the most appropriate literary model for these young writers, had not been available to them during the Nazi years. Besides, the emphasis placed by expressionism on experimentation with language, imagery, and form was too "art-and literature-centered" to be adequate for the immediacy that the times demanded. Nevertheless, some poets reached back to expressionism to give shape to the horrors of violence, war, and suppression. Nelly Sachs, in her nightmare vision of the human being as a marionette caught in the web of destructive forces (*Welche geheimen Wünsche,* 1945; *What Secret Wishes*), draws from expressionism:

> Arms up and down
> legs up and down
> And in the moving ash-grey horizon of fear

gigantic the Star of Death
standing there like the clock of time.

(230, I, 31–32)

But none of the poets reached the sheer power of Paul Celan's *Todesfuge* ("Death Fugue"), ". . . death is a master from Germany . . ." in which the expressionist cry links the theme of "death and the maiden" with mass destruction in the concentration camps. Alongside Picasso's painting *Guernica*, Celan's poem stands as a great cultural monument to human suffering, tangible and universal at the same time.

The writers who were able to draw from an established moral context had an easier time finding the words to express what had happened in Germany. Foremost among them was Heinrich Böll, a Catholic born in 1917. He brought his moral strength to bear on the problem of Nazism. His novel *Wo warst du Adam?* is a characteristic example of the early output of Böll and the *Gruppe 47*. It is, among other things, the story of an SS officer in charge of an extermination camp. He has the task of carrying out the extermination of the inmates expeditiously, and he considers it his public duty to do the job well. Thus in public life he is the perfect bureaucrat whose supreme value is the smooth functioning of the state. He is the quintessential average man who fits into the dominant patterns of the society into which he happens to be born. (Years later Hannah Arendt pointed out in her book on Adolf Eichmann, one of the most notorious extermination agents, that psychological tests showed him to be an "average human being"). In his private world the SS officer is a different person altogether—sentimental, almost sensitive, and a great admirer of traditional German songs. To cultivate his private cultural interests, he forms a choir of talented singers from the inmates of his camp, ignoring the discrepancy between his private interests and his public duties. The bureaucrat in charge of extermination and the lover of music live in different worlds. Finally, when Maria, a beautiful Jewish girl with a fine voice auditions before him by singing the *Sancta Dei Genetrix (Holy Mother of God)*, he is personally touched and the walls between the two worlds begin to crumble inside him. He reaches for his pistol and shoots the girl on the spot. This bizarre narrative drives home Böll's intense moral outrage. He explains Nazism in part as a result of the moral collapse of bourgeois values, which were predicated on a basic split between the private "humane" sphere and the public sphere with its social laws.

Like Böll's moral paradigms, Günther Eich's lyric poetry also captures the postwar years most effectively. His *Kahlschlag-Lyrik* is often cited as the first significant lyric utterance of the postwar generation. He was one of the first to introduce into his poems a gentle tone evocative of mundane things, a modern elegy for normal daily existence and the stability it could bring. After the upheavals of the war, such words as *window, clothes line, Danube bridge,* and *roofs* formed a wistful hope, even a promise of normalcy and good cheer: "Our life, it passes fast as if we were flying away, and hidden in the abyss, happiness dwells" (*Augenblick im Juni,* "Moment in June"; *189, 96*). Other poets also attempted to capture the nightmare of the war and the bombing raids. For instance, Ingeborg Bachmann's *Nachtflug* ("Night Flight," 1952) already shows a symbolic transformation of the war experience generally not found in the poems composed immediately after the war.

Radical simplicity in poetic language (we need poets who call "a tree a tree, a woman a woman, poets who say yes and who say no; loud and clear and three times without subjunctive," Wolfgang Borchert, *Manifesto; 230,* I, 12), coincides with the existential discovery of the isolated self after the war:

> Behind everything that you call God, stream and star, night and mirror or cosmos or Hilde or Evelyn—behind everything there stands always you. Icy and lonely. Pitiful. Grand. Your laughter, Your distress, Your question. Your answer.
>
> (*230,* I, 13)

During its formative years between 1947 and 1950, the *Gruppe 47* provided a social and cultural focus for a group of authors and critics who were trying to write and speak in spite of the violence done to the German language by the Nazis. They were attempting to come to grips with themselves as individuals and survivors, and they grappled with the overwhelming events that had overtaken the Germans whom the war had uprooted: "They wander from North to South, from East to West and from West to East. In part, they have lost their homeland and are now living in railroad stations and trains" (Richter, *Unterhaltungen am Schienenstrang,* 1946; *Conversations Along the Railroad Track; 230,* I, 46).

## THE PROBLEM OF MASTERING THE PAST: FRIEDRICH MEINECKE, THOMAS MANN, LEO LÖWENTHAL

Several attempts were made by sociologists and cultural historians to come to grips with the Nazi past (*Vergangenheitsbewältigung).* Most instructive are three divergent analyses of Nazi totalitarianism presented by the great German historian Friedrich Meinecke, by the sociologist and cultural critic Leo Löwenthal, and by Thomas Mann, who appeared in the spring of 1945 before the United States Congress to present his views of Germany.

In his book *Die deutsche Katastrophe (The German Catastrophe;* 156), Meinecke assailed the optimism of the Enlightenment for having encouraged a "false striving for unattainable happiness in the masses." He believed that this encouragement was directly responsible for the two great waves of nationalism and socialism in the nineteenth century that later merged in Nazism. He advocated a return to a cultural conservatism in which religion as well as culture—the latter signifies Weimar classicism for him—provided a sufficient moral base for building a new Germany. His argument overlooked almost all social and psychological determinants of the Nazi rise to power. His insistence on the "Purification and making inward the life of our soul" (*156*, 164), perpetuated the apolitical attitude of the Germans that Hitler had exploited so effectively just a short time before.

Leo Löwenthal, a member of the Frankfurt School of Social Thought, in 1945 described the psychological characteristics of totalitarian terrorism *(141)*. He defined dehumanization as a "total integration of the population into a collective that paralyzes all interpersonal communication" (*141, 26*). Subjected to the whim and the omnipotence of the state, the individual broke down because on a deeper psychological level his experience lost its continuity. The normal rhythms of the individual's life were disrupted. As a result he became a bundle of spontaneous reactions to overwhelming traumas (*141, 28*), which turned him into putty in the hands of the dictatorial exploiter. In this way a fatal link was forged between the oppressor and the oppressed. Löwenthal concluded that terror was as much a part of history as the "dream of freedom and happiness." In spite of the detailed information that had just become available about concentration camps, Löwenthal's conclusion was optimistic. He broke with Sigmund Freud's starkly dualistic standoff between the death instinct and life instinct (*Civilization and Its Discontents,* 1936) by affirming that enlightened reason will and must win out in the long run. Although he did not state it specifically, the origins of Löwenthal's optimism in the face of modern totalitarian dictatorships can be found in the eighteenth-century Enlightenment, which Meinecke condemned as the root of modern political excesses. The two merely stress different aspects of the Enlightenment. For Löwenthal the emergence of reason made emancipation and individual responsibility possible, whereas for Meinecke the eighteenth-century notion of a general popular will fueled modern totalitarian states. Löwenthal did not ignore the general popular will; he merely brought it up to date and analyzed its modern mutation, namely, mass culture and its leveling effect on the individual.

In his congressional address Thomas Mann spoke of Germany in metaphors (*"Deutschland und die Deutschen"; 50,* 225 ff.) and evoked before his American audience the dark side of German culture. He drew a picture of the irrational and romantic German and his penchant for hysteria, medieval in origin. Mann pointed to an inwardness that attracted the Germans to music, poetry, and fantasy but not to social and rational discourse. He turned to the French novelist Honoré de Balzac, who said in 1839, "The Germans don't know how to play the great instruments of liberty, but they are naturally adept at playing all the instruments of music." Mann's complex analysis stressed the contradictory element in the German character. For him Faust's pact with the devil was a paradigm of Germany in the twentieth century. Mann presented intuitive and artistic insights into Germany but, just like Meinecke, he barely acknowledged the social determinants of collective behavior. He was more interested in creating a myth of a national character than in a rational analysis of Nazism.

Thomas Mann saw Nazism as a German problem to be understood as part of Germany's intellectual and cultural history. Meinecke explained Nazism in a European context. Löwenthal related Nazism and totalitarian terror to modern mass society in general. These immediate postwar efforts at coming to grips with the past did not find a receptive public in West Germany, absorbed as it was in the all-consuming task of survival. With the advent of the "economic miracle" under Adenauer, the Nazi past was repressed for almost two decades.

Between 1945 and 1949 the pattern for contemporary German culture and society emerged; most important, the division of Germany was determined. The origins of this division can be found in the different policies put into effect by the wartime Allies in their occupational zones despite their agreements about a united Germany: the West opted for economic recovery; the East, for political integration. In due course politics in the western zones developed in consonance with a Western economic orientation; in the East political developments brought about eventual economic integration under the Soviet sphere of influence. Yet the primacy of economics over politics in the West and of politics over economics in the East defines the relationship of the two German states to each other, and it continues to contribute to their self-images.

After the division of Germany, postwar West German culture eventually developed an antagonism toward the all-embracing consumer society under Konrad Adenauer. The promising beginnings of an antifascist literature based on emigré writers in East Germany became for decades a handmaiden of the rigid Marxist-Leninist regime under Walter Ulbricht. Finally, in the immediate postwar years there was a short-lived openness, cooperation, and experimentation in all spheres of the decentralized social, cultural, and political life. Although it was a period of deprivation and uncertainty, for a time high hopes bloomed that a united Germany might be established within a group of peaceful and cooperative European nations.

# Chapter III

# ERA OF RECONSTRUCTION: THE ADENAUER YEARS (1949-1966)

## 1. Personalities

The period of reconstruction overlapped with "the economic miracle." During this time entrepreneurs, politicians, and institutions of the Weimar Republic returned to power and "a restored world of money and materialism and militarism" emerged (*42*, 124). Reconstruction also democratized the government, brought integration with the Western Allies, and, later, rapprochement with the Eastern bloc.

To rise from the ashes of a bomb-scarred country within a decade would not have been possible for the West Germans had it not been for several important factors: (1) the people's eagerness to rebuild their lives and gain prosperity through hard work—millions of refugees helped provide a pool of cheap labor that kept wage demands down; (2) the currency reform of 1948; (3) economic help in the form of Marshall Plan aid; (4) the strengthening political cooperation between the Allies and the budding German state, especially at a time of threatening Soviet expansion westward—e.g., the Berlin blockade of 1948; (5) a relatively small percentage of the GNP had to be paid for the stationing of occupation forces; (6) the "social market economy" and private initiative, particularly in the field of exports; and (7) skillful guidance by three distinguished leaders who secured economic and political stability for the FRG: President Theodor Heuss, Chancellor Konrad Adenauer, and Minister of Economics Ludwig Erhard.

Heuss was a liberal politician from Swabia who had served as a member of the Weimar Parliament and as a lecturer on political science in Berlin before his writings were prohibited by the Nazi regime. A modest but charismatic personality, he was appointed professor at the *Technische Universität,* Stuttgart, in 1947. When he assumed the federal presidency in 1949, a position without political power, no one could anticipate that Heuss would considerably influence the political climate of the republic for a whole decade.

The most important statesman since Bismarck, Konrad Adenauer led his people out of a desperate situation, ended suspicions among West European nations, and won back respect for his country in the eyes of the world. François Seydoux, the French ambassador to West Germany, remarked about Adenauer: "He stands in history like a monument" (*123,* 139). Adenauer was already 73 years old when he took over the chancellorship, yet he remained in office longer than the combined twenty-one cabinets of the Weimar Republic and longer than Hitler's Third Reich. He achieved most of his goals during his first term (1949–1953), taking up the work of reconciliation among former enemy states where Gustav Stresemann had left off before WWII.

Adenauer was born in Cologne in 1876 and studied at the universities of Freiburg, Munich, and Bonn before he became a lawyer. From 1917 to 1933 he served as lord mayor of Cologne and as president of the Parliamentary Council. Removed from his positions by the Nazis in 1933, he was arrested after the coup of July 20, 1944, in which he was suspected to be involved. When after the war the American forces looked for reliable Germans to govern Cologne, he was reinstated as mayor. Dismissed by the British for "incompetence," he cofounded the CDU and became president of the Parliamentary Council that drafted the *Grundgesetz* (Basic Law) in 1949. By the time he became chancellor, Adenauer's political career had already spanned three distinct eras of German history: the *Kaiserreich,* the Weimar Republic, and the Hitler years. By the time he retired, he had served his country in fifty public offices.

A summary of German achievements under Adenauer provides the framework for the following sections. During this time West Germany experienced an unprecedented reconstruction—internally through its miraculous economic recovery and externally through its growing international importance. Economic revival occurred simultaneously with the recovery of political sovereignty as the FRG became integrated into the economic and political organizations of the Western democracies. For Adenauer this was the only road to autonomy and prosperity. Thus his foreign policy was firmly based on friendship with France and Britain, and strict alignment with the U.S. An effort at reconciliation with Israel followed.

The rapid realization of his goals can be explained partly by Allied good will at the height of the Korean cold-war confrontation, partly by the dynamism of the German people, but above all by Adenauer's experience, character, and methods. As a man he was rational, steady, cautious, devoted to duty, and endowed with a ready wit. He was a tough, realistic, and persuasive negotiator. He wielded power skillfully and employed a patriarchal authority in his management of men. In the face of great odds, he used his power of persuasion more than anything else to influence political opponents and to win the trust of Germany's former enemies who, from 1945 were represented by the occupation authorities. "Both as chancellor and foreign minister, Adenauer applied himself to cultivating the friendship and esteem of foreign politicians and diplomats" (*123, 33*). His style of government came to be known as *Kanzlerdemokratie* (chancellor democracy)—a mixture of authoritarian control and grudging recognition of democratic institutions only insofar as they did not hamper his legal right to "determine the direction of politics"—perhaps not surprising from a man who between 1951 and 1955 was his own foreign and defense minister. But this style convinced his countrymen "that the authority for which they longed could be found in a democratic government under his leadership, and they never seriously wavered in that faith until his retirement" (*42, 44*).

The "wise old fox" Adenauer survived a number of domestic and international crises, but toward the end of his rule he suffered a considerable loss in stature. After ten years in office, his ambition apparently got the better of him; he decided to have himself put up for nomination for the federal presidency in the belief that he would be able to run things from behind the scenes by means of a handpicked successor to the chancellorship. His fall was hastened by his failure to fly to Berlin in 1961 when the Wall was built and when people wanted to know where he stood on the question of German reunification. The final blow came a year later with the "Spiegel Affair," the illegal arrest of the editors of the influential leftist magazine under suspicion of treason in October 1962. This incident became the occasion for the middle class to demonstrate publicly its displeasure with a breach of democratic processes. It stood up for freedom of the press against the dictatorial measures taken by the police and by Secretary of Defense Franz Joseph Strauss. Adenauer's government fell and it took him six weeks to form a new cabinet.

In foreign relations the chancellor suffered severe setbacks too. Perhaps "the worst blow that Adenauer's diplomacy ever suffered" (*123, 39*) occurred when a plan for a supranational European defense community failed to pass the French Assembly in Paris in 1954. Instead, rearmament came through West Germany's accession to NATO. A further setback for Europe, not so much for Adenauer personally, occurred when de Gaulle vetoed British entry into the Common Market in 1963.

As a *Realpolitiker* Adenauer secured peace, prosperity, and respect for the FRG as well as membership in the European Community and the Atlantic Alliance. But this integration of West Germany into the West was achieved at the expense of Germany's future reunification, a goal more vigorously pursued by his SPD opponents Kurt Schumacher and Erich Ollenhauer, who had aimed for a neutral and demilitarized Germany between the superpower blocs. Adenauer denigrated his opposition and adhered rigidly to his dogma of the nonexistence of a second German state, the so-called Hallstein Doctrine, by which the FRG did not maintain diplomatic relations with any nation (except the Soviet Union) that recognized the GDR. Although he remained hostile toward the Soviet Union, he went to Moscow in 1955 to restore diplomatic relations and to negotiate the release of the last 10,000 German prisoners of war.

# 2. The Economy

## THE ECONOMIC MIRACLE

Although Adenauer was largely responsible for the rapid political emergence of West Germany as a sovereign country, his minister of economics, Ludwig Erhard (later vice-chancellor and chancellor), deserves much of the credit for the recovery, the *Wirtschaftswunder*. Adenauer did not conceal his animosity for the popular Erhard, yet together they laid the groundwork for the ensuing prosperity in West Germany—Adenauer by negotiating the Petersberg agreement with the high commissioners in November 1949 (this halted the further dismantling of German industries and opened the way for Germany's membership in international organizations); Erhard by standing up to the high commissioners when he decided to lift the economic controls that hampered industry in the trizonal region. As Britain and France still had wartime-controlled economies, the military governors could not have taken such a farsighted and courageous step (*200, 40*). Along with the currency reform of 1948, it enabled Erhard to establish his *soziale Marktwirtschaft* (social market economy). This formed the cornerstone of the "miracle" that was to transform West Germany within a decade from what the French newspaper *Paris Match* in 1952 called a lunar landscape into a flourishing beehive. Particularly Americans credited Erhard with West Germany's return to prosperity and helped him to his reputation as "champion of international economic freedom."

What were the characteristic features of this system? Since 1948 the German economy was characterized by the rejection of the laissez-faire doctrine and of major government intervention in favor of free play of market forces: supply and demand, competition, private initiative, efficiency, and profit. Erhard believed in "as little state as possible, as much state as necessary," because the marketplace should decide prices, wages, and products. Entrepreneurs received incentives, such as tax deductions, for innovations and investments, the state enacted a *Kartellgesetz* (law against restraints of competition) in 1957 to prevent a lack of competition through mergers. This policy allowed enterprise to invest and to profit optimally; at the same time it ensured full employment and worker participation in the new prosperity, including collective bargaining. Market prices were freely negotiated between suppliers and consumers, who secured a wide choice of goods. High performance of the system was ensured by the competition to win customers. And the resultant consumerism and materialism provided individuals with increased leisure and freedom once their basic needs were satisfied.

Ludwig Erhard had a messianic belief in the social justice of his economic system. In his view, consumerism not only allowed for a lightened workload at home (through household appliances, prepared foods, and the like) but, more importantly, also for a rapprochement between classes. He hoped that "prosperity for all" would overcome the old class structure in which a wealthy elite could afford many luxuries but the purchasing power of the lower and middle classes was rather limited. Through stimulating competition Erhard wanted to increase this purchasing power and thereby eliminate exploitation.

It was clear to him from the start that his free-enterprise economy needed some management or regulation by the state. In addition, "concerted action" by various agencies was used to harmonize the regulatory functions of the federation, the states, the trade unions, and the entrepreneur associations. This created a certain balance between the free-enterprise economy and state incentives to export and hold consumption down as required by the "macroeconomic management." Beside these early checks and balances, an economic policy was enacted by the Stability and Growth Act of 1967 which tried to reach four objectives at the same time: stable prices, full employment, adequate growth, and equilibrium in foreign trade (65, 166).

From 1948 to 1949 the German economy was still in shambles. There were tremendous shortages ranging from housing and food to cars, telephones, tables, and beds. With one bold stroke Erhard removed economic controls along with the old currency:

> The change that took place overnight was unbelievable. Stores that had been all but empty, suddenly had their shelves filled again, and a business recovery started that still continues and which has resulted in

West Germany becoming one of the greatest industrial countries in the world.

(*200*, 41)

The dimension of the "German miracle" can be appreciated not only in statistical terms but also in terms of its effects on West German society and the Free World.

It is easy to measure West Germany's prosperity—or "crass materialism," as critics put it—in statistical terms. Whereas initially there was considerable unemployment (11 percent in 1950) because of the destruction and dismantling of industries and the influx of 16 million refugees from the east, an era of full employment was achieved by the late 1950s; unemployment sank to about 1.3 percent by 1960 after about 9 million new jobs were created. Large numbers of refugee workers kept wages down and provided competition with local workers. The first 30,000 foreign workers were hired in 1960. Between 1950 and 1960 industrial production rose by about 150 percent. Three years after the founding of the republic the production level of the prewar period had been reached. "In 1949 an industrial laborer worked 4 hours, 13 minutes to earn one kilogram (2.2 lbs.) of butter; in 1960, 2 hours 19 minutes" (*151*, 143). In September 1950 there were 10 million housing units for the 50 million people in the FRG, but by 1961 the figure had risen to more than 16 million, with half a million new dwellings added each year. Automobile ownership was rare after the war— only 9 people in 1,000 had a car. By 1960 this number increased to 70 per 1,000, and by 1963 to 128 per 1,000. By 1964 West German car production was second only to the United States, and there were 4,500 miles of freeway as opposed to the 1,300 miles in 1949. By the early 1960s many families owned a car, refrigerator, television set, and an apartment of their own.

Between 1950 and 1963 . . . exports increased nearly sevenfold, automobile production rose twentyfold, and Germany's merchant marine grew to more than seventeen times its former size. By 1963 the Federal Republic was economically the strongest power in Europe except for the Soviet Union; it was the world's second largest exporting country.

(*79*, 195)

Germans were proud of their achievements, and foreigners tended to look with amazement and sometimes envy on the economic miracle of the defeated nation. In comparing the economic and social conditions in West Germany with those in England, an essay in the London *Economist* of October 15, 1966, titled "The German Lesson," concluded that Germany had developed into "a heartening decent society" thanks to its economic policy, whereas the English had barely "muddled through" (p. 111 f.).

Whether or not Erhard's dream of social justice was realized, nevertheless a consumer society came into being in which workers merged with the middle class to a large degree. Moreover, this strong performance of the West German economy allowed for the "greatest peaceful redistribution of wealth that has ever taken place" (*123*, 88) without disrupting the economic system as a whole. In 1952 the West Germans introduced a *Lastenausgleichgesetz* (burden-sharing law) aimed at equalizing burdens and integrating refugees who had suffered during or after the war or as a result of the currency reform. The program was financed by the state, the *Länder*, and the citizenry who were taxed up to 50 percent of their pre-1945 assets over a period of thirty years. The strong economy was, of course, a decisive factor in its success. Within a matter of years the refugees were integrated and their shattered lives rebuilt.

In the same year the flourishing economy made it possible for Adenauer to offer financial restitutions to the Jewish people for the crimes committed against them by the Nazis. The FRG undertook to pay a sum of 3.5 billion DM within twelve years to those Jews who had fled from German-occupied territories to make their home in Israel. Jewish refugees living elsewhere and other individual survivors were also given financial assistance; the Jewish Material Claims Conference handled their claims until 1966. These reparations to Israel in the face of an Arab boycott "had a decisive effect on the recovery of respect for Germany throughout the world" (*123*, 92).

In 1949, when President Truman announced his "Point Four" program for assistance to developing countries, West Germany was still in dire need of development aid. But ten years later it ranked second to the United States in productivity and world trade. This favorable situation moved Erhard to declare in 1959 that West Germany's prosperity should not be restricted only to improve the living conditions of its own people, but should also consider the needs of underdeveloped countries (*200*, 405 f.). Thus the FRG joined the United States in extending financial assistance to Third World nations for building large industrial projects such as dams, power plants, and factories. Later on the FRG found it more effective to emphasize technical assistance, training of foreign students, and missionary and Peace Corps work. Also, a policy of West German trade with developing countries has been so successful that a number of them have been able to build up an export surplus to the FRG since 1972.

The "German miracle" set an example of successful free trade for the Western world. It was Erhard who believed in "the long-range importance of a free market to a free society and a free world" (200, 41). He advocated liberalization of trade, free convertibility of European currencies, economic integration of free Europe, and the creation of an Atlantic economic community. Through its prosperity West Germany contributed to the economic stability of the Western world, and its essentially free-trade zone still functions as Erhard envisioned.

The economic miracle, which depended on the German people and the farsightedness of their leaders, on peace between labor and management, and on the rapid integration of West Germany into international organizations, made progressive achievements on domestic and international fronts possible. But its negative side effects should not go unmentioned: by concentrating almost all efforts on economic recovery, energies were diverted from long overdue social reforms and from reckoning with the Nazi past.

## LABOR PEACE

Before Wilhelm Leuschner, one of the leading trade unionists of the Weimar Republic, was executed by the Nazis, he wrote a letter to his friends admonishing them to remain united and to reconstruct the labor movement *("Einig bleiben und wiederaufbauen!")*. This call became the motto for the new trade unions of the postwar period. The working men and women in the reopened factories provided a starving population with the essentials necessary for survival. In cooperation with the Allied authorities, they halted the dismantling of factories and created a "worker's paradise" in partnership with management. Although the SPD had opposed the "social market economy" during the first legislative period (1949–1953) as subservient to capitalist interests, workers to a large degree supported it wholeheartedly. The SPD leadership realized this belatedly and adopted Erhard's economic principles after 1955. An SPD representative declared in that year: "We are proud to be able to state that the unique development of the German economy during the last ten years has been the fruit of a political, economic, and social order based on the principle of freedom" (200, 428).

From the beginning of the FRG, this advocacy of free play in the economic sphere was rooted in the Federal Constitution as the individual's right "to the free development of his personality" (Article 2) as well as to "freedom of association" (Article 9). In particular, "The right to form associations to safeguard and improve working and economic conditions is guaranteed to everyone and to all trades, occupations, and professions" (Article 9, Paragraph 3). These constitutional guarantees led to the reorganization of the trade unions and to the stability of the economic system in general.

The DGB (*Deutscher Gewerkschaftsbund*, German Trade Union Association), consisting of sixteen individual trade unions, was founded in 1949. By its restraint and by its responsible and cooperative policies it "has become one of the foundations of our society" (Helmut Schmidt, *151*, 135), particularly as membership was no longer based on political, religious, or ideological restrictions.

The key to the transformation of war-torn West Germany into a worker's paradise lay in the preservation of social peace. This was achieved by means of *Mitbestimmung* (codetermination), which over the last three decades has been introduced into all branches of industry. Codetermination refers to a system of worker participation in industrial management ("industrial democracy") that gives employees a share in corporate decision making and profits. It was first realized in the coal-and-steel industry in 1951 by the Codetermination Act. Here labor has come to enjoy parity of representation with shareholders on the supervisory board, which influences factory management. Workers elected to it secure labor's participation in basic policy decisions such as mergers, takeovers, and manpower. Since codetermination was not extended to other industries until 1976, and then only to near-parity, this 1951 law concerning heavy industry was a decisive and progressive first step unique in the Western Europe of the fifties. That codetermination was introduced in this branch was largely due to Allied pressure on West Germany to decentralize its heavy industry. The Allies wanted to eliminate any possibility of reviving war production. To this end trade-union participation and some degree of decartelization provided sufficient safeguards. In the case of I.G. Farben, however, "Each of the four companies into which it was divided produces more chemicals, dyes, and medicines than the entire firm had done under Hitler" (*172*, 323F.).

Passage of the *Betriebsratsgesetz* (Works Constitution Act) in 1952 constituted a second important step in the direction of industrial democracy. Although the supervisory board is limited to overall strategy, through their *Betriebsrat,* workers play a considerable role in the daily operations of their company. This law may also be called The Shop Organization Act because it is on the shop floor that corporations with more than 500 employees allow "work councils," which also take an active part in running the factory. These councils have a voice in work rules, production schedules, new technology, and job evaluations. Industrial democracy works, therefore, on various levels at once: on the supervisory board as well as on the shop floor, in the plant (works-council bargaining) as well as in the industry-wide union (trade-union bargaining).

The Codetermination Act and the Works Constitution Act combined to give West German industry a measure of labor peace enjoyed by no other West European country. Legal concessions resulting in voluntary wage restraints and the settlement of disputes through collective bargaining ("shared responsibility") were important cornerstones in laying the foundation for the economic miracle. Since management-labor cooperation was enhanced, strikes and lockouts were kept to a minimum. The rising prosperity of blue-collar workers has virtually eliminated militancy and class struggle. In statistical terms, in "1975 the Federal Republic registered three strike days per 1,000 workers, Great Britain had 262 strike days, France 209, and the U.S. 399 strike days" (627, 54). Although a degree of class differentiation continued in education, achievement, income level ("meritocracy"), and social mobility (172, 329 f.), the hereditary upper class was weakened and the prewar social class structure in Germany gave way to a more egalitarian society after the fall of Nazism, which proved advantageous to West Germany. It has minimized labor confrontations compared to other Western Europe countries where worker participation in management has been a growing trend. Germany has also been helped in this regard by its traditional subservience to authority, by comprehensive and generous social-welfare legislation (since Bismarck) and by the Germans' sheer enjoyment of work and efficiency.

# 3.  Politics

## THE EUROPEAN IDEA AND WEST GERMANY'S INTEGRATION

West Germany's rapid economic reconstruction would not have been possible without its simultaneous integration into Europe. As a political idea, the "United States of Europe" harks back to Charlemagne's Holy Roman Empire and the medieval Church. De Gaulle and Adenauer knelt together in the Cathedral of Reims in 1963 to indicate symbolically a cultural and political unity based on medieval "Catholic" European universalism. In the Middle Ages, "Germany," and even "Europe" were not significant political concepts. Like the knights of the crusades in the Middle Ages, the humanist elite later on regarded itself as cosmopolitan or supranational. Luther's Reformation helped transform the religious and political landscape of Europe into smaller entities, ruled by absolute princes according to the maxim cuius regio, eius religio ("The religion of the prince determines the religion of his subjects," Religious Peace of Augsburg, 1555). Despite the emergence of these individual rulers, the Holy Roman Empire continued to exist, if precariously, as a federation until 1806.

Europe began to take shape as a concert of nations in the sixteenth century. But the balance of power it sought was to break down again and again after the Thirty Years War (1618–1648) be-

cause of the persevering strength of nationalism. After the end of
WWI in 1918, the idea of a "United States of Europe" was conceived by Aristide Briand of France at the League of Nations in Geneva, 1929 and by Gustav Stresemann of Germany in the Treaty of
Locarno in 1925. It took another self-destructive war (WWII)
between the European nations to convince more than a few statesmen that the time was ripe for a restructuring of Europe. Churchill, in a historic speech in Zurich in 1946, called for the foundation of a United States of Europe based on friendly cooperation
between France and Germany. Two years later Adenauer realized
that integration within Europe was the only hope for Germany
(August 28, 1948, CDU Party Congress). His plan provided for an
interweaving of the German, French, and Benelux economies
(*124*, 224). Repeatedly he pointed to Churchill as the father of the
postwar European movement *(europäische Bewegung)*, founded
in 1948. Adenauer and Churchill were joined by Léon Blum
(France), Alcide de Gasperi (Italy), Richard Nikolaus Coudenhove-
Kalergi (Austria), Robert Schuman (France), and Paul Henri Spaak
(Belgium). This impressive team for the unification of Europe was
moved by three main factors:

1. The devastation of WWII was an urgent reminder that a cooperative system had to be evolved to prevent wars between
neighboring nations.

2. Squeezed between the United States and the USSR, the countries of Western Europe foresaw the loss of self-determination if
they did not stand together. In the face of the Soviet presence in
the center of Europe, survival and security of nationhood depended on Western European solidarity.

3. Nazism revealed the horrors of extreme nationalism. Where
once national glory, heroism, and loyalty to the fatherland had
ruled, there was now an ideological vacuum. It was to be filled by
enthusiasm for Europe, especially among German youth, in "reaction to the horrid experience of extreme nationalism [that] had first
made Germans receptive to the idea of a united Europe; now they
were able to see it as a cooperative venture. Hence the paradox of a
nation that having first been pan-German, was now the most pan-
European." (*172*, 316).

The "birth hour" of the "Europe of the Six" came in 1950 when
Robert Schuman, the French Foreign Minister, proposed the formation of a European Community for Coal and Steel (Montan-
Union). For Adenauer, who only a few months earlier had become
West Germany's leader, this first step towards a European Federation, with a supranational Commission in charge of heavy industry, provided the necessary leverage to gradually free the FRG
from the restrictions imposed on it by the Allies. It meant "the
dawn of a new life," because it would hasten the day when the

FRG would become a sovereign and equal partner. Schuman's proposal was completely in line with Adenauer's thinking: "Common economic interests in my view are the most secure and best foundation for a rapprochement of the people and for securing peace" (*124,* 236). In March of 1950, Adenauer pursued this idea when he suggested a political union between France and Germany, to be headed by a single parliament (interview, 7 March 1950, ibid., 238f.). This, in turn, led to Schuman's plan (letter of 9 May 1950), strongly supported by Jean Monnet, who argued that French industrial reconstruction would be jeopardized if the question of German production and its competitiveness was not settled. "If we do nothing, we face another war, not caused by or against Germany, but because "of Germany" *(162).* Fear that a Germany having regained her former strength might again dominate Europe was at the heart of the French initiative, but it worked also in favor of European integration. This treaty of 1952 represented the strongest renunciation of national sovereignty made by Western European nations. Adenauer wrote:

> I was convinced that the *Montanunion* in its results would change not only the economic relations of the peoples of our continent but also the whole way of thinking and political feeling of Europeans. I was convinced that it would lead the Europeans out of the confines of their nation-state existence into the broad reaches of the European area, and this would give the life of the individual a greater and richer meaning. The youth of all European peoples have longed for this . . .

> *(42,* 46).

In 1958 a second, and more decisive step followed—the founding of the European Economic Community (EEC or Common Market) with Belgium, France, West Germany, Italy, Luxembourg, and The Netherlands as members. These countries intended to create a "supermarket" for the exchange of goods and labor without artificial trade barriers. Its customs union would serve as a model for reducing restrictions in international trade and provide a motivating force for a future political federation. Indeed, the last customs tariffs within the Community disappeared after a decade. During its first phase, the EEC achieved what it set out to do: economically, it advanced as a whole and thereby contributed to strong revivals in all its partner states. It created a huge market of 260 million people, which was first in world trade, ahead of the US. The member nations developed a sense of solidarity that had been lacking since before the Reformation. Through pooling limited economic resources of each country, the EEC gained the strength to survive among the superpowers.

The Treaty of Rome in 1957 created a number of permanent European institutions. Important among them was the European Council of Ministers *(Ministerrat)*, responsible for taking action necessary to achieve the goals of the treaty. It is also in charge of the budget and of international negotiations. The European Commission, with head-quarters in Brussels, is responsible for proposing legislation, fixing prices, and watching over member states' adherence to European laws. To the dislike of some countries, such as Britain, the Commission has mushroomed into a huge bureaucracy with executive powers in the economic sector. Unfortunately, bureaucratization has grown since Euratom (European Atomic Community) and the ECSC (Montan-Union) merged with the EEC in 1967.

The Commission president is not directly responsible to any electorate, but rather works for an through the Council. His personal style and diplomatic skill are important in the EEC's effort toward greater unity. If laws have been broken or if disputes arise, it is the European Court of Justice in Luxembourg that has jurisdiction and thereby plays a substantial role in the process of integration. The Council, the Commission, and the Court are complemented by the European Parliament in Strassbourg. Its members were initially appointed by the national parliaments between 1958 and 1979. It consisted of 142 members and functioned as an advisory and debating body.

Next to the creation of the Common Market, perhaps the most important achievement of European integration has been the establishment of this supranational administrative system. With its economic success, the system would need little more than some strengthening through further appropriation of national rights, in order to function as a truly European government.

Due to Adenauer's and Erhard's success in strenghtening West Germany's economy, the Allies considered the lifting of the occupation statute even before full sovereignty was extended to the FRG. The fledgling Republic was invited to join the North Atlantic Treaty Organization (NATO) in October 1954, and this move was ratified in May 1955. The fear of a possible Russian attack on Western Europe during the Korean War (1950–1953) hastened the military integration of the FRG into NATO. The Allies feared the Soviet Union more than the possible reemergence of German military might. Germany's entrance into NATO jolted the Eastern bloc and raised suspicions in some quarters of the West—particularly in France, whose anxieties were allayed only by the promise of the US and Britain to station their troops in West Germany. Even many Germans were taken by surprise. WWII had ended barely ten years earlier. The neutralist opposition represented by the SPD bitterly opposed the formation of a new German army, but it failed to reverse the decision. Ultimately, the West German army *(Bundeswehr)* proved not to be a financial or military disadvantage for the Allies.

The *Bundeswehr* was conceived as a member of an alliance, and from the outset its half million men were placed under NATO command. Apart from its territorial units, this army can act only jointly with the Allied armies. In the light of German military history, great care was taken to insure its being under parliamentary control (article 87 of the Basic Law). After careful screening, about 10,000 officers of the old *Wehrmacht* were commissioned, but in contrast to the former army democratic control was established through a series of laws and institutions. The civilian military commissioner and his staff serve as intermediaries between the army and Parliament. Civil courts have jurisdiction over military offenses. Recruitment is based on general conscription. But article 4 of the Basic Law, which states that no man may be compelled against his conscience to bear arms in military service, allows conscientious objectors to opt for alternative service.

Since its beginning, however, the *Bundeswehr* has suffered from problems of legitimacy. How could a democratic army be built with officers and generals from the *Wehrmacht?* Even the "tradition decree" *(Traditionserlaß)* of 1965 could not solve this dilemma, praising, as it did, the soldierly virtues, such as sense of duty, obedience, and loyalty. The debate about military tradition was not to subside until the 1980s despite the facts that the FRG has become the closest ally of the US and the biggest contributor among European nations to defense spending. The *Bundeswehr* provides all the naval forces in the Baltic, fifty percent of all NATO ground forces in Central Europe, and it is also deployed alongside other NATO troops within its own borders. This commitment has helped considerably to stabilize the balance of conventional forces vis-à-vis the Warsaw Pact (1956, *see 42, chapter* 11).

Integrating West Germany into NATO, however, was not the main achievement of the Adenauer years. Rather the carefully de-designed Franco-German rapprochement, against the background of a tragic history of disastrous confrontations, was, in the words of one contemporary, a "Copernican change" of which Jean Monnet, Robert Schuman, and Konrad Adenauer were the principal movers. The initial impetus for closer formalized links between the ancient enemies on the European continent came after Adenauer visited de Gaulle in 1958 and the General made a triumphant tour of West Germany in 1962. The Friendship Treaty of 1963 sealed the cooperation of the two governments on all levels. Youth exchanges, sister-city arrangements, and efforts to edit hatred out of the history books were to proceed apace.

Franco-German friendship worked better than anyone anticipated, although it did not solve the recurrent policy conflict between West Germany's interest in the Atlantic alliance and de Gaulle's dream of a great France free of American and Russian influence. Additionally, friction continues to exist between West German industry and French agriculture in the EEC. 1963 was a euphoric year in Franco-German relations, yet seeds of trouble were sown at the same time: de Gaulle built his own *force de frappe* (deterrent force) and vetoed Britain's entry into the EEC. In 1964 he withdrew French forces from NATO and during Adenauer's last year (1965–66) he even withdrew France from the EEC commission in Brussels for a year in protest against the organization's desire for greater supranational controls.

Since 1960 de Gaulle appraised Adenauer of his plans for a European Union of sovereign states under French leadership; actually, he wanted to invalidate earlier treaties which assigned nothing but an integrated role, that of an "extinguished" nation, to France (*124,* 235). Adenauer was torn between his desire for the support de Gaulle promised against communism and the American military presence in Berlin and the nuclear umbrella NATO provided. Finally, he acted in favor of de Gaulle who had taken a strong stand on Berlin in 1958–59 and who wanted to strengthen the Franco-German ties. However, the West German Parliament restored the precarious balance between the Atlantic Community and the French-German friendship with a preamble to the Friendship Treaty that stipulated the primacy of previously concluded covenants and advocated membership for Britain as well as for other states. In the long run, however, this Friendship Treaty contributed to a strong political, economic, and cultural interrelationship between France and West Germany within the EEC. West Germany became France's most important trading partner, and through the Youth Exchange Program, young people of both nations developed a surprising trust in each other. According to polls taken in the seventies, the West Germans trust the French more than any other people within the EEC, and the French consider the Germans their best friends in the world. The frictions of the Gaullist era subsided altogether when Helmut Schmidt and Giscard d'Estaing took office in 1974 and became close personal friends *(178).*

West European integration proceeded at the expense of Germany's reunification goal written into the West German constitution: "The entire German people are called upon to achieve in free self-determination the unity and freedom of Germany." Several impediments stood in the way of German reunification. The Soviets insisted on communist control of the GDR while the FRG's Hallstein Doctrine made it practically impossible to establish contact with any government that had established diplomatic relations with the GDR. Also, Adenauer believed that reunification would only come as a result of his West European integration strategy. And despite their official support of the FRG's drive toward unification, neither the Allies nor Adenauer were seriously interested in it. The Allies wanted a strong NATO with superiority over the War-saw Pact if at all feasible. A Germany as a central European power, united and neutral but possibly under Soviet influence, was there-fore not desirable to the Allies or to Adenauer. In Adenauer's view, freedom came before peace and unity, especially if unity meant neutrality: "neutrality is only possible for a country so strong that it can defend this neutrality against any attack. But where a vacuum exists, it will be filled by Russia" (January 13, 1965; *124,* 286). Ade-nauer also wanted to prevent a rebirth of expansionism, which had characterized Germany during much of his own lifetime.

Nevertheless, Adenauer toyed with the preconditions for reuni-fication. Since 1951 he and his government declared categorically that the first step would have to be free and secret elections in East and West Germany under UN supervision. But the GDR refused to admit a UN commission in 1952, and although the German ques-tion was taken up again at several international conferences (Ber-lin, 1954; Geneva, 1955 and 1959; Paris, 1960; Vienna, 1961), meaningful progress came to a quick halt whenever the questions of reunification, elections, and neutralization were raised. Ade-nauer put forward his original proposal for a solution without reu-nification in 1958 by suggesting that the GDR be neutralized as was Austria. This was followed by the so-called Globke-Plan for reunifi-cation in 1959–60, but the superpowers hardly responded to either.

Should Adenauer be blamed for not reaching his professed goal of wresting central Germany from the Soviet grip—as Dr. Thomas Dehler of the FDP alleged, when he claimed that Adenauer did not really want a unified Germany: "Do you believe that this man has the will to bring about the German reunification?" (January 23, 1958; *124,* 290). The question remains whether reunification was a real possiblity under any circumstances. In fact, nothing short of "neutralization" would have been acceptable to the Soviets. Yet from the outset, Adenauer torpedoed any attempt by the Left to of-fer such a solution. Neutralization would require the removal of all NATO forces from the FRG, which would make it subject to Soviet influence and possibly even a military take-over. Political consider-ations made the "Catholic Rhinelander" reluctant to include Prot-estant East Germany in his plans. It took more than a decade for his SPD opposition to conclude that there existed no other choice for the FRG but to remain within the Western alliance and to subscribe to Adenauer's foreign policy (see Herbert Wehner's speech, 30 June 1960 in Parliament).

SPD leadership had tried desperately for a decade to prevent the FRG from being integrated into the West. "At one point Schuma-cher called Adenauer 'the Chancellor of the Allies,' for which he was suspended from the *Bundestag* for two weeks" (*172,* 290).

Debates in Parliament became heated whenever the Soviets came forward with a unification proposal of their own, which usually coincided with a further step in West Germany's integration. For example, in 1952, when it was on the verge of joining the European Defense Community (EDC), Stalin offered reunification, elections (but not free and secret ones under international supervision), and neutralization, but unfortunately in the wrong sequence to be acceptable! Had the West accepted Stalin's proposal, the FRG's integration into the Western Alliance would have been undone according to Adenauer. He therefore did not ask Stalin what the price would be for reunification, a failure that was to haunt him and his party for a long time. By the time the Berlin Wall was erected in 1961, every attempt to find acceptable solutions to the German question had failed. A decade of inter-German and international haggling came to an end without results, and reunification ceased to be an active issue. Even the West Germans, "the children of the economic miracle," were not sure anymore "whether they really wanted to be reunited with their poor eastern brothers" (*172, 299*). With the abandonment of reunification as a central policy issue, another question came to the fore: what could the FRG do to stimulate liberalization in East Germany? "In this quest," Adenauer proclaimed on October 9, 1962, "humane concerns play a larger role for us than national considerations" (*124, 291*). Almost a decade later Willy Brandt's *Ostpolitik* tackled this issue with some measure of success.

## POLITICAL SYSTEMS OF
## THE GERMAN-SPEAKING COUNTRIES
### West Germany

The FRG is the most liberal and democratic state in German history and its *Grundgesetz* (Basic Law) goes further than any earlier constitution in the protection of human rights and civil liberties. The Grundgesetz was drafted by the Parliamentary Council, chaired by Adenauer. The members of the Council drew important lessons from the various German constitutions passed between 1848 and 1919. These lessons prevented West Germany from sliding back through a pseudo-legal process into a dictatorship, as happened in 1933 when Hitler became chancellor. The postwar Basic Law was partially designed to avoid the mistakes of the Weimar Constitution.

It received the name "Basic Law" (*Grundgesetz,* not *Verfassung* = "constitution") because the Allies had not signed a peace treaty and consequently the West German parliamentarians acted only provisionally "for a transitional period" on behalf of the Germans in the tri-zonal area as well as for "those Germans to whom participation was denied" (Preamble). For the same reason the various federated *Länder* parliaments, not the electorate, ratified the Law. Apart from the choice of "Grundgesetz," the traditional nomenclature—*Bundeskanzler* (1871), *Bundesrat* (1871), *Bundestag* (1915) —had its roots in German constitutional history, above all in the Basic Rights of the *Paulskirche* Parliament set down in Frankfurt in 1848, which never became political reality. Far more significant than the respect for tradition were the innovations that made the West German constitution stand out among those of the Western democracies.

The 19 articles of the first section guaranteeing Basic Rights are of primary importance. These human rights "shall bind the legislature, the executive, and judiciary as directly enforceable law" (#1). Article 19 stipulates that "in no case may the essential content of a basic right be encroached upon." In contrast to the Weimar constitution, this represents a great advantage in protecting the rights of the individual since emergency laws can no longer suspend Basic Rights. The FRG guarantees freedom of faith, expression, movement, education, and the development of personality without qualification. Conscientious objection is a human right, and capital punishment is abolished (#102). All persons are equal before the law regardless of sex, race, homeland, faith, or political conviction (#3). Those who abuse these freedoms "in order to combat the free democratic basic order" shall forfeit them (#18). Clearly, all these basic rights safeguard against the revival of a totalitarian system such as Nazism. Moreover, in contrast to the traditional supremacy of the state *(Obrigkeitsstaat),* it is the first time that "all state authority emanates from the people" who exercise that authority "by means of voting in elections and by specific legislative, executive, and judicial organs" (#20). Unlike the plebiscites of the Third Reich, the people do not exert their power directly but indirectly through their elected representatives in Parliament, in the regional elected bodies of the *Länder,* counties, and communes. "This means that the state's authority comes from below and flows to the top" (*151,* 103), reversing the traditional view of authority from the top.

As in all Western democracies, government rules according to the division of power. It must observe the constitution, preserve the Basic Rights, and allow for open competition of parties and candidates in the electoral process. Article 20 states: "The FRG is a democratic and social federal state," (*Bundesstaat,* not *Staatenbund*) based on federalism which has deep roots in German history all the way back to the Holy Roman Empire, but which has received strong impulses from the US constitution. This system is based on checks and balances in government. As a reaction against the centralized *Kaiserreich* and Hitler's Third Reich, self-governing federal states (*Länder*) were organized, among them three newly created ones that previously had not even existed as regional or provisional entities: Niedersachsen, Baden-Württemberg, Rheinland-Pfalz. These *Länder* had jurisdiction within their own boundaries, over education for example, and codetermination in federal affairs, such as budget matters. Some of the *Länder* such as Bayern and Hessen had existed before the founding of the FRG, and Bayern for example, afraid of too much centralism, did not ratify the Basic Law in 1949.

As in the US, federal law supersedes *Länder* law (#31), and in accordance with earlier historical patterns central control and most legislative power rests with the federal government while the states are responsible for primarily administrative functions (see *103, 213*). Similarities to the US government are quite apparent when it comes to comparing constitutional branches and their offices: Parliament *(Bundestag, Bundesrat)* corresponds to a large extent to Congress (House, Senate), the Federal Constitution Court to the US Supreme Court, the Chancellor to the US President and thus in some measure "Chancellor's democracy" to presidential democracy. The federal president retains a ceremonial function much like the American vice president.

However, the division of power is structured in a different manner from the United States. The *Grundgesetz* not only prevents the concentration of power within any one branch; it also requires the president to work closely with the chancellor, and the chancellor with the *Bundestag* (House), the *Bundestag* with the *Bundesrat* (Upper Chamber). In addition, all government departments depend on close cooperation with the *Länder,* which have a large measure of cultural, educational, and police autonomy and receive 65 percent of their revenue from nationally raised income and corporation taxes. They, in turn, have to collaborate with the cities and communes *(Gemeinden)* which have been self-governing since the Middle Ages. Thus, the effectiveness of the Federal system depends on political codetermination.

The *Bundestag* enjoys political preeminence as the only institution elected by the people. Its major function, after the election of the Chancellor and the federal judges, is control over the government. Although the administration usually introduces new legislation, the *Bundestag* may also initiate bills. Most of the work of the *Bundestag* is done on the committee level where tradition allows the opposition party to chair the powerful budget committee.

The *Bundesrat,* as the Council of Constituent States, is a unique institution among Western democracies. The constitution stipulates that "the *Länder* shall participate through the *Bundesrat* in the legislation and administration of the Federation" (#50). As a "continuous congress of state *(Land)* ministers who vote in accordance with their governments" (*103,* 204), this institution is a throwback to German tradition between 1815 and 1919 *(Deutscher Bund, Weimarer Verfassung).* Yet it is a "more effective instrument in shaping federal affairs than the *Länder* had in the *Bundesrat* of the Kaiser era" (Karl Erdmann, "Ein historischer Glücksfall. Entstehung und Zukunft des Bundesrates," *Die Zeit,* November 16, 1981). In representing federated and state governments, it differs from the U.S. Senate with its regional, partisan, and electoral interests. Further, its members (*Land* ministers or their delegates) are not elected by the people. Although party conflicts sometimes extend to the *Bundesrat,* party affiliation is often not as decisive as a bi-partisan stand taken by the *Länder* against the central government. Its codetermining function in the field of legislation and administration determines its power. Frequently it mediates "conflicts either between the executive and the *Bundestag* or between the federal and *Land* governments" (*103,* 205). The president of the *Bundesrat* acts as the federal president's deputy.

The *Bundespräsident,* the figure head of state who stands above party politics, exerts more symbolic than political power as he represents, mainly through his personal style, the Republic. Elected indirectly by a federal convention, he appoints the chancellor according to the wishes of the majority in parliament. He signs bills and treaties with other countries, but his signature requires validation by the countersignature of the chancellor, who exercises the real power. The chancellor sets the guidelines of government policy and assumes command over the *Bundeswehr* in case of a national emergency. The FRG has been called a democracy of chancellors *(Kanzleidemokratie),* who are, however, responsible to parliament. The Weimar Republic had suffered from too strong a president—Hindenburg had appointed Hitler—too weak a government, and a parliament that lacked a majority and failed to adhere to the constitution. The executive powers of the Weimar presidency (which had appointed the chancellor without consulting parliament, issued emergency decrees, and served as commander-in-chief) were shifted to the FRG's chancellor. At the same time, the Basic Law provides safeguards against the emergence of coalition governments constituted of minority or splinter parties. Article 67 states that a chancellor can only be dismissed by the election of a successor with "the majority of its members," that is, by a constructive vote of no-confidence. By contrast, a simple vote of no-confidence could topple a chancellor at any time under the Weimar constitution.

The Weimar Parliament consisted of many small parties which impeded the formation of a clear and durable majority. Only a drastic move towards totalitarian rule seemed to show a way out of this chaos. Three safeguards were built into electoral law to avoid a similar fate for the FRG:

1. A combination of proportional and majority representation in the election system replaced the purely proportional representation of the Weimar Republic which had allowed minute splinter parties to gain seats. Today, each voter casts two ballots: one for district deputy according to plurality voting, another for a party list of candidates according to proportional representation. This provision has allowed the FDP (Free Democratic Party), which otherwise fails to carry a district, to obtain seats in the *Bundestag.*

2. A "five percent debarring clause" excludes smaller parties from Parliament.

3. Political groups that seek to "impair or abolish the free democratic order or to endanger the existence of the FRG," are unconstitutional (#21). These devices present a formidable hurdle for the fringe parties (DKP = German Communist Party with c. 4,000 members, NPD = National Democratic Party; each received 0.2 percent of the popular vote in 1983). "For example, in 1968 the five percent clause caused 1.4 million NPD votes to be 'wasted' because not a single NPD candidate entered the Bundestag" (*103, 169*). For this reason, and because the majority party led by Chancellor Adenauer incorporated the splinter groups, only three out of the original ten parties have survived since 1949.

The SPD was founded in 1875 when the General Workers' Association under Ferdinand Lasalle and the Marxist Socialist Worker Party merged. After a period of banishment (see Bismarck's Socialist Laws, 1878–90), the KPD split off from the SPD in 1918. The latter established itself as a nonrevolutionary, democratic party during the Weimar period. Labor-oriented, it was the strongest party before 1933 and next to the KPD, the one most decisively opposed to Hitler. After WWII the SPD never left the opposition benches until it broke with Marxist theory in 1959 (see the Godesberg Program, *90,* 219f.). Then it gained an appeal for the middle class and especially the intellectuals, most of whom were civil servants. As a majority party with broad voter appeal, it finally joined the Grand Coalition in 1966 and participated in government for the first time since Weimar. Its platform supports the "social market economy" *(soziale Marktwirtschaft),* based on private ownership, social reforms, reconciliation with the East, and European integration on all levels.

Neither the CDU/CSU nor the FDP are based on their Weimar predecessors. For instance, the CDU is not a revival of the earlier Catholic *Zentrumspartei.* Instead, this new party appealed to all denominations and a broad social spectrum to bring about a rapprochement between various segments of society. The CDU's political platform is not much different from the one adopted by the

SPD later on although its anticommunist stance, for example, its initial opposition to *Ostpolitik,* and its lack of major social reform programs stamp it as a conservative party.

Apart from the Christian Socialist Union (CSU) of Bavaria, which in federal elections allies itself with the CDU, the FDP is the decisive third political force, tipping the scale in favor of either the CDU or the SPD in the formation of government coalitions. Although numerically weak, the FDP lays claim to the heritage of German liberalism and is attractive to many young progressives who disdain the major parties. The latter have invariably provided the chancellors, while the FDP has often supplied the federal president (e.g., Theodor Heuss, 1949–1959) and/or the foreign minister (e.g., Hans-Dietrich Genscher).

## East Germany

The former German Empire is partitioned in a complex manner, so that Germans now live in several different regional entities, divided by religion, dialect, history, and political systems. Aside from the Main River line between northern and southern Germany, there is the border between the GDR and the former Eastern provinces of prewar Germany (beyond the Oder-Neisse) ceded by the GDR in 1950 and the FRG in 1972 to Poland and the Soviet Union. The GDR and the FRG in turn are separated from each other by the "wall." After the war two different social, political, and economic systems emerged in the two German states.

Because of its economic success, the GDR has been called "the other German miracle." Yet for decades West Germans proud of their economic superiority looked down on the nation of 17 million people as *der doofe Rest* (the dumb remainder) for its oppressive communist regime. Günter Gaus, former head of the FRG mission in East Berlin, put it succinctly: "We turned the DDR into our Ersatz-KP" (i.e., substitute communist party, *Die Zeit,* 18 IX 1981). Although GDR communism is not totally orthodox (e.g., privately owned homes, automobiles, and small businesses are allowed), still the Ulbricht era between 1946 and 1971 was Stalinist in orientation, contrasting sharply with West German democracy under Adenauer.

Walter Ulbricht claimed that his "democratic" style corresponded to the "dictatorship of the proletariat" and that it would help bring about a classless society. In reality, however, he was a puppet of the Soviets who ruled the country through the party bureaucracy of the Socialist Unity Party (SED). Tragically his dictatorship incorporated totalitarian measures analogous to those of the Nazis—for example, *Gleichschaltung* (coordination) forced all parties and social classes, the media, the judiciary, and the professions to conform politically. The FDJ *(Freie Deutsche Jugend)* has taken over the functions of the HJ *(Hitlerjugend)*. Those who do not participate in such party-controlled socialist organizations are discriminated against. The police (SDS: *Staatssicherheitsdienst* = state security police) served the SED through intimidation and coercion. Open criticism or deviation from party policy leads to denunciation and police action. Overt opposition still is out of the question; moreover, the SED considers it impossible by definition in a classless society. Thus, although with an antifascist slant, a system has evolved that has many characteristics of the totalitarian Third Reich.

In addition to Soviet domination, the Russians also created the GDR as a state whose power does not emanate from the people but exclusively from the party-controlled government. "The chief instrument in creating the foundation of socialism is the power of the state" (SED Party Congress, 1952; *228, 532*), in some respects a throwback to the *Obrigkeitsstaat* which has dominated German political history. Although the GDR constitution has been changed twice since its first 1949 version—by the Ulbricht constitution in 1968 and the Honecker constitution in 1974—the supremacy of the state has never been called into doubt; rather, it has been strengthened. The first constitution derived from the Weimar constitution in its emphasis on liberal democratic principles, on basic rights, and its inclusion of federated *Länder* in the legislative process. Yet the concentration of power in one institution, the *Volkskammer* (Lower Chamber), indicated the direction East German political development was taking towards one-party control.

Since the socialist element in the revolution is of paramount importance to the GDR, Basic Rights, as defined in the West, are secondary. In the socialist system (#1–18) Basic Rights are not guaranteed to the individual but to the collective. In contrast to the Basic Rights of the FRG, the GDR does not grant: freedom of movement, freedom to strike, the right to object to military service, to dissent. Also freedom of research, of assembly, and of speech do not exist. For instance, GDR citizens, especially party members and political workers *(Betriebskampfgruppen)*, if not officially sanctioned, may not converse freely with Western tourists and journalists. Justice is completely embedded in socialist laws. As Lenin said: "New power creates new laws" (*54, 16*).

In keeping with this interpretation of the basic rights, the initial federal structure of the GDR was gradually dismantled in favor of a centralized state. In 1952, the same year the zonal border was sealed off from the western parts of Germany, the states were dissolved altogether and replaced by 14 districts. In 1958 the upper chamber *(Länderkammer)* was abolished, and in 1962 the State's Council created. Accordingly, government does not rule by division but by concentration of power *(demokratischer Zentralis-*

*mus).* In practice, a chain of political and economic command was formed, stretching from the top level (Councils; SED Central Committee or Political Bureau) to the community council.

Each level of government controls the one below, the central one the districts, the districts the counties, these in turn the cities, and so forth. Paradoxically, as power has been concentrated in the hands of one man, there has been a move towards colleagial governance which modifies, at least outwardly, the strict totalitarian system of the GDR. Arnold Heidenheimer calls this process of decision-making "consultative authoritarianism" (*103,* 297). The presidency, which was discontinued in 1960, was replaced by a 24-man Council of State, similar to the Presidium of the Supreme Soviet. This Council of State supervises domestic and foreign policy. In the 1960s this institution became Ulbricht's most important instrument to run the government, since all its members also belonged to a SED steering committee.

Originally conceived as the Cabinet of the minister president, the Council of Ministers *(Ministerrat)* had to give up much of its political function when it became dependent on the Council of State in 1963. Until Ulbricht's death in 1971, it was in charge of the economy and the development of science and technology. However, it regained its former status with the accession to power of the more flexible Erich Honecker.

The *Volkskammer* (People's Chamber) is by law the most powerful ruling body in the GDR since the constitution provides it with both legislative and executive functions. However, its power is actually rather limited: "In practice the *Volkskammer* has transferred almost all of its powers to the Council of State and other executive bodies. Its sole remaining function is that of acclamation; it meets only on symbolic occasions" (*103,* 301). There are at least two reasons for its lack of power: first, the electoral process provides for only one slate of candidates. Even the quota of parliamentary seats has been preassigned to the individual parties of the National Front. These elections merely confirm those who are already in power and they demonstrate the ideological unity of the working people. The East German government's preference for introducing "new bills as administrative ordinances rather than as laws via the legislative route" (*103,* 302), weakens the *Volkskammer*'s constitutional right to take the initiative in legislating. According to article 1 of the 1968 constitution, one "State Party" controls all political institutions and the economy. The SED claims to be the only source of political legitimacy and the sole instrument for achieving a socialist society. "The Party directs the work of the State apparatus with the help of the party members working in this apparatus; these have to execute the party decisions in a disciplined manner" (Party Congress, 1950; *228,* 531). The party considers itself to be "the executive organ of history," and it is thus entitled to plan and guide social developments according to the most progressive criteria of Marxist-Leninism.

## TWO FLEDGLING GERMAN STATES

Ever since the end of WWII, two different systems have been in the making, reaffirming the dominant historical trend of Germany as a diverse and divided country that had been shaped by international developments. Aptly, the French used to refer to Germany in the plural as "Les Allemagnes" (*152*, 1036). Political and economic competition has also characterized the precarious relationship between the FRG and the GDR since their inception as occupational zones. Each state, in its own turn, has reacted to the other's moves as Prussia used to respond to Austria in the past. But this time, the gap has widened in economics, politics and ideology.

Particularly during the first two decades of their existence, the Cold War of the superpowers deepened the division between the two Germanies, their leaders, and their parties. The foundations of the split were already laid at the conclusion of WWII and the immediate postwar years (see Chapter II). More decisive was the accession to power of intransigent government leaders such as Adenauer and Ulbricht, who personified the cold war stand-off in Germany. To be sure, Adenauer with his Western outlook (Golo Mann calls it, "Rhenish, South German, not all-German," *152*, 1041), with his authoritarian methods and with his insistence on "no experiments" soon led the FRG into a corner over the German question. "His policies and his character wrenched German politics, but he also gave the state stability" (*172*, 297)—at the expense of a constructive dialogue with Ulbricht.

A survivor like Adenauer, the East German leader not only came through the Nazi period unscathed in Moscow (1933–1945) where he became a Soviet citizen and an orthodox follower of Stalin; he also survived the many power struggles and purges within the Communist Party (KPD) to whose Central Committee (ZK) he had belonged since 1923. Ulbricht was wily and uncompromising in eliminating his SED opponents and in putting through his policies. He combined in his person the offices of General Secretary of the SED, Head of State (Chairman of the State's Council), and Vice-Chairman of the Council of Ministers, a feat not even achieved by Stalin himself. Thus he was at the same time in charge of ideology, of the executive, and of representing his state internationally. Long after the death of Stalin in 1953, he ruled almost absolutely into the early 1960s without initiating a de-stalinization as Khrushchev did in the Soviet Union after 1956.

Despite several international East-West meetings between 1954 and 1961 and a general "thaw" within the East bloc, Adenauer and Ulbricht—genuine cold war warriors—neither recognized each other's existence nor ever talked to one another.

Whereas the FRG has become firmly bound to the Western Alliance, the GDR has been completely integrated into the socialist camp (see its constitution of 1974, paragraph 6). While Westerners usually view 1961, the year of the erection of the Berlin Wall as the historical turning point, the SED's periodization of GDR history is different. It begins with a transitional phase of an "antifascist democratic order" from 1945 until 1949, followed by the "planned building of socialism" until 1958, which in turn lead to the years of "completing the socialist basis" until 1963. The next eight years (1963–1971) have been officially designated the phase of "the comprehensive building of socialism." With Ulbricht's resignation from SED leadership in 1971 under Soviet pressure, the period of "the developed socialist society" began (54, 14f.). This nomenclature covers almost 40 years and marks a decisive step toward a communist restructuring of society, often with tragic consequences for the individual.

In 1950 the GDR joined COMECON (the Council for Mutual Economic Help), the Eastern counterpart of the Marshall Plan and the EEC. The GDR was thus integrated into the economic order of socialist-controlled Europe. This entailed nationalization and collectivization. "About the same time that the West moved to decentralize economic control through adoption of the 'social market policy,' the East began to move energetically in the opposite direction" (103, 57). By 1961 about 87 percent of the private sector of the economy had been collectivized. Thus, GDR industry became integrated with the East bloc. (Military integration had already been accomplished in 1955 when the GDR entered the Warsaw Pact).

In the face of political and economic pressure from the top, people "voted with their feet" (Herbert Wehner) against the system. Three and one-half million East Germans, especially professionals, peasants who had lost their land, and members of the armed forces and border patrol, fled the country between 1946 and 1961. After 1957 and the Law Against Fleeing the Republic, more severe sentences were meted out to those caught. An order to shoot anyone crossing the closed border without permission has been in effect since 1952.

Entire social classes disappeared during the forming of the GDR. The nobility and the old intellectual elite no longer exist; the middle class has lost its influence in the "worker-farmer state." Yet despite the dismantling of industries, the enormous reparations, the continuous population- (and brain-) drain, and the political as well as economic restructuring of what was the former Soviet zone, the

GDR succeeded in producing a second "German miracle." "Between 1950 and 1970, the GDR managed to increase production by almost 500 percent, becoming the world's eighth largest industrial power," ranking second in industrial output to the Soviet Union in the Eastern bloc, but outstripping it in per capita national income (*103*, 54f.).

To achieve this feat with barely 17 million inhabitants, the leadership had to shift emphasis from agriculture to industry and, especially since 1961, to place particular importance on incentives and profits for higher skills and greater industrial output (based on the Lieberman Plan developed in the Soviet Union to encourage and reward individual initiative). Although smaller in area than Cuba, East Germany now produces more than Hitler's prewar Reich. International recognition of the socialist Republic has acknowledged its economic might. First, the Arab States recognized the GDR (1969f.), then normalization of relations with the FRG in 1972, and diplomatic recognition by the Western powers (the US in 1974) followed. Finally, the GDR (and West Germany) joined the UN in 1973.

"Career advancement has been found to be as primary a motive in the determination of job behavior among top-management personnel in the GDR as among corporate executives in the United States" (*103*, 60). A technical elite has been gaining ground since the 1960s, helping to bring about an East German economic boom. This development contradicts Soviet claims that the USSR has reached a higher plateau of social performance (the so-called "creation of the material-technical basis of Communism") than any other East bloc partner.

Relations between the FRG and the GDR during the Adenauer and Ulbricht era were shaped by policies and political events. Because of the Federal Republic's refusal to recognize the GDR, official contacts at the government level did not come about until after Adenauer's death in 1966. On the other hand, the GDR desperately strove to break out of its political isolation. Paradoxically, it desired recognition by the "imperialistic" FRG and at the same time proposed a confederation *(Staatenbund)* between two equal partners. Nothing much changed until the end of the Ulbricht era in 1971.

Relations between the two states were sharply jolted twice during the time of cold war confrontation. On June 17, 1953, shortly after Stalin's death, East German miners, machinists, construction and steel workers went on strike against poor food distribution and the policy of lower wages for higher production. To begin with, the strikers made only economic and social demands, but at the height of their protest, they added sweeping political demands which included a call for Ulbricht's resignation, free elections, and the reunification of Germany. From East Berlin, unrest spread to all major GDR cities, and some party centers, police stations, and prisons were stormed. Although the strikers did not have the entire population behind them, they dealt a significant blow to the system which had prided itself on its popular support. Soviet tanks had to come to the aid of the beleaguered state, even before it had become sovereign. The uprising ended with shootings in the street, mass arrests, and executions. It left about 500 dead and 1,100 convicted. June 17 is remembered in West Germany as the "Day of (lost) German Unity." It was the first major unrest to surface in the Eastern bloc, to be followed by others in Hungary in 1956, in Czechoslovakia in 1968, and in Poland in 1981.

How did the SED hierarchy react to this challenge to its authority? Minister President Otto Grotewohl, a former SPD member, admitted serious mistakes in "the method of administration, of police encroachments and of judicial harshness." He added: "If people turn away from us, then this policy must be wrong" (45, 450). However, the SED did not make any important changes. Its proclaimed "New Course" consisted of reaffirming its hard line to bring the unstable situation under control. The State Party proceeded more cautiously, yielding in details without jeopardizing its blueprint for the future development of the state. It postponed, for example, enforced collectivization and laid the unpleasant reality of June 17 to rest by labeling it a "fascist putsch," staged by "counterrevolutionary agitators and provocateurs infiltrated from the FRG."

The second event to jolt the West was the building of the Wall, beginning on August 13, 1961 during the "completion phase of the socialist foundations" from 1958–63. With the resumption of wholesale collectivization and socialization of private enterprises in 1960, the number of refugees soared—155,000 left between January and August 13, 1961—20,000 in the last week alone. The GDR leadership stemmed this tide by building a 30-mile wall through Berlin, the only remaining open door to the West. The 260 miles of the intra-German border had been fortified earlier. The People's Police (Volksarmee) sealed off East Berlin from the Western sectors. The "Wall of Shame" sealed the division of Germany for the foreseeable future. A crude measure, it nevertheless brought about the end of Cold War confrontations over Berlin, which had culminated in Khrushchev's Berlin ultimatum of 1958 that the Western Allies should rescind their occupation status and transform Berlin into a free city.

The Western Allies protested but were forced to watch as the Wall was erected. President Kennedy was reputedly relieved that Khrushchev stopped short of occupying West Berlin, leaving the Western Powers' rights of access untouched. Adenauer continued in his election campaign almost as if nothing serious had happened. The GDR regime achieved thereby a significant coup in two respects: it nipped resistance in the bud through its show of military force, and it also compelled its subjects to make the best of prevailing conditions by removing the possibility of escape. For the GDR a period of consolidation followed which paralleled a gradual decline in opposition as well as a shift in priorities from politics to consumerism and economic growth.

The SED's claim that the Wall narrowly circumvented imperialistic aggression from the West was hardly credible. Yet a "period of comprehensive build-up of socialism" followed that was only mildly disturbed by the Czech uprising in 1968. Rebellions against the party's social-development plan not only proved futile but also served to confirm the party's infallibility and deepen the East Germans' resignation. Nevertheless, Ulbricht's "anti-fascist bulwark" did not stop East Germans from trying to flee their country. About 190,000 have fled since that time; 50,000 are estimated to have been caught and imprisoned, 8,000 applied for exist visas and were put behind bars, and at least 180 have been shot trying to escape across the Wall or the border.

While the economy improved and internal politics consolidated in the GDR, the economic miracle ran its course in the Federal Republic, although Ludwig Erhard, its principle architect, took over the reins of government from Adenauer (1963 to 1966). In political terms, the shock of the Berlin Wall brought home to the new government the realization that the status quo had been made permanent by this event and that therefore new ways had to be found to deal with the reality of a divided Germany. "By the mid-1960s, the bitter truth was that the FRG's policy of strength as a means of securing German reunification had been a total failure" (*103*, 345). Although the SPD had anticipated this, it was neither able to change the course of Adenauer's policy nor to provide ready solutions of its own.

One of the first to draw serious conclusions from the Wall was Foreign Minister Gerhard Schröder, who tried to develop a more flexible approach to the communist East. He worked out a trade agreement with Poland in 1963, which was followed by similar treaties with Hungary, Rumania, and Bulgaria. (Because intra-German trade had been uninterrupted since 1946 in the absence of tariff barriers between the two Germanys, the GDR is virtually a partner in EEC).

Unfortunately, free trade does not mean free movement. After the border was sealed off, West Berliners could not visit their relatives in the East for twenty-eight months. Backed by Chancellor Ludwig Erhard, lower-level talks between West Berlin and the GDR resulted in a passport transit agreement *(Passierscheinab-*

*kommen)* that enabled millions to cross the border for limited periods. Of utmost importance for the FRG was the requirement that this be achieved without giving political recognition to the GDR.

The two fledgling states continued their animosities throughout the mid-sixties; the first official exchange of notes between their leaders did not take place until the Grand Coalition of 1967. The general "thaw" between East and West had not yet weakened the resolve of political diehards in both Germanies to achieve unity only on their own terms. From the start each side refused to grant legitimacy to the other, and each upheld its right to be the sole representative and spokesman for all Germans. According to West German governmental and legal opinion, the German Reich of 1937 (i.e., minus Hitler's conquests), continues to exist, with the democratic FRG its only heir. Like West German Basic Law, article 8 of the 1968 GDR constitution (article 1 in the 1949 version) also expresses a desire to reunite both parts of Germany (after the eventual defeat of the West German "imperialist" system).

Ulbricht, as much as Adenauer, believed in the continuity of one German nation and he saw in his GDR a German core state *(Kernstaat)* based on socialism, which would in due course extend its socialist "achievements" to West Germany and bring about "a peaceful future of socialism for the entire German nation" (Constitution of 1968, Preamble). Until 1969 the GDR and the FRG subscribed to the same tenet of a single German Nation but two different states *(zwei Staaten—eine Nation).* For the SED and Ulbricht, the idea of reunification on the basis of socialist principles constituted an inevitable historical law.

A first breach in this thinking occurred when the GDR codified its citizenship laws in 1967 and excluded West Germans from consideration. The FRG on the other hand has always extended citizenship to all Germans regardless of birth place due to its belief in one German nation, one language, and on the basis of family ties that relate 40 percent of the citizens in both German states. While Brandt's *Ostpolitik* attempted to bridge the widening gap between the two Germanies, in the GDR since Ulbricht's death, a policy of separation *(Abgrenzung)* has taken root in SED thinking. It has resulted in a declaration of an independent "socialist worker-farmer state." The Erich Honecker constitution of 1974 has deleted references to a "German" state or nation, and to reunification of the two states.

## AUSTRIA'S RECONSTRUCTION

Austria belongs to the German-speaking countries but not to the German nation. In 1945, Austria was almost as devastated as Germany. A serious shortage of housing and food existed, and a million men had not returned from the war—250,000 were dead or missing, and 750,000 were prisoners. The country was divided into four zones of occupation ruled by an Allied Council in Vienna which was to retain supreme authority until 1955.

> The Germans emerged from the nationalist paroxysms of World War II with a monumental hangover; nor were the Austrians exempt from it. Their flirtation with Hitler, for which they had paid so dearly, left many of them with a desire to build a future unencumbered by constant reminders of an incriminating past.
>
> (*201*, 149)

This proved a difficult moral and political undertaking, since the majority of Austrians had favored Hitler's *Anschluß* (annexation) in 1938. As early as 1943, the Moscow Conference of Allied Foreign Ministers reminded the Austrians of their responsibility for participation in the war at the side of Nazi Germany. At the same time there had been a broadly-based active resistance against the Nazis, and many Austrian Catholics, communists, and socialists had died in the concentration camps for their resistance. A strong guerilla organization had fought the SS in the Austrian Alps. The Allies decided to reestablish a free Austria, independent of Germany, whose first victim it had been. But it took a decade until Austria regained its sovereignty. These years from 1945 to 1955 represented the first phase of postwar reconstruction, a period with severe restrictions on Austrian freedom because of the Allied occupation.

As early as April 1945 a provisional government was formed which was immediately recognized by the Soviets. The constitution of the First Republic of 1920 was declared in force again, and elections were held in November 1945. While the Austrian president is elected by popular vote, the Chamber of Deputies *(Nationalrat)* is chosen by proportional representation. During elections, Austria is subdivided into nine districts which overlap with the nine Federal Provinces. Seats in the *Nationalrat* are allocated to individual parties according to the apportionment of seats within each electoral district. The federal president appoints the chancellor who is put forward as a candidate by the majority of the National Council. The chancellor suggests his cabinet and the president appoints its members. As in the FRG, the Federal Council *(Bundesrat)* represents the interests of the federated provinces which have their own constitutions and regional governments.

After WWII difficult tasks lay ahead for both government and people. Apart from the battle for survival, a struggle for political tolerance, for the hearts and minds of the defeated people, and for a renewed pride in an independent Austria had to be won. Furthermore, a constructive relationship had to be worked out with the

Allied Council. Luckily, Austria found a solution to its political, social, and economic problems: a Grand Coalition of the two major
political parties—the Social Democrats (SPÖ) and the Peoples'
Party (ÖVP, Österreichische Volks-Partei equivalent to the CDU)—
ruled the country from 1946 until 1966. About the time Willy
Brandt formed the first SPD-led government in West Germany in
1969, his Austrian counterpart, Bruno Kreisky—like Brandt an exile returned from Sweden—became Federal Chancellor and Chairman of the SPÖ.

In 1955 all three German-speaking countries—the FRG, the
GDR, and Austria—regained their sovereignty. For Austria independence marked a major turning point in its postwar development. Occupation forces departed, the last prisoners returned
home from Russia, and a permanent neutrality in foreign affairs
was decreed. Austria had to pay 150 million dollars to the Soviets
to get back its "German assets," which included oil fields, industries, and shipyards claimed as war reparations.

Since the Allies considered Austria a victim of Hitler's aggression, they signed a State rather than a Peace Treaty with her. In
1980 Chancellor Kreisky called this document the first significant
step toward postwar detente between the superpowers. Austria
also joined the UN in 1955 and has played a major role in international peace efforts, particularly since its former Foreign Minister,
Kurt Waldheim, was Secretary General of the United Nations from
1971 until 1981. Austria's desire for peace and neutrality was put to
a severe test during the 1960s when a border dispute erupted between Austria and Italy over self-rule in German-speaking South
Tyrol. After a campaign of nationalist terror by Tyrolean extremists, Italy agreed to grant regional autonomy to South Tyrol in
1969.

Accompanying its political reconstruction, economic revival
aided by the Marshall Plan between 1948 and 1961 resulted in a
modern industrial society and an economic miracle similar to those
of the two Germanies. This surprising success is generally not well
known, perhaps because Austria is not widely regarded as a strong
industrial nation. Indeed, its industrial base was weak when a nationalization law was passed covering public utilities, basic industries, and manufacturing. Austria's economy was formerly oriented
towards Germany and the member states of its old Hapsburg Empire. Landlocked, its trade with foreign markets was limited. Furthermore, Austria's dependence on West Germany's economic
performance might have been to its disadvantage. On the positive
side, its size worked to its advantage, because "it is always easier to
keep a small house in order" *(Austrian Info* 33, No. 3–4, p. 3). The
Austrian tradition of relaxed cooperation and pragmatism aided
economic reconstruction. Austria has not had a general strike since

WWII, mainly due to its unusual political and social interaction. For instance, the country benefits greatly from a Parity Commission on Wages and Prices, a unique behind-the-scenes bargaining agency which strengthens social ties.

> The Constitution does not provide for a Parity Commission, no Austrian law mentions it, and the body has no legal power to enforce its decisions. Yet in its twenty-year existence, the commission has achieved enough clout to make its views on such matters as demands for wage or price rises stick.
>
> *(The New York Times-Austrian Info* 30, 1977, I, 2)

Economic growth started in the 1950s and continued at a fast pace into the 1970s, reaching an all-time high in 1978, when Austria dismantled its tariff barriers with the EEC. Since 1960, real annual growth amounted to 4 percent, total productivity (1960–1978) per worker increased by 115 percent, as compared to 104 percent in the FRG, while labor costs were about 50 percent lower than in the FRG. Among all industrial nations belonging to the Organization for European Economic Cooperation (OEEC), only Japan shows a higher annual per capita growth (seven percent versus four percent in 1979). Although, as a highly dependent economy, Austria's industrial productivity has been subject to fluctuations in the FRG's economy, with which it has been synchronized for some time (e.g., fixed schilling - DM exchange rate), Austria has managed to keep its inflation, labor costs, and unemployment rate lower than the FRG's. As the London *Economist* put it: "When West Germany sneezes, the Austrian economy cannot avoid a slight touch of flu" (*Austrian Info* 33, No. 3–4, p. 12). Inspite of West Germany's recession, Austria's economy continued to grow. In terms of overall living standards, the differences that existed in 1960 have virtually disappeared. In economic competitiveness, e.g., export volume per capita, Austria has even developed a slight edge over the FRG.

## THE UNITED STATES AND WEST GERMANY (AMERICANIZATION)

In the same year (1963) that the Franco-German Friendship Treaty was ratified, President Kennedy made a triumphant tour through West Germany assuring all Germans, particularly West Berliners, of the US commitment to keep their country free. "Ich bin ein Berliner," he asserted. A few months later, Adenauer stepped down and Kennedy was assassinated in Dallas. With Kennedy's death an era of close German-American relations ended. None of Kennedy's successors achieved a similar degree of

popularity in West Germany. His visit symbolized a "special relationship," once reserved only for England, and pointed to the importance the FRG had gained as America's strongest European ally.

During the first fifteen years of the Republic, the FRG gradually
developed from its postwar status as an American protectorate to
an almost equal partner and best friend. Furthermore, an economically strong and militarily armed FRG became an important element in the US containment strategy towards the Soviet Union. In
the sixties, both the US and West Germany constituted "essential
pillars of an international system that they wished to preserve"
(211, 12). In the process of solving postwar problems, the FRG
sought to fulfill the American notion of the "good life," and enthusiastically embraced many of its fashions and trends.

The German-American partnership began right after the war
when the German population, longing for liberty after the years of
Nazi oppression and hate propaganda, was pleasantly surprised by
the humane treatment it received from the American G.I.'s, by the
help that arrived in the form of CARE packages, and, later on, by
Marshall Plan aid. By 1949 West German-American friendship had
turned into something like "the second Basic Law" for the FRG
(121, 154). And during the Adenauer years this alliance bore many
of the characteristics of a father-son relationship.

John Foster Dulles, US Secretary of State during the 1950s,
shared with Adenauer a deep faith in Christian principles as an answer to communism. Both firmly believed that Truman's containment policy could only be realized if the Western European
nations would transfer much of their sovereignty to supranational
political and economic institutions (see Dulles' book *War or
Peace,* 1950). Dulles and Adenauer turned their friendship into an
important asset for close US-West German ties. Dulles helped to
overcome anti-German prejudice in American public opinion, and
Adenauer promoted German acceptance of the US as the dominant
partner in the Atlantic alliance. Political frictions arose in 1955
when Adenauer saw in the Radford Plan for the reduction of US
troops in Europe a sign of a possible US-Soviet rapprochement at
the expense of West Germany. He put German-American relations
on ice until Dulles assured him of his opposition to such a possibility. Before meeting Adenauer in 1953, Dulles had been frightened
by German militarism and by a possible resumption of Germany's
former Rapallo-politics of 1922—a seesawing between the superpowers for political advantage. But Adenauer's steadfast pro-
Western stance helped Dulles overcome any lingering distrust.

De Gaulle did not subscribe to the pro-US stance of Adenauer.
Chiefly concerned with the glory and independence of France, he
sought the dissolution of NATO and the abolishment of all supranational agencies of the Common Market. As de Gaulle attempted

to use the FRG to achieve his own goals, Adenauer's will to defend his West European integration policy was put to a severe test. Alarmed by de Gaulle's vision of a Europe defended by a Franco-German alliance, the German chancellor tried to dissuade the General. But pressured by de Gaulle and unable to find a compromise between American and French plans, Adenauer finally signed the Franco-German Friendship Treaty in 1963. He remained convinced, however, that this agreement could not be a substitute for the American nuclear umbrella.

While relations between Bonn and Paris grew closer, those between the US and West Germany were set back on the personal level when a new administration took over in Washington in 1961. President Kennedy proclaimed a strategy for peace, based on a strong Atlantic alliance but aimed at a detente between East and West. To him the security of the Western world was indivisible. Yet the chancellor thought Kennedy much too flexible toward the Soviets while the President was unhappy with Adenauer's rigidity. Despite Kennedy's triumphal tour through West Germany, American-German relations did not regain their former strength at the official level until Ludwig Erhard became Chancellor.

Erhard was "Atlantic-minded" and disagreed, like the Americans, with de Gaulle's EEC boycott of 1965–66. Erhard's "social market economy" struck a responsive chord in the US. As George Ball, Secretary of State, explained: "that phrase compressed in three words some basic American convictions as to the dynamic force of free competition, yet explicitly recognized the need of government to fulfill its social responsibilities" (200, 359). There were financial difficulties in supporting 230,000 US soldiers in West Germany, and the FRG's contribution had to be renegotiated almost every year until the 1970s. But both Erhard and President Johnson opposed de Gaulle's wish to withdraw French forces from the integrated military NATO command in 1966.

When Johnson decided to improve East-West relations, Erhard supported him, convinced that the prospects for a unification of Germany might increase. However, both leaders failed to anticipate the rapid decline of US popularity in West Germany during the late 1960s as a result of the Vietnam war.

In the economic sphere, German-American relations developed at a quickening pace. American financial aid helped rebuild West Germany's industrial capacity and also helped establish a liberal free market system, the antithesis of a Soviet-style planned production-based economy. By the time Adenauer renewed the 1923 trade agreement with the US in 1953, it had become clear that the FRG could only regain its lost world markets with US help, but its later successes cannot be explained solely by American assistance. The US and the FRG have been vying for preeminence as exporting countries for quite some time. West Germany usually takes second place to the US, with Japan a close third. Until 1967, the US was West Germany's most important trading partner, but thereafter fell back to fourth, fifth, or even sixth place as more goods and commodities were exchanged within the EEC, following the removal of tariff barriers. US exports to the Federal Republic were also affected, sinking to fourth place in 1982.

It is not surprising that America has ambivalent attitudes toward the Common Market. Washington supports it for political and military reasons but is critical of what it regards as preferential trade agreements (*121,* 174f.). In spite of this, trade between the two states has increased: in 1960 US imports from West Germany totaled $.89 billion, while exports to West Germany reached $1.42 billion; this compares with $12.6 billion in US imports and $11.5 billion US exports to Germany in 1981. Among the main items exported from Germany are cars, machine tools, machinery, chemical products, and electrical appliances.

Direct investment in each other's economies has developed concurrently. For some time, the US has been the major recipient of West German business investments ($9 billion by 1981), while US investment in the FRG surpasses all other countries at $7.8 billion. By 1967, US multinational corporations had bought, established, or participated in large oil, automobile, or computer firms such as Esso (Exxon), Opel (GM), Ford, and IBM. Almost no sector of the West German economy is without some American involvement.

US-German cooperation is significant in three major areas of science and technology: microbiology, high energy physics, and space exploration. German-born microbiologists perform research in American universities while their American counterparts teach and experiment in West German institutions. With American help, the FRG constructed an electron-synchroton ("Desy") that led to the discovery of some nuclear particles. Of great significance were Wernher von Braun's efforts in space exploration starting with the Redstone rocket in 1953 and climaxing in Saturn V, which enabled the first moon landing in 1969. The twelve-nation European Space Agency (ESA) built the Space Lab for NASA's reusable Space Shuttle, which was sent into space in November of 1983; it launches its own communication satellites with its Ariane rockets. In 1978 Ulf von Zahn became the first non-American to contribute an experiment to the US Venus mission which probed the chemical make-up of the planet's outer atmosphere.

While the GDR turned into a defender of Stalinism and came completely under the Soviet sphere of influence, the FRG was increasingly "Americanized" by its political, military, economic, and cultural interaction with the US. By 1963, with over 3,000 US companies established in Europe, and over 750 in the FRG by 1977, the US was bound to exert an appreciable influence on its closest European ally.

Depending on the political climate of a country, "Americanization" will have different meanings. It runs "the scale from implications of openness and freedom, or ingenuity and high quality, to grossness, bad taste, even a certain vague but inherent evil" (*148*, 1). Some governments in the East (e.g., USSR) and the West (e.g., France) have tried to stem what they have called the "Americanization" of their respective countries on the grounds that it would bring about undesirable changes in society, language, and young people. In West Germany change was desired and accepted long into the 1960s. Germans admired the US and became "Europe's Americans," as the French saw it. That the Federal Republic had become the strongest ally and trading partner of the US clearly had an influence on values, customs, fashions, language, and social attitudes, since "the very 'cultural essence' of a people [is] in large part a reflection of their economic past and present" (*148*, viii).

But West Germany's "economic miracle" cannot be explained simply by postwar American assistance nor can the rise of a consumer society and mass culture be attributed solely to the US model. After all, the FRG's economy grew increasingly independent of the US, eventually outperforming it. Partly due to its leading role in the EEC, the FRG assumed a political role not always in harmony with Washington. Many West Germans regarded the Vietnam War as a cause of the decline in US authority as a world power. During this period, "Americanization" took on a negative meaning. Still the flow of American mass culture and goods to West Germany was uninterrupted.

From the arrival of the first G.I.s in 1945, chewing gum, chocolate, coffee, Lucky Strikes, Coca Cola, jazz, jeans, and nylons have been favorites among German youth and young adults. Such products symbolized a distant affluent world about which the defeated Germans could only dream. After the currency reform of 1948, people no longer needed to barter for these things on the black market; they could buy them in the stores. Leather jackets, motor bikes, boots, and army uniforms became teenage status symbols. Kitchen gadgets, plastic products, instant foods, refrigerators, and televisions are now standard items in German households. What was stimulating and emancipating at first, filling a need for entertainment and consumption after the spartan Nazi years, was in time taken for granted. Today West German children watch Sesame Street, John Wayne movies, and Bonanza on TV, they read "Peanuts," and they eat at McDonalds or Kentucky Fried Chicken. Teenagers dance to rock and disco music.

But there is more to "Americanization" than is evident on the surface of mass culture: "Both Americans and Germans value their democratic institutions and their free way of life" (*211*, 80). The West German political system is largely based on the US model. In the business sector, American marketing techniques were studied, adapted, and developed to meet German tastes and standards. The West German entertainment industry has imitated Hollywood to a great degree and continues to flood TV and cinema with American myths, legends, ideals, and stereotypes. Characterized by a greater sophistication, the New German Film has had a more differentiated view of America, and has revealed a German love-hate relationship to things American.

The impact of American mass culture is most apparent in the jargon and the idioms of the teenage world, especially in the fields of music, fashion, cosmetics, and dating—as any employment page, marriage-advertisement page, or a German TV guide confirms. The following condensed example of teen slang is exemplary:

> Die *Boys* und *Girls* in ihren *Jeans* und *Boots* und mit *Buttons* und ihren *T-* und *Sweat-Shirts* aus den *Second-hand-Shops* erscheinen zum *Comeback* der *Band,* deren *Sound* so viel *Feeling, Power* und *Drive* und deren *Show* ein so starkes *Timing* besitzt, daß sie keine *Publicity* nötig hat: Bei den *Teenagern* und den *ausgeflippten People* aus der *Szene* ist sie solch ein *hit,* daß all die *relaxten Fans* und *coolen Freaks* beim *Run* auf die *Tickets* in der *City* ganz *happy* sind . . .
>
> (Dieter Zimmer, *Die Zeit,* 23 April 1981)

After WWII there was a great influx of American loan words into West Germany: e.g., "teenager" for *Backfisch,* "sample" for *Muster,* "story" for *Geschichte,* "city" for *Stadt.* Some old romance loan words have been replaced by US terms: e.g., "team" for *Ensemble,* "manager" or "boss" for *Impresario,* "band" for *Kapelle.* English adjectives and nouns have received German endings: e.g., *recyclebare Spray-Dosen.* A variety of mixed forms and compound words have also developed. Many phrases now bear an American imprint: *im gleichen Boot* ("in the same boat"), *jemandem die Schau stehlen* ("to steal the show"), das Gesicht wahren ("to save face"), *Gehirnwäsche* ("brain washing").

Not only vocabulary, but also morphology, structure, and style have been affected. Among the morphological innovations: the extension of the English plural s-form to German: e.g., *Fans, Flirts, Treffs, Tiefs, Hochs;* singular derivations ending in -o or -i: e.g., *Porno, Disco, Memo, Info, Profi;* and compounds with "super-," "co," and "mini": e.g., *Superbombe, Kopilot, Minirock.* Traditional complex sentences, consisting of several main and subordinate clauses with the verb (or part of it) at the very end, are also on the wane, and finally, written German is approaching everyday oral speech ("Germanistik," *Der Spiegel,* November 1968).

Trends toward simplification have been inherent in German linguistic developments since the nineteenth century. The postwar influx of US mass culture and consumerism accelerated this process, particularly in advertising, colloquial and teenage speech, and business terminology, all of which have come to rely heavily on language "made in the USA."

# 4.   The Cultural Scene

## GRUPPE 47 AS ELITE

The *Gruppe 47* was the primary focus for the literary and cultural activities in the era of economic recovery and political restoration under Adenauer and his successors from 1949 to 1968. The writers of the group varied greatly in their political orientation, cultural prominence, and literary style. Yet they also had much in common. For one thing, their rise and decline parallels the rise and decline of the Adenauer era. Although the antagonism between many of their members and the materialist society around them was strong, there nevertheless existed a deep connection between Adenauer's FRG and the *Gruppe 47.* Both believed in individualism, which they defined without ideological focus as self-reliance. This German version of American individualism had no deep roots in the cultural and political experience of either the old politicians such as Adenauer or the mostly young writers now gathering together in well publicized yearly meetings. The *Gruppe 47* developed into a powerful cultural elite that set norms for German writers in the Federal Republic for the next two decades.

*Gruppe 47* writers underestimated their impact as an institution. Individualism merely became an ideological screen that hid from them the effect of the marketplace on their literary activities. Similarly, the free-wheeling entrepreneurial society of the early Adenauer years following upon postwar experimentation became in the mid-sixties Ludwig Erhard's *formierte Gesellschaft,* an economically efficient and politically integrated society, rigid in shaping its economic and political life. Despite the parallels between Adenauer's Germany and the *Gruppe 47,* some of the most prominent writers did not agree with the majority who accommodated themselves to the Adenauer restoration.

The transformation of the group from an intimate circle of writers to a powerful cultural institution was reflected in the regular meetings. These gatherings were originally intended for reading, criticism, and discussion as acts of self-definition. As time passed, however, and certainly after 1960, the meetings became important cultural events with an emphasis on public reading and criticism as a representative social act. A Munich broadcast of the sixth meeting on October 22, 1949 captured the spirit of the group's early activities, calling it a "literary workshop, a carpenter's shop *(Schreinerei)* in which the workman's aspect of writing played a central role" (*135,* 47). The writers stressed the process of writing over the end product and saw their group as a workmens' guild. Their emphasis on the process contrasted with the older bourgeois tradition that did not stress the craftsmanship of the creative arts but rather the results. Further, the *Gruppe 47* was democratic in the sense that the writers communicated directly with one another while they were in the process of writing. They also agreed in general about what kind of literature should be written and what role it should play in society. In the mid-sixties their best-known literary and cultural critic, Marcel Reich-Ranicki, aptly characterized the ethos of the *Gruppe 47* in political terms: "A literature not of protests or the scream, but rather of reflection and self-analysis, not one to attack but to contemplate" (*135,* 214). In commending the group of its choice of the 1965 prize recipient Peter Bichsel, a Swiss writer, the same critic praised the winner's prose as, "representative of a large part of German literature of our day—a literature, that, in soft tones and a knowing smile, speaks of the life of small people" (*6,* 14).

## LITERARY GENRES IN THE 1950s

The literary activities in the fifties and the early sixties can still be assessed in terms of traditional genres—the drama, lyric poetry, and the novel.

In the drama of the fifties, the Swiss playwright Friedrich Dürrenmatt stands out with his *Besuch der alten Dame* (1956; *The Visit,* 1958). In the tradition of Aristophanes and Bertolt Brecht, he presents an exemplary event of moral significance: an impoverished small town is visited by one of its former inhabitants, who is now a billionairess. She has returned from the United States to demand that the lover who jilted her in her youth be turned over to her in return for a financial bail-out of the town. The town, gradually corrupted by easier times and an excessive reliance on financial credit, acquiesces. The moral of the story is neatly balanced by ribald wit and a sense for the bizarre.

Lyric poetry with its inwardness and subjectivity was a popular genre in the fifties. It attempted to catch up with developments abroad—surrealism, mannerism, and the German Expressionism of the twenties. Hans Arp, for example, combined in many of his most successful poems descriptive elements of destruction with esoteric metaphors and he infused them both with the urgency of the expressionist:

> The darkness of the earth is getting darker
> In the dark there multiply like vermin
> Noise-people
> Bomb cooks
> Copulators with machines
> Centaurs, half man, half machine
> People with soccer ball heads
> People without a trace of a heart
> Unfathomed.

"Dunkler wird das Dunkel" (1955; "The Dark Is Getting Darker," 7, 187)

Also Günther Eich, whose poem, "Inventur" with its radical departure from tradition typical of German literature immediately after the war, developed in the fifties an intimate and an inwardly lyrical style. In his *Botschaft des Regens* (1955; The Message of Rain, 1955), Eich mixed lyric sentiments of isolation and despair with the magic charms of nature. In his 1958 volume of poems, Alexander Fried captured most eloquently the spirit of inwardness and magic characteristic of the cultural scene under Adenauer:

> What the wind has sown
> His brother, the storm harvests
> What the storm harvested
> Is drunk by his sister the sea
> At the edge of the clouds
> Stars dive for pearls:
> Soon the crown will
> Be in heaven again.

"Rückkehr," ("Return," 74, 27)

Magic realism, precious baroque conceits, the grand gestures with which Klopstock had evoked nature in his "Frühlingsfeier" almost 200 years earlier—all appear in this remarkably eclectic poem. When Fried issued this volume of lyric poetry in 1968 during the heyday of the cultural and political revolution in Germany, he apologized for the lyrics, which lacked a political-social dimension: "It is not in my character to censure old poems by rewriting them. . . . Thus I have not dropped any of my 'odd-ball' or 'apolitical poems of the old volume' " (74, 5).

German prose in the fifties was heavily indebted to Albert Camus, James Joyce, Jean-Paul Sartre, and Ernest Hemingway. Especially the novels and stories of Franz Kafka—*Der Prozeß* (1925; *The Trial,* 1937), *Das Schloß* (1926; *The Castle,* 1930), "Die

Verwandlung" (1915; "The Metamorphosis," 1936)—spoke to the personal and social dilemma of an entire generation of writers after the war. Kafka saw his protagonists trapped in a world of inexorable laws and buffeted by incomprehensible and traumatic events. But the limits that defied understanding also stimulated a spirit of inquiry and quest for freedom. Kafka's paradoxes became a magic incantation for survival in a hostile world.

Camus called Kafka's *The Metamorphosis* the greatest story of the twentieth century, and German prose writers of the fifties agreed with him. With the emergence of the cultural and political revolt in the late sixties, however, Kafka's exclusive concern with the individual's plight and quest became less interesting, and his influence waned. A renewed interest in subjective experiences in the seventies no longer owed much to Kafka.

One of the most significant prose writers indebted to Kafka was Ilse Aichinger, a recipient of the literary prize of the *Gruppe 47.* In 1952 she published her first major work, a series of short stories, under the title *Rede unter dem Galgen* (1952; *Speech Underneath the Gallows).* In these stories she portrays the helplessness of the individual confronted with the world's inextricable laws. Other prose writers, Gerd Gaiser (*Schlußball,* 1958), and Wolfgang Koeppen—*Das Treibhaus* (1953; *The Rome Parliament,* 1955)— wrote noteworthy novels and short stories. The almanac of the *Gruppe 47,* which chronicled their meetings, events, and criticized representative works, supported the generally held belief that literature should be primarily a private endeavor. Many of the titles revealed the orientation of the authors and their audience: *Mit dem Kopf durch die Wand* (1959; *With the Head through the Wall)* by Wolfgang Weyrauch, (*189,* 392); *Ein Fall von Kalten Füßen* (1959; *A Case of Cold Feet*) by Klaus Roehler (*189,* 420 ff.); *Bedauern über ein Postamt (1959; Regrets Concerning a Post Office*) by Walter Höllerer (*189,* 438). In sum, it was a literature with "soft tones and a knowing smile."

The political upheaval of the late sixties and the subsequent retrenchment and reaction in the early seventies brought into sharper focus the political profile of some of the most prominent writers of the *Gruppe 47.* Heinrich Böll, Günter Grass, Martin Walser, Hans Magnus Enzensberger, and Peter Handke not only influenced the scope and substance of postwar literature, they also participated increasingly in political activity. These writers also began to concern themselves with Germany's unintegrated past *(unbewältigte Vergangenheit).*

Günter Grass's *Die Blechtrommel* (1959; *The Tin Drum,* 1962), the major postwar prose work brings to life the Nazi period from the unique perspective of a dwarfed boy, Oskar Mazerath, who after having taken a good look at the world of the adults around him, decides to stop growing. He is a devoted, even fanatical drummer and communicates with the world in this nonverbal way during the days of the Nazis and the war. He also possesses a voice shrill enough to shatter glass. Towards the end of a novel filled with brilliantly presented scenes, episodes, and characters, the Russians arrive evoking one of the high points of the novel: huddled in the cellar together with friends, neighbors, and family members, the dwarf Oskar observes his father who does not know where to hide the metal Nazi insignia on his lapel. As the Russians approach the cellar, the father chokes to death desperately trying to swallow the Nazi emblem. The novel contains many other scenes of memorable precision: Mazerath's naive contemplation of Christ on the cross as the greatest athlete of all times, grandmother Kowalski crouched in a potato field hiding fugitives under her skirts; a four-man card game that cannot be concluded because one player sits motionless in their midst, killed by shrapnel—a galling turn of events for the player holding the winning hand. Such scenes express the earthy humor of Günter Grass and his gutsy sense for story-telling. Very much in the tradition of the picaresque novel (for example, Hans Jakob Grimmelshausen's *Simplicius Simplicissimus),* Grass tells an epic tale in which the protagonist could easily fall prey to circumstances, were it not for his undaunted will to survive. A key to Mazerath's character can be found in his ability to see everything and to deal with traumatic experiences and events without really understanding them, let alone integrating them into a coherent view of himself and the world around him. Grass provided a thematic focus for Peter Handke's *Kaspar Hauser,* which restated Mazerath's dilemma a decade later in more radical terms. Grass shared with most of his contemporaries the view that there could be no moral response commensurate with the Nazi crimes. Thus he ridiculed the powerful and rooted for the survival of the lowly.

*The Tin Drum* represented a radical departure from the middle-class development novel (*Entwicklungsroman* or *Bildungsroman*) that had been central to German literature since Goethe's *Wilhelm Meister* and was very much alive in Thomas Mann's *Der Zauberberg* (1924; *The Magic Mountain,* 1927), which was the last great representative of the genre. The novel's hero, Hans Castorp, recuperates from tuberculosis in a sanatorium in the Swiss resort town of Davos, where, far removed from society, two mentors of highly contrasting world views initiate him into a complex analysis of the society they had all left behind. Castorp's real intellectual and spiritual breakthrough, however, does not occur in the sanatorium but high in the mountains during a snowstorm, where in hallucinatory vision he comes to realize the power of love over death. He returns to society at the beginning of World War I to join the army. In *The*

*Magic Mountain*, Mann articulates lofty intellectual positions from which to comprehend societal forces. By contrast, Günter Grass's protagonist never emerges from the daily flow of violent experiences and events down in the flatlands of the Polish border region. Mann portrays the discrepancy between intellectual insights and the vagaries of social existence, including war. Grass is not interested in this discrepancy. Instead he uses his vitality and prodigious artistic imagination to depict brutal events and so writes a blueprint for survival. While Mann emphasizes in his elegant prose the culturally representative function of his writing, Grass breaks syntax, just like his dwarf breaks glass, opening his discourse up to the unconscious. Hans Castorp grows intellectually and emotionally; Mazerath literally decides to stop growing as an act of protest against the world, but also as a strategy for survival.

Grass's novel is the first masterpiece of postwar West German literature for its exuberance and expressiveness. It also was the first major German work to deal with the Nazi past with consummate artistry. Grass not only broke new ground in his creative play with language, imagery, and character, he also challenged the assumption of the Adenauer era that writers should write positively about the great materialistic accomplishments of postwar West Germany. With Grass's novel, literature had become for the first time since the Weimar Republic a visible and effective vantage point from which the political and social sphere could be critically assessed.

Next to Günter Grass, Heinrich Böll was the most important writer to articulate the critical function of the cultural sphere. Although he was an established author before Grass, Böll's first novel to have a major impact on postwar German culture was his *Billiard um halbzehn* (1959; *Billiards at Half Past Nine,* 1962), a moral allegory that narrates the experiences of a family throughout three generations, from Wilhelm II's Germany to the postwar years. The novel approaches the problems of the German past by means of a tightly constructed plot, which centers around St. Anthony's abbey. The abbey was constructed by the grandfather in 1908. The son, also an architect, became a demolition expert during World War II. He remarks:

> . . . by rights I should be putting houses up. But I've never put any up, I only blow them down. And the same goes for churches too, which I used to draw on nice soft drawing paper when I was a boy, always dreaming that someday I'd build real ones like them. But I never did build any.

> *(22, 62)*

Finally, towards the end of the war he blows up the abbey his father had built in protest against the Catholic Church and its cooperation with Hitler. After the war, his own son rebuilds the abbey. Böll's moral intensity shapes the characters and the plot, and the narrative remains a complex message.

Böll provides the most rigorous criticism of the Adenauer era in his novel, *Ansichten eines Clowns* (1963; *The Clown*, 1965) in which the son of a wealthy family rejects a lucrative career in order to become a dunce and jester, a position that enables him to tell the truth freely.

Grass and Böll belong to the generation of writers who found themselves increasingly alienated from a West Germany that repressed its Nazi past and concentrated on building a consumer-oriented materialistic society. It is a curious fact that hardly any of the writers of the *Gruppe 47* became involved in the issue of the divided country, either in their writings or their personal commitments. The Nazi past and the emerging materialistic society overshadowed the problem of Germany, now separated into two states that were growing farther and farther apart in all spheres of life. A refugee from East Germany, Uwe Johnson, brought this problem to the fore.

Johnson's novels focus on the problems of Germans living in a divided country. The best-known of them, *Mutmaßungen über Jakob* (1959; *Speculations about Jakob*, 1963; *116*), deals with the relationship of the individual to the state. As is characteristic of much East German writing in the wake of Brecht, the story is shaped by a specific political issue that has general applicability, in this case the Hungarian uprising of 1956. Jakob, a train dispatcher, has been killed crossing the tracks, and the reader knows Jakob only through what others remember about him, and their memories are hazy and their reports conflicting. We can only make assumptions about Jakob, as the title of the novel indicates. We do find out, however, that "Jakob always walked straight across the railroad tracks" (*116*, 7). He was a nonconformist, yet he remained loyal to his socialist convictions. Ultimately, Jakob's story points towards the GDR's unfulfilled promise to grant individualism an important place in a socialist society.

Uwe Johnson deliberately tells the story from a variety of perspectives as if to suggest that truth is a matter of perspective. Although he was one of the first prominent writers to flee from East Germany, his simple socialist-realist style ran counter to West German literary taste with its preference for a reflective complexity, and he never played an important role in the cultural scene of the Federal Republic.

Innovative experiments and a turn towards documentary dramatization characterized the West German drama in the early sixties. In 1963, Rolf Hochhuth's play *Der Stellvertreter* (1963; *The Deputy*, 1964), seized upon the historical controversy about the cooperation between Hitler and Pope Pius XII. Hochhuth's concerns about the German past are raised in the tradition of a Schillerian historical drama built on conflicts and moral issues.

Peter Weiss, an altogether avant-garde dramatist, portrays events of the French Revolution in his play, *Die Verfolgung und Ermordung Jean Paul Marats dargestellt durch die Schauspielgruppe des Hospizes zu Charenton unter Anleitung des Herrn de Sade* (1964; *The Persecution and Assassination of Jean-Paul Marat as Performed by the Inmates of the Asylum of Charenton under the Direction of the Marquis de Sade,* 1965) as seen through the musings of the feverish Marat shortly before his murder. The play is directed by the Marquis de Sade and performed by the inmates of an insane asylum. Weiss's play within the play removes historical action from dramatic directness, suffusing it with reflection, commentary, and analysis—in sum, the entire play represents "history" on various levels of abstraction and alienation. While the play lacks the immediacy of Hochhuth's concern with specific issues of the German past, it raises for the audience larger questions of history and its meaning. Whatever the differences between the simple historical *exposé* (Hochhuth) and the complex drama of history's meaning (Weiss), both heightened the awareness of historical issues and the problem of moral accountability.

## CRITICISM OF THE LATER ADENAUER YEARS

In the early sixties when everything was still relatively quiet in the FRG, the cultural sphere began to foreshadow the political activism and social change to come later in the decade. Two years after Günter Grass's *The Tin Drum* was published, Martin Walser articulated a new, slowly emerging political attitude when he asked in 1961 in the title of his essay, "Die Alternative oder Brauchen wir eine neue Regierung?" ("The Alternative or Do We Need a New Government?"):

> We are well off again, but the state that we have today could only have been invented by a self-satisfied petit bourgeois whose horizon and standards are determined by a disinterest in problems because of a self-perpetuating wealth.

In newspapers, pamphlets, and manifestoes cultural critics sharpened their attacks on a society that had become wealthy and morally complacent:

> How is it possible that a society, having experienced in the span of half a century such extraordinarily profound and existentially destructive changes . . . that such a society, two decades after the end of the war, generally behaves as if nothing had happened, as if one were protected

and comfortably embedded in a continuous development full of sentiment and feeling.

(*85*, 16)

Stirrings outside the cultural sphere soon made obvious that
change was in the air. In the famous *Spiegel* affair of 1962, for example, the Defense Minister Franz Joseph Strauss was forced to resign over a freedom-of-the-press issue, having seized the Hamburg
offices of this influential journal on flimsy spy charges. By the mid-
sixties the economic reconstruction of West Germany was slowing
down. Free-wheeling entrepreneurial expansion had come to an
end. This flattening of the economy was an unusual experience for
the Germans who since the war had become accustomed to a constant increase in living standards and wealth. Political diversity was
stifled more and more by the fact that only one party had been in
power since the founding of the FRG, namely the CDU-CSU, giving
rise to fears that a one party state with a cooperative state bureaucracy, was emerging once again in Germany. When finally in 1966
the SPD joined the CDU to form a grand coalition, more and more
Germans felt that a one-party state was actually in the making, or at
least a state in which there would be no significant alternative to
the entrenched political party system. At the same time, a postwar
generation was beginning to emerge with a profoundly different
historical experience than the two generations before it. Raised in
an era of general global peace and economic stability, younger
Germans did not share the crippling traumas of the war and the
deprivation suffered by their parents. What made the political activities of this younger generation initially so effective was the considerable support they received from the middle generation before
them. This middle generation had been politically silent during the
era of economic reconstruction:

> For several years a new development has been taking place in the Fed-
> eral Republic which can be called "Filled with a future," a new genera-
> tion is gaining in importance, reputation, and influence. It is not the
> younger generation. It is the thirty- to fifty-year olds, who after 1945
> were suppressed in a patriarchal manner.

(Hermann Glaser, 1965; *85*, 113)

This middle generation, which by the mid-sixties had gained
considerable influence in the media and the universities, provided
some measure of legitimacy to the radical student revolt: "What is
it to be politically left today? It is whatever one claims it to be; it
sits around beer tables or stands by champagne bars. . . . We are
approaching the one-party state which will allow a few left little

wings to flutter" (Heinrich Böll, *Was heute links sein könnte,* (1962; *What could be politically left today; 86,* 535ff.). In the course of the sixties the SPD became the home of the political left and it provided literary spokesmen with an outlet for their political dissatisfactions. Finally, on June 2, 1967 a student was shot during a demonstration protesting the Shah of Iran's visit to Berlin. Botho Strauß, an important avant-garde dramatist and cultural critic, described this event with the exaggeration that was typical of the times as a turning point for West Germany: "This day—one would say—marks the end of the German postwar era, the end of a way of thinking that was intertwined with the past. . . . This kind of thinking determined official politics as well as art and literature" (*219,* 61). The title of Strauß's essay may be seen as a manifesto for the entire sphere of culture in the late sixties: *Versuche ästhetische und politische Ereignisse zusammenzudenken (Attempts to bring together in thought aesthetic and political events,* in *Theater Heute,* October 1970). The title characterizes the weakness and the strength of this short-lived trend towards political and cultural change. On the one hand, the interdependence of the political, economic, and cultural sphere was stressed; on the other hand, this new way of thinking comprehensively about the various aspects of German society in its entirety—emphasized theory over pragmatic action.

When finally in 1967 the *Gruppe 47* gathered for one of its traditional meetings at the Pulvermühle near Nuremberg, the writers and critics who had shaped German literature for two decades were confronted by a student demonstration. The students declared the literature of their elders irrelevant and demanded that the writers show their colors in the political arena. Thus the end of traditional literature was pronounced, and culture was now to serve the political transformation of society. The social theorist Herbert Marcuse justified political activism on the theory that individual liberation and the end of foreign oppression should be linked through visible but largely symbolic acts of civil disobedience. In many respects, however, the students ignored the more thoughtful reflections of their intellectual mentors. Theodor Adorno and other prominent members of the Frankfurt School of Social Thought did not intend to reduce literature to a political tool. They remained cultural elitists, viewing great literary works as islands of resistance against mass culture and simplistic politicizing. The utopian function of literature existed for them as an open-ended historical possibility, not as a specific politicial blueprint.

The students' attack on the *Gruppe 47* did not differentiate between the nonpolitical writers and those writers who had a clear political commitment. Günter Grass had joined the SPD and organized the *Wählerinitiativen* (voters' initiatives), Heinrich Böll was a prominent spokesman of the Left, Hans Magnus Enzensberger's influential journal, *Kursbuch,* provided a critical analysis of the prevalent political and economic order, and Reinhard Lettau became known for his fight against the United States' involvement in Vietnam. The student attack and the writers' own reassessment of their political role ended the effectiveness of the *Gruppe 47* as arbiter of literary norms. In the students' opinion, the *Gruppe 47* had not lived up to the promise made by Günther Eich as early as 1950 to, ". . . be uncomfortable; be sand and not oil in the machines of the world."

With the announcement of the "death of literature" (*Kursbuch* 15, 1968), the question arose as to what should replace it. New literary forms were demanded, fiction was to be replaced by documentation, and poetic diction was to give way to everyday speech. Symbol-making and the idea that literature may have a function beyond the social sphere was vigorously attacked as elitist. There was no shortage of theoretical pronouncements, but the only tangible suggestion that emerged out of these theoretical considerations was the advocacy of documentary literature over traditional fiction. The proletariat was to replace the old *Bildungsbürger* (intellectual) and constitute its own public sphere for this new documentary writing. Two major theoretical works marked the transition from a middle-class definition of culture to a proletarian one: Jürgen Habermas, in his *Strukturwandel der Öffentlichkeit* (1969; *Structural Change in the Public Sphere)* outlined the social context within which bourgeois literature flourished. The result of this far-reaching sociological probe was to explain the cultural norms that the German middle class had cherished as absolutes in terms of their institutional function. Three years later, two writers, Oskar Negt and Alexander Kluge, went a step further with their *Öffentlichkeit und Erfahrung: Zur Organisationsanalyse von bürgerlicher und proletarischer Öffentlichkeit* (1972; *Public Sphere and Experience: Organization Analysis of the Bourgeois and Proletarian Public Sphere*). It advocated a proletarian public sphere in which the new radical literature could flourish. These works were both highly theoretical and all-encompassing. While Negt and Kluge attempted to replace, and Habermas radically to modify the cultural sphere, both approaches had in common an unshakable faith in theoretical interpretations. Both shared an optimism that a comprehensive *Systemanalyse* was the only road to a new consciousness and to the radical transformation of society. This optimistic faith was shared by the students rebelling in the streets and university halls. It was to bring universal emancipation to all. Exaggerated expectations that far exceeded possibilities were not unknown to twentieth-century Germany. This optimistic faith in systems was replaced in the seventies by a crisis of all sorts—ecological, social, interpretative, and economic.

The amount of theoretical speculation about the function of literature in society contrasted with a minimum of literary productivity. There was a brief flurry of documentary literature that emphasized proletarian issues. In 1961 several writers founded a *Gruppe 61* that made the world of labor its central theme. Max von der Grün's *Irrlicht und Feuer (Will-O-Wisp and Fire)* described the life of workers in the mines. However, he remained a middle-class writer who saw himself as an independent creator of fiction, which happened to deal with the world of work. Günther Walraff, a much more prominent representative of workers' literature, created a *Dokumentarliteratur* in which the speech of laborers and the simple man's problems replaced poetic diction. Erika Runge, a GDR writer, increased the popularity of workers' literature in West Germany with her *Bottroper Protokolle.* Enzensberger joined the trend with his *Das Verhör von Habana* (1970; Havana Hearings) in which he documented the trial of American prisoners caught during the Bay of Pigs invasion in 1962. Klaus Tscheliesnig's *Lehrlingsprotokolle* (Apprentices' Protokols; with a foreword by Günther Walraff) consisted of documentary montages depicting the experiences of apprentice workers. Documentary montages, however, proved to have only limited "transfer value" outside their own specific proletarian context. The student revolution of the late sixties altered the cultural sphere and changed long-held assumptions about literature, but it did not initiate a literature that reflected its own values, let alone those of West Germany as a whole.

Many writers of the *Gruppe 47* expressed a solidarity with the student revolution. Martin Walser declared in 1968 that political engagement should be a "required subject for writers." But despite the student revolution and the political activism of key literary figures, few lasting literary works emerged from the political turmoil.

Several obstacles prevented the emergence of a radical literature concerned with social issues and the world of the laborer. First of all, there was no proletarian sphere in West Germany. The German laborer who was to be the subject of these literary endeavors (the worker as writer) simply did not care. He remained loyal to his factory and devoted to mass culture, whether in the soccer stadium or in front of a TV set. Some of the educated middle class remained devoted to traditional cultural norms, while others readily embraced mass culture. In spite of its sympathy for political radicalism, ultimately the intelligentsia also favored the complexities of traditional fiction and poetry. Also, a new proletarian literature did not become prominent because it lacked a tradition of its own. It was no longer feasible to build a politically conscious literature both in theme and diction on the works of Bertolt Brecht alone. East German literary culture was largely not applicable since, during the fifties and sixties East German writers were part of the state-directed Leninist-Marxist system that determined what could be written in support of the established socialist state.

A much more significant break with traditional literary forms was made by the Austrian Peter Handke, one of the outstanding dramatists and novelists of the postwar period. During the Princeton meeting of the *Gruppe 47* in 1966, Handke created a literary sensation with his dramatic happening, *Publikumsbeschimpfung* (1966; *Offending the Audience*, 1969), in which his literary message was simply an attack on his audience. The main issue was one of language. Handke concluded that traditional literary language, no matter how experimental it seemed, did not come to grips with the fundamental links that exist between traditional language patterns, individual identity, and social cohesion. As long as this link was not examined, no radically new literature would be created. The 1966 literary happening at Princeton foreshadowed Handke's fundamental reexamination of the conditions that shaped human communication. His dramatic piece, *Kaspar Hauser* set the stage for the West German literary style of the seventies.

# FROM DEVASTATION TO ECONOMIC MIRACLE

The Allied Zones of Administration and the Division of Germany and Austria after the Second World War.

British   American   French   Soviet   Polish

Brandenburg Gate in Berlin on May 8, 1945. (Courtesy of the German Information Center)

The Reichstag in 1945 devastated by bombing and looting. (Courtesy of the German Information Center)

Berlin Airlift of 1948-49 broke through the Soviet blockade of the city by nonstop supply shipments to beleaguered garrisons and 2¼ million civilian population of West Berlin. (Courtesy of the German Information Center)

Uprising of June 17, 1953, in East Berlin for economic, social, and political reasons including reunification of Germany. (Courtesy of the German Information Center)

Reichstag and the Wall. (Courtesy of the German Information Center)

Sign at the Wall calling for Unity, Justice, and Liberty. (Courtesy of the German Information Center)

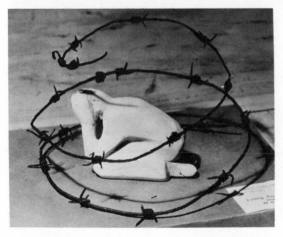

A 13-year-old West German boy's artistic response to the Wall. (Courtesy of the German Information Center)

Konrad Adenauer, 1949-1963.
(Courtesy of the German Information Center)

Ludwig Erhard, 1963-1966. (Courtesy of the German Information
Center)

Kurt Georg Kiesinger, 1966-1969.
(Courtesy of the German Information
Center)

# WEST GERMAN
# CHANCELLORS

Willy Brandt, 1969-1974. (Courtesy of the
German Information Center)

Helmut Schmidt, 1974-1982. (Courtesy
of the German Information Center)

Helmut Kohl, 1982-
(Courtesy of the German Information Center)

Konrad Adenauer and John F. Kennedy consolidate German-American Friendship in 1961. (Courtesy of the German Information Center)

## TIES TO THE WEST— COOPERATION WITH THE EAST

In order to document the historical significance of Franco-German reconciliation, Konrad Adenauer and Charles de Gaulle attend Mass together at Reims Cathedral in 1962. (Courtesy of the German Information Center)

Soviet Communist Party Chairman Leonid Brezhnev with Chancellor Willy Brandt and Mrs. Brandt during his visit to the FRG. (Courtesy of the German Information Center)

Chancellor Helmut Kohl and French President François Mitterrand seal Franco-German friendship in 1984 with a joint commemorative ceremony for the war dead at Verdun. (Courtesy of the German Information Center)

Chancellor Helmut Kohl and GDR Council of State President Erich Honecker emphasize in 1985 that war must never again originate on German soil. (Courtesy of the German Information Center)

# Chapter IV

# THE LATE SIXTIES AND EARLY SEVENTIES: ERA OF SOCIAL AND POLITICAL EXPERIMENTATION

## 1. West Germany as a Global Power

Twenty years after the end of WWII, the Adenauer-Erhard era came to a close. Under the first Federal Chancellor, foreign policy was securely anchored in *Westpolitik,* dominated by the US. It was a period of confrontation with the East Bloc during which Adenauer never revised his set of political priorities: strength through western integration. Towards the end of the 1960s the time was ripe to replace the policy of confrontation with negotiations and accomodation with the East. Detente between the superpowers gave the FRG a chance to develop its own more flexible foreign policy towards its eastern neighbors.

*Ostpolitik,* designed by Willy Brandt (foreign minister in 1969 and federal chancellor from 1969 to 1974), became the keyword of the late 1960s and early 1970s in international politics, as the world focused its attention on the FRG and its relationships with Central Europe (GDR, Poland, and Czechoslovakia) as well as Eastern Europe (Soviet Union, Romania, and Bulgaria): "An essential ingredient of our *Ostpolitik* was that we applied ourselves to our own affairs in a new and more positive manner instead of relying solely on others to speak for us" (*30,* 168). The success of Brandt's *Ostpolitik* attested to the FRG's status as a global power.

In his quest for reconciliation with Eastern Europe, Brandt had two German models: Bismarck, who had feared an anti-German coalition and therefore had resorted to a complex set of treaties to ensure peace; and Gustav Stresemann, who after WWI hoped to make friends with Germany's foes (Locarno) and emphasized a policy of common sense (*30,* 152). West Germany's *Ostpolitik* was

151

late in coming because "The FRG was the last major Western power to climb out of the Cold War trenches" (*115*, 164).

Easing tension with the Soviets had been Eisenhower's aim. Kennedy accepted the status quo in Berlin and did not interfere with the construction of the Wall in 1961; he initiated the Nuclear Test Ban Treaty in 1963. Despite the Vietnam War, Lyndon Johnson pursued a policy of "bridge building." Under Nixon, the pace of detente quickened with the Berlin Agreement. SALT I and troop reduction talks started in 1968. These endeavors in the area of international security spurred the FRG's reconciliatory moves toward its eastern neighbors. "Germany and the United States moved on approximately similar schedules toward détente, even in the early period of 1963–1965, and more when later détente flowered. At times, the United States was moving faster. At other times Germany was" (*211*, 27). Even before Brandt's *Ostpolitik,* Gerhard Schröder had encouraged such a policy, which climaxed in Chancellor Erhard's renunciation-of-force offer *(Gewaltverzichtserklärung)* as the best approach to East-West problems. Shortly thereafter, the "Grand Coalition" of CDU and SPD brought to power a new chancellor, Kurt Georg Kiesinger (1966–1969) and a new foreign minister, namely, Willy Brandt. There was no more room for a parliamentary opposition, because this coalition contained virtually the entire political spectrum ranging from former Nazis (Kiesinger, Finance Minister Schiller) and army officers of the *Wehrmacht* (Strauss) to exiled politicians (Brandt and Herbert Wehner, a former KP member).

Born in Lübeck, Willy Brandt soon displayed his capacity for leadership. At sixteen he joined the SPD and led a young socialist group until Hitler's takeover in 1933. Hunted by the Gestapo, he fled to Norway, and, after it was invaded by the Nazis, to Sweden in 1940 where he worked in the resistance. He reentered Germany only once, on a secret mission that took him to Berlin. After the war, in 1945, he returned to Germany with a Norwegian passport as a correspondent covering the Nuremberg war trials. Next, he went to Berlin as an attaché of the Norwegian Embassy. He regained his German citizenship in 1947 and entered Berlin politics as an SPD member. He rose rapidly to become mayor of West Berlin (1957–1967). In this capacity he distinguished himself in the struggle against Soviet attempts to take over the city and became internationally known as a symbol of Western resistance. He was a prime mover in the SPD's rejection of Marxism (Godesberg Program, 1959), a precondition for its transformation into a broadly based popular party. Twice defeated for chancellor by Adenauer, his party finally won enough votes to be accepted by the CDU as a coalition partner. As chancellor, Brandt launched his *Ostpolitik*. In 1967 he established diplomatic relations with Romania and a year

later with Yugoslavia. Kiesinger exchanged the first official correspondence with Willi Stoph, Chairman of the GDR's Council of
Ministers. But the Czech uprising of 1968 brought a temporary halt
to the first phase of his Eastern policy.

Brandt's historic reconciliation effort met with success for three
reasons:

1. His political record was above suspicion. He was universally
acknowledged to be a social democrat who had actively resisted
the Nazis. His policy was founded on a combination of idealism
and common sense. He acknowledged the status quo in Europe,
emphasizing publicly that Germany had lost WWII and the lands
beyond the Oder-Neisse. He admitted that there was little possibility for either a reunification of Germany through free elections or
a peace treaty with Poland to revise the eastern borders. Sober
judgment, political pragmatism, refusal to rely on escapist illusions, and a charismatic personality were the qualities that stood
Brandt in good stead in his negotiations with the East. For him,
"the recognition of realities entailed, first and last, sufficient
courage to acknowledge our own history and its consequences"
(30, 181). He believed a politics of realism (Realpolitik) to be the
best hope for survival in the nuclear age.

2. Brandt renounced the use of force against all existing frontiers, the GDR's included. This reduced suspicion from the outset.
Further, he made sure that solutions were not just bilateral or national but comprehensive and European, based on a recognition of
the Soviet Union's dominant role in Europe. He was sensitive to
Soviet security needs and negotiated the Moscow Treaty of 1970
as a framework for dealing with Eastern European nations individually. In the treaty with Poland, for example, he adopted the Oder-
Neisse line as Poland's western frontier on the basis of the Moscow
Treaty.

3. He believed that acknowledging the political realities would
actually strengthen the Atlantic Alliance. West German security
and economic stability would continue to depend on its place in
NATO and in the EEC, but Ostpolitik would reduce tensions and
eliminate possible military confrontations in Central Europe. All
this would also be in America's interest.

Brandt's signature to the Moscow Treaty, which renounced
force and declared existing European borders inviolate, improved
relations with other members of the Warsaw Pact, especially the
GDR. Anticipating opposition on the domestic front, Brandt stated
on Moscow television: "Russia is inextricably involved in the history of Europe, not only as an enemy and menace but also as a partner. Nothing is lost with this treaty that was not gambled away long
ago. We have the courage to turn over a new page in history" (29,
107).

This remark applied to Poland in particular, which at the end of the war had expelled millions of Germans, some of whom wanted back their lands. But the Warsaw Pact fixed the western Polish frontier along the Oder-Neisse, putting an end to the "chain of injustice" (Brandt) by declaring that the FRG had no territorial claims. This was a courageous decision because it admitted that the traditional German homelands such as East Prussia and Silesia were permanently lost (90, 465). "Escape from reality creates dangerous illusions" (29, 113), and Brandt was ready to say farewell to them. Normalization of relations with Poland could not proceed, however, without an act of atonement for the Nazi crimes committed in Warsaw and Auschwitz. On behalf of Germany, Brandt knelt down before the Warsaw Ghetto Memorial in 1970 in an attempt to rebuild a bridge with the nations upon which Germany had inflicted so much suffering.

The Treaties of Moscow and Warsaw smoothed the way for the subsequent Four Power agreement on Berlin in 1971 and the *Grundlagenvertrag* (Basic Treaty) with the GDR in 1972. Negotiations on Berlin had begun primarily at American initiative in 1969. They were urgently needed since the GDR repeatedly levied tolls on traffic, required passports and visas of West Germans and West Berliners in transit through the German Democratic Republic, and restricted travel by West German government officials to and from Berlin.

Following Brandt's first meeting with Premier Stoph in Erfurt, East Germany, quadripartite talks on Berlin produced a contractual agreement which confirmed its Four Power status as well as "the ties between the Western Sectors of Berlin and the Federal Republic of Germany"—a bone of contention for a long time (Part II of the Berlin Agreement; 37, 195). Final authority for unimpeded transit traffic was returned from the GDR to the USSR; residents of West Berlin were allowed to visit East Germany. As a result of these guarantees, Berlin was unlikely to become the catalyst for an international crisis in the future (206, 126), but this compromise was only possible at a steep price: West Berlin would not be "a constituent part of the Federal Republic of Germany and not . . . be governed by it."(37, 195)

As a result, the communist idea of Berlin as "an independent political unit" had to be given up. Now West Berliners obtain passports from the Berlin Senate on behalf of the three Western city commandants. The FRG represents West Berlin internationally. But the city is not legally a *Bundesland,* even though it is administered as such. In West Berlin an exceptional case has become the rule: "it is half a city, at the same time an incomplete *Bundesland,* fully integrated into the social, economic, and legal system of the Federal Republic which, however, is not allowed to govern it; an area under military occupation 36 years after the war ended" (D. Schwarzkopf, *Die Zeit,* June 26, 1981; *42,* chapter 12). Berlin belongs to the Common Market and participates in West German government agencies and bodies, but it lacks full voting rights. Plenary meetings of the Federal Parliament are not permitted in the city, neither is conscription for the army. It is a complicated legal, political, and geographical situation, made permanent by the 1971 agreement. While East Berlin men under 65 and women under 60 cannot enter the West except for major family affairs (births, deaths, weddings), the Wall is not as impermeable for West Germans and West Berliners. Commercial traffic flows back and forth between West and East Berlin. Partial telephone links have been reestablished between the two halves of the city.

The Berlin Agreement was one of the pillars on which the ratification of the Moscow and Warsaw accords and the subsequent treaties with the GDR, Czechoslovakia, Hungary, and Bulgaria rested. A milestone in Chancellor Brandt's quest for a comprehensive, negotiated settlement of outstanding issues was his first personal encounter with Stoph in Erfurt and Kassel in 1970. Their exchange of views formed the groundwork for the Treaty on the Basis of Relations Between the Two Germanys (1972)—countries which for two decades did not even recognize each other's existence. Article 6 of the treaty reads: "They shall each respect the other's independence and autonomy in its internal and external affairs." This stipulation does not involve diplomatic recognition of the GDR by Bonn, because the GDR is not considered a foreign country according to the West German Basic Law. Accordingly, only missions, not embassies were exchanged. Brandt used the formula of "two states within the German nation" to get the treaty ratified. Additional negotiations achieved a transit and traffic agreement, facilitating travel across the border and the settlement of family problems. Even younger East Germans are now allowed to travel to the West on urgent family business. Nine additional road and rail crossing points have been opened.

All these accomplishments were of such a sweeping nature that Brandt was awarded the Nobel Peace Prize in 1971 while negotiations were still going on. But reactions at home and abroad to his *Ostpolitik* were mixed. An American study alleged that the early phase of West German detente initiatives fostered the political "spring" in Prague and the subsequent Soviet-East German invasion of 1968 (*30,* 215). Although Kosygin and Brezhnev were interested in relaxation of tensions, Soviet hardliners distrusted détente as a device to tempt East European satellites away from Moscow. The U.S. on the other hand encouraged *Ostpolitik* at first as a parallel move in a joint diplomatic offensive.

Things were different in the two Germanys. Having gained neither political recognition by the FRG nor sovereignty over the access routes to West Berlin, Walter Ulbricht proclaimed a policy of further *Abgrenzung* (separation) from the West, a GDR counterthrust to neutralize the friendly overtures of the FRG and the United States. Ulbricht put up more resistance to détente than the Soviets expected, and this contributed to his fall in 1971. The new Erich Honecker government still had to be coaxed by Moscow to accept the Basic Treaty.

Major trouble greeted Brandt upon his return from Moscow to Bonn. The CDU attempted to torpedo his initiatives on the grounds that he would sell out East German territories and normalize relations with the GDR without getting anything in return. It challenged the GDR treaty as unconstitutional because it would perpetuate the division of Germany. The Federal Court in Karlsruhe, however, ruled that the treaty was compatible with the *Grundgesetz* which considered the GDR part of Germany similar to a *Land*. Franz Josef Strauss of the CSU advocated the rejection of the Moscow and Warsaw treaties, but the opposition abstained in the final vote. With 248 votes for, 238 abstentions, and 10 no votes, the treaties passed in 1972, but Parliament was dissolved for lack of a majority. In the ensuing election, Brandt, running on the issue of *Ostpolitik,* regained a majority for the next term of the federal assembly. But he was forced to resign only eighteen months later because East Germany, ironically enough, after all these efforts, had planted a spy among his personal aides (the Guillaume Affair, 1974).

The impact of *Ostpolitik* was far-reaching and continues to affect the political, economic, and social life of central Europe. Along with the recognition that postwar de facto borders were inviolable, the obligation to use peaceful means to settle outstanding issues was established by the treaties. The FRG normalized its relations with the GDR and eased family transit as well as East bloc restrictions on the emigration of its ethnic Germans. About 200,000 of them were allowed to leave Eastern Europe by the late 1970s, and about 50,000 East Germans joined their families in the West (*115,* 168). In addition, West Berlin ceased to be a useful instrument for blackmail. In turn the GDR by virtue of its grudging cooperation finally won international diplomatic recognition as a state. The Basic Treaty between the two states of Germany became the precondition for their membership in the United Nations.

For Germans of sober judgment, these negotiated successes were manifold and tangible, even if their main effect was to destroy illusions that distorted the political climate between the European nations in the East and West. CDU diehards had voted against *Ostpolitik* and even against the FRG's entry into the United Nations because of their deeply entrenched reunification dogma.

The Soviets, and perhaps Brandt himself, were somewhat disappointed. Both parties had expected more to come out of *Ostpolitik* than some legal documents. Above all, everyone had hoped for broader contacts of all kinds in an atmosphere of trust. But this was not the case. The mills of state bureaucracy in the USSR dealing with ethnic Germans turned slowly, and the GDR deliberately misinterpreted the Quadripartite Agreement on Berlin and stonewalled any further erosion of its separation policy.

In actuality, "normalization" has turned into a mixed blessing, if not occasionally into an embarrassment. It translates into new individual freedoms for GDR citizens to tune into TV-West, for their youth to wear long hair and jeans, and to dance to rock and disco music. On the other hand, those privy to state secrets (members of the SED and *Betriebskampfgruppen*, worker's militia) are not allowed to maintain contacts with the West, and even factory workers are not supposed to be visited by West German relatives. Crossing the intra-German border is easy for West Germans. The long lines and traffic checks have largely disappeared, but in return the FRG must prosecute the organized refugee trade, because use of Berlin transit for escape is an abuse of the Basic Treaty. Noncommercial efforts to help East Germans escape are not subject to prosecution; West Germany is also permitted to buy the freedom of 1,200 political prisoners each year. On the other hand, GDR spies, agents, and functionaries roam the FRG with surprising freedom.

The success of Brandt's *Ostpolitik* has other ramifications. It resulted in a major departure from Adenauer's policies, which during the Cold War period moved largely in tandem with the all-powerful US ally. It brought about the final phase in the political growth and development of the FRG by the official acceptance of the inviolability of East Germany's borders. Thus the FRG became an identifiable state. Accepting the inevitable amounted to the demise of the sacrosanct Hallstein Doctrine and its fixation upon the unification issue. From then on, there would exist "two States within one German nation" (Brandt). Moreover, détente signalled the return of West Germany (and the GDR, for that matter) to the world stage after a quarter century of West German's submission to the political will of the Allies. Brandt observed: "we became the advocate of our own interests vis-à-vis the governments of Eastern Europe. By doing so we strengthened our voice inside the bodies devoted to West European, Atlantic, and international cooperation. The Federal Republic became more independent—more adult, so to speak" (*30,* 168 f.).

The FRG's economic strength has been translated into political power, or—to use a fashionable term—"ecopolitics." Rousseau said, "Where there is trade, there is peace," and this axiom has emerged as a key principle in West Germany's peace policy in East and West, dependent as it is on flourishing international trade. *Ostpolitik* has been a definite stimulus to trade, particularly with the nations to the east.

In the EEC, an ironic situation developed on the heels of *Ostpolitik*. Detente lessened the desire of its member states to seek greater unity to the same extent that political and military pressure from the Soviet Union waned. But Brandt used his influence to exert pressure on the EEC to develop beyond the original Six to the European Nine by including Britain, Denmark, and Ireland in 1973; he believed that only in this way could the Community assert its place beside the superpowers. Britain's entry into the EEC in 1973, the year of Brezhnev's visit to Bonn, proved that the chancellor had not neglected the Western basis for his *Ostpolitik*. One of the final steps of his East policy was to restore diplomatic relations with China in 1972, which in turn led to a major West German industrial exhibit in Peking in 1975.

Equally important as its economic muscle was West Germany's political weight. In step with a steady decline of US global power and authority during the Vietnam War era, symbolized by the weakening dollar, the Federal Republic, through its *Ostpolitik,* managed to lighten its dependence on the West without loosening its ties with its allies. It gradually rose to become a full partner in a special relationship to the US that has been described as an "interdependent equivalence" (*211,* 14). This has enabled it to play a mediating role between members of the Atlantic community as well as between East and West.

Brandt was also instrumental in preparing the European Security Conference at Helsinki (1972–1975), an outgrowth of détente with its guidelines for human rights and for improving relations between East and West. Not only was German used as a lingua franca among the various representatives from 35 nations, but the US became at Germany's insistence a guarantor of the European status quo (*172,* 355).

Although the FRG had cooperated with and considerably contributed to UN agencies since 1950, its official admission to the UN in 1973 was a turning point, as was true even more so for the GDR. It was Brandt's policy of reconciliation that had made their acceptance by the UN possible. Soon afterwards, the FRG became a member of the Security Council (1977–78), and it presided over the UN General Assembly in 1980–81. It was as if the dark chapter of Nazi horrors was symbolically closed and simultaneously the division of Germany confirmed. At the same time Brandt's *Ostpolitik,* by its efforts on behalf of peaceful cooperation, brought greater international respect to West Germany than had been achieved by "those

German governments that conspicuously" sought world power for so many years (*211,* 13).

# 2. Equal Opportunities in Education

## THE OLD SYSTEM: SCHOOLS AND UNIVERSITIES

The German education system remained essentially unchanged for centuries. Almost to the present day, an education in the classical humanistic tradition has been considered superior to one in mathematics and the sciences. The same school curriculum from the Weimar period was pursued through the Hitler years into the FRG. Small wonder then that its rigid traditions came under attack in the late 1960s when its failure to resist Nazism was belatedly recognized.

The cultural experience of the Middle Ages provided the structure for the modern university, while the Reformation shaped the secondary schools. Luther's friend Philip Melanchton, as *Praeceptor Germaniae* (educator of Germany), created the German classical grammar school, the forerunner of the *Gymnasium.* This "medieval" college prep school and university was modernized by Wilhelm von Humboldt, director of Prussian culture and education from 1809 to 1815, who emphasized German studies and mathematics without neglecting the classical languages. He conceived of the *Gymnasium* as a school that offered a general education without professional training, because its main function was to prepare students for more specialized work in graduate school *(Universität).* Since Humboldt's reforms the German education system has followed the Western tradition of a tripartite division into primary, secondary, and tertiary education, with further subdivisions in secondary schools and universities based on intellectual capacity, financial needs, and parental class background.

The hierarchical educational structure, which generally did not permit students to transfer from one type of school to another, had its roots in a centuries-old, three-class system reinforced by a sliding civil-service salary scale for appointment and promotion after schooling was completed. Only the *Grund-* or *Volksschule* (elementary school) was a democratic institution, because all children, regardless of sex or social status, had to attend (grades one to four). After that, at age ten, their paths diverged when their parents and teachers chose between three possibilities for them: the *Hauptschule* (main school or secondary modern, grades five to nine, with an emphasis on technical skills and crafts, and one foreign language), the *Realschule* (intermediate school, with one additional

year of study, grades five to ten, a greater variety of foreign languages, natural sciences, and commercial and practical subjects),
and the *Gymnasium* (grades five to thirteen). The main school led
(and still leads) its graduates to blue-collar jobs after a transitional
period of attending a part-time *Berufsschule* (vocational training
school) while they complete their apprenticeship; the intermediate
*Realschule* enables graduates to enter white-collar jobs in the middle echelon of the civil service (e.g., postal or railway supervisors),
while the *Gymnasiast* with an *Abitur* (diploma) in hand may
either prepare himself for a senior position in the civil service or
opt for continued education at a university.

Admittance to the *Gymnasium* depended on a decision made at
the end of the fourth grade, regardless of the child's social background and promise of future development. At an early age then,
the pupil's entire educational, financial, and social future was determined by the appropriate authorities. Because of the hierarchical system, placement at a certain level usually meant the pupil
was "stuck" in that track.

The *Gymnasium* was, and to a large extent still is, an elitist
school out of the reach of the working class (tuition was in effect
until 1959). Before 1968 only about 7 percent of an age group
achieved the *Abitur,* in contrast to the American high school,
which is a comprehensive institution offering educational opportunities to all children regardless of class or sex. The majority of
German children either had to be content with the intermediate
maturity diploma *(mittlere Reife)* at the end of ten years or the
*Hauptschule* examination. Students who left the *Gymnasium* after
the completion of the tenth grade also received the *mittlere Reife.*

What was it like to attend a traditonal German *Gymnasium?* Pupils went to school six days a week from 8 am to 1 pm. They
studied fourteen required subjects and no electives. Failure in two
subjects or in German studies alone usually put an end to university aspirations. Pupils remained in one classroom throughout the
school day while the teachers moved from class to class. Social life
was minimal. Afternoons were reserved for two to four hours of
homework. Lunch breaks, PTA's, libraries, and lounges for socializing did not exist. But the advantages were tangible. Instead of a
school spirit, a class spirit developed over nine years; for students
who passed the last three years (*Oberstufe* or college prep), the
highest positions in the army, in government, and in teaching were
open.

Statistics reveal the elitism of this school system: In 1966 almost
66 percent of all pupils attended a *Hauptschule,* 10 percent a *Realschule,* and 15 percent a *Gymnasium;* but this does not imply that
the 25 percent in the two higher schools graduated. Only a third of
the *Realschüler* made it to the *mittlere Reife* and only a handful of

*Gymnasiasten* attained their *Abitur,* which is still all-important. To leave school without it was considered a disgrace. Transfer to a lower school resulted in loss of status as well.

The character of German universities has changed only slightly since the 1500s. Wilhelm von Humboldt reformed the institutions of higher learning after the defeat of Prussia at Jena in 1806. The reforms he introduced at the University of Berlin in 1809 imbued the Prussian universities with a new philosophy of education without transforming the traditional power structures. His changes involved three major principles:

1. *Autonomy,* that is, self-government for the university, freedom from the shackles of the state as it had freed itself from the chains of the churchmen earlier. This autonomy is symbolized by the university's privilege of awarding academic diplomas and of appointing faculty.

2. *Academic freedom* gave the professors the right to teach any courses they chose and to carry on research in any field. The German university was interested only in theoretical knowledge *(Wissenschaft),* not in practical applications. Hence, musical theory (or musicology) was taught, but teaching the playing of instruments was left to the conservatory. The university taught economics and political science, but business administration and applied economics were left to professional institutes.

For students the principle of academic freedom meant the privilege of working independently, the freedom to choose any subjects offered, and to transfer from one university to another to hear outstanding scholars in their fields of study.

3. The *authority of professors* to govern every aspect of academic life was paramount. Unlike the collegial department system in the US, the equivalent German academic unit had only one full professor *(Ordinarius)* who chaired his department like a god: he collected tuition from the students, appointed his own successors, and selected his Ph.D. candidates. He could not be dismissed nor instructed by higher authority. For generations, the standard German lecture-hall scene consisted of a snowy-haired professor reading from his latest research project, refusing to answer student questions. Seminars in which professor and students discussed the lecture material were rare. The German university of the nineteenth century was a place in which "pure" research or knowledge for its own sake was sought, discovered, and handed down. Humboldt believed in the ideal of self-development *(Bildung)* which German educators and writers of the *Goethezeit* had formulated. The university was to be an association of a small elite of professors and students dedicated to the pursuit of *Wissenschaft.* They would be financially supported by the state but otherwise remain independent of it. Such an academic community, it was thought,

would further the development of politically responsible citizens (*66,* chapter 3).

Although the German university was not concerned with the preparation of students to enter professions, the faculties of law and medicine did train lawyers and doctors. Agriculture too somehow entered the sacred precincts of pure learning. In general, the state-operated university did train upper-class students for the civil-service elite. And with the rise of the physical and biological sciences in the nineteenth century, the vocational goals of university study became increasingly emphasized.

But the pursuing of knowledge for its own sake and the emphasis of the positivistic aspects of science led to the serious consequence that ethical values and moral standards were generally relegated to the sidelines of scholarly endeavor. The application of knowledge to the problems of life and the effect of knowledge on human behavior were largely ignored in the educational system or were twisted to the support and promotion of nationalistic, reactionary goals; this facilitated the National Socialist takeover of the universities *(Gleichschaltung)* in 1933. A frequently antidemocratic, strongly patriarchal elite was easily kept in line by Nazi students and party functionaries (*42,* chapter 8). Overseen by Hitler's Ministry of Culture, professors belonged to the Nazi party. Students were not permitted to question them, nor did they question the new wave, unless they were willing to risk their jobs and lives. Max Horkheimer, a Frankfurt sociologist, called professorial lectures "secularized sermons," because they were not based on communication between professor and student, or on the practical purpose of learning and knowing.

After WWII and in spite of the upheavals that Nazi years brought, West Germany's education system remained largely unchanged. In the postwar years students and scholars alike had to concentrate on sheer survival and on the rebuilding of interrupted careers. These conditions did not favor a major overhaul of the old educational system. This was left to the second postwar generation.

## THE STUDENT REBELLION

To understand the German student rebellion of the late 1960s, it should be kept in mind that the baby boom of WWII produced serious overcrowding twenty years later in the educational systems of the western hemisphere. The reconstruction of the shattered European cities and economies brought about affluent societies in both the victorious and defeated nations, and also student populations with high aspirations for upward mobility. President Kennedy's assassination in 1963 destroyed the hopes that an entire generation in the United States and abroad had placed in this young leader with his zest for the future.

"The great catalyst of the new mood has of course been the civil-rights campaign. It gave the campus generation the cause it had been waiting for: a cause of conscience" (*Harper's Magazine*, May 1968, p. 15). "Conscience" and "sincerity" were the catchwords of the student riots at Berkeley in 1964 which protested social injustices and the insensitivity of large bureaucratic institutions. Inept university management and lack of communication fueled the students' anger. Freedom of speech and assembly denied them by the impersonal university machine were the pressing issues. Hard-hitting political speeches exposed the society's sexual hypocrisy. Eventually the emphasis shifted from an attack on the institutions to the hated Vietnam War, especially after 1967, when Congress subjected college-age men to the draft.

The situation for German students was similar in some ways. Baby boomers raised during the economic miracle saw no place for humanistic values in a materialistic society. When the CDU and SPD formed the Grand Coalition in 1966, Rudi Dutschke, leader of the radical SDS (Socialist German Student Organization, founded in 1960), appealed for "extraparliamentary opposition" (APO) to the existing political party structure. Anti-Vietnam demonstrations took place in Berlin, followed by protests against Chancellor Kiesinger, an ex-Nazi and by demonstrations against the visiting Shah of Iran. One of the demonstrators, the student Benno Ohnesorg, was shot by police on June 2, 1967, an event that radicalized (*146*, 117) young people and persuaded them to fight the "system," that is, the social institutions and the educational structure, which directly effected them. In contrast to the US Civil Rights Movement and the Berkeley Free Speech and Sexual Freedom Movements, the German student rebellion focused its attention on the educational system and the press, both of which were still believed to be permeated by Nazis.

The causes for unrest and rebellion lay deeper than any single political event. International in scope, there was general disillusionment in Berkeley, Berlin, Tokyo, Paris, and London. Students were dissatisfied with the prevailing materialism, with authoritarian structures, and with a bureaucratized and institutionalized world that did not foster individual growth. In addition, affluence stimulated utopian thinking. Especially in Germany, students often reacted with great fervor and chiliastic expectations to an institutional world they were now setting out to transform radically (*42*, 210).

The various phases of the German student movement reflect this mixture of diffuse romantic longings and social realism. "In its anti-authoritarian stage, the rebellion had much more the character

of an existentialist revolt in Sartre's or Camus' sense than the hallmark of a political revolution" (*146,* 128). At the same time, it also
had roots in Expressionism (after 1910), an idealistic movement
that promoted democracy and equated personal change with social progress. This first phase lasted no more than one year
(1966–1967) and was directly chiefly against the educational establishment, personified by autocratic professors. A militant Marxist period followed (1967–1969), during which shots fired at
Dutschke (on Easter in 1968) led to a consolidation of all APO
groups. In May 1968, student demonstrations took place in a number of university towns. In Berlin, Frankfurt, and Munich, youth
rebelled against the ratification of the Emergency Laws of 1968,
while in Paris a general strike by students and workers toppled de
Gaulle. Student unrest spread to Italy and Spain and contributed to
the "Prague Spring."

Contrary to the expectations of Marxist students, German workers did not generally go along with their demands as they had different social backgrounds and also different aspirations. Their
ways of speaking and acting resembled more closely the middle
class than the antiauthoritarian students, who felt called upon to
represent the workers' interests. In Berlin trade unions demonstrated against the students. Despite some degree of collaboration
between the two groups in cities such as Hannover, the students'
dogmatism, which the workers rejected, and ideology contributed
to the dissolution of the SDS in 1970. A third phase, sometimes la-
belled the "New Subjectivity," followed, during which weary and
disillusioned students distanced themselves from Marxist collectiv-
ist views and returned to the individualistic beginnings of 1966. A
few years later, serious unrest erupted once more at many universities when the restrictive University Outline Law was adopted in
1976. More disturbances followed when the Baader-Meinhof gang
was brought to trial in 1977 and when President Reagan visited
Berlin in 1982.

As the antiauthoritarian movement unfolded, two main concerns seemed to reflect the divergent aspirations and methods of
the students: "One . . . operated chiefly in the field of university
policy . . . the other . . . of the 'anarchists,' was ready to oppose
every norm and requirement of social and university insitutions"
(*183,* 77). In 1969 the united Student Left split into three factions:
the first was a hippie-type movement inspired by the American
counterculture which concentrated on romantic ideas of individual freedom. A second group worked for change "within the system" (i.e., Social Liberals or Christian Democrats), and a third
consisted of communist radicals organized in *Spartakus,* a Marxist
group, and in Red Cells. Within the SPD the *Jusos* (Young Social
Democrats) were poised to return the party to its Marxist origins,

which the SPD had rejected at the Bad Godesberg convention in 1959. They opposed the SPD leadership and demanded an end to the consumer-based economy in favor of a centrally planned system of "democratic socialism." The *Jusos* enjoyed a large following, particularly in universities, but they presented anticapitalist resolutions, many of which turned out to be utopian. The Red Cells' activities ranged from pamphleteering to physical violence. Inspired variously by Soviet ideology and Third World leaders such as Che Guevara and Mao Tse-tung, their small but militant cadres used direct action to confront the authorities, particularly in the Free University of Berlin (FU) and in Munich. They organized strikes, disrupted lectures, and destroyed property and careers, alienating professors and administrators alike. As the majority of the students did not participate in student parliament (ASTA) elections, these militant minorities exerted an influence far beyond their numbers. Their tactics of disruption spilled over into municipal council meetings (Hamburg), court trials (Hamburg, Berlin, 1968), and confrontations with police.

Even the Frankfurt sociologist Theodor Adorno, assumed by many to be the mentor of the APO, was embarrassed by radical, antibourgeois students and critical of their activism. A split between theory and practice plagued the German student movement more than its US counterpart. During the heyday of the student revolution, numerous radical splinter groups were organized, ranging from the Social Democratic Left and unorthodox dogmatic groups all the way to so-called *Chaoten* ("chaoses"), anarchistic groups such as the Red Dawn and Red Flag, which specialized in destroying German institutions. *Time Magazine* of May 14, 1973 reported the existence of 390 assorted communist groups in West Germany.

Why was Marxism suddenly so popular among West Germany's youth in the face of the dismal human-rights record in Eastern Europe? Intellectually, Marxism had never been totally discredited in Germany since leftist intellectuals had opposed nationalism in the Second and Third Reichs (for example, Wilhelm Liebknecht and Rosa Luxemburg), and the protest movement of the 1960s saw in Marxism a tradition of idealism to oppose the deepening US involvement in Vietnam, which was interpreted as imperialist, capitalist, and quasi-fascist. The Shah's visit to the FRG in 1968 and the resultant death of Benno Ohnesorg in Berlin also crystallized the student's feeling of alienation toward the West German government. Under the Marxist banner the young generation turned against the establishment to vent its frustration with a rigid industrialized capitalist society. They were joined by leftist professors, journalists, union and church leaders, who demanded the ouster of US forces, a reduction in the defense budget, German reunification under a socialist regime and finally, a restructuring of the educational system. By marching through the institutions, they tried to wrest physical control from the authorities. Some universities and streets looked like battle zones while many groups and subgroups struggled with each other more fiercely than with their alleged oppressors. East Germany and Moscow backed some Marxist cadres financially.

As Friedrich Heer states (*102,* 218), youth movements believe in a "great act of creative destruction [of] all living idols and institutions," but in the end are crushed by the forces in power. From the ashes, however, a more humane society may arise. The results of the German student rebellion of the 1960s and early 1970s are debatable. The rebellious students succeeded in destroying a few taboos and brought about an education reform that was long overdue; the movement as a "literary-cultural revolution" (*146,* 129) has survived. Many rebel leaders ended up as members of the establishment in universities, government, and business, or they disappeared in the alternative "counterculture." According to Paul M. Lützeler,

> . . . the student movement neither reached the goals of its antiauthoritarian phase nor that of its Marxist dogmatic period. The authorities in state and society have hardly been changed. . . . Social structures, property conditions, and government bodies have withstood the violent attacks of those exciting years unchanged.

> (*146,* 128)

The rebels' numbers were too small, their objectives too vague, their ideological differences too large: *"Geschlagen ziehen wir nach Haus"* ("defeated we go home").

After their defeat, the conservative reaction to the period of unrest was swift in coming. The establishment dealt with political dissidents by outlawing extremist organizations (e.g., the SDS at Heidelberg University in 1970) and by preventing radicals from obtaining civil-service jobs. Rebel leaders had attacked these positions in earlier days, but many of them, now weary, desired to secure the same jobs for themselves. However, as the political pendulum slowly moved from Left to Right, the *Radikalenerlaß* ("Extremists' Decree") of 1972 was passed which decreed that right-or leftwing extremists hostile to the democratic order would be excluded from civil-service jobs. Opponents at home and abroad interpreted this directive as a revival of the Nazi *Berufsverbot* (professional or career ban). And in fact, a McCarthy-like witchhunt got under way which discriminated not only against radicals, but progressives as well, especially prospective teachers, but also mailmen, railroad engineers, lawyers, doctors, police, soldiers, and ministerial bureaucrats. For example,

Teacher X lost her chance at a school job when she failed a cross-examination that ran like this:

Q. Is your apartment a commune?
A. I sublease my place from. . . .
Q. Do you have contact with the other subleasees?
A. I know the other subleasees. . . .
Q. Do you have political conversations with these people?
A. No. I'm hardly ever at home. . . .
Q. Are you familiar with the group of International Marxists?
A. Yes, I once read their flyers. Otherwise, I don't know anything about this group.
Q. Do you know a prominent member of this group?
A. Yes, Ernest Mandel.
Q. How do you know him?
A. From TV.
Q. So you saw this broadcast, did you?
A. Yes, part of it.
Q. Where, in your apartment?
A. No, at the home of a colleague from my school. . . .
Q. Did the people in your apartment also see this broadcast?
A. I don't know . . .

(Elizabeth Pond, *The Christian Science Monitor,*
December 7, 1978, p. B11)

Although long-standing German civil-service laws have traditionally required loyalty oaths from career civil servants, the widespread practices of hearings and cross-examinations, sometimes based on denunciations by fantasizing school children reminiscent of medieval witch trials, violated the civil rights of the applicants by putting the "unlimited burden of proof of comprehensive innocence" (ibid., B 12) on them. They generated a climate of suspicion and eroded the country's constitutional guarantee of freedom of thought. It was not surprising then that this decree was viewed with suspicion in neighboring countries such as France, where in 1975 François Mitterand set up a committee for the defense of civil and career rights in the FRG. The German Left reacted with paranoia, exploiting the issue for its political gains. But blame for its unfortunate results must rest with the commando-like wording of the decree itself and with its vigorous application by the states.

Since 1972 the *Verfassungsschutz* (Office for the Protection of the Constitution) was inundated with inquiries requesting political information on applicants for civil-service appointments. CDU/CSU-ruled states screened these applicants more stringently than states governed by the SPD/FDP. "Between April 1973 and December 1980 Bavarian authorities submitted 186,111 inquiries. In 1,250 cases there was a file on applicants; 1,189 were leftwingers, in 114 cases applicants were rejected" (*Nürnberger Nachrichten,* January 26, 1982). All in all, out of a million applicants, between 2,000 and 4,000, mostly teachers, were rejected between 1972 and 1978. In spite of the relatively small numbers affected, an atmosphere of uncertainty and fear pervaded the political climate of West Germany. In 1979 the controversial Extremists' Decree was rescinded on the federal level although security-checks are still practiced on a case-by-case basis, particularly in CDU/CSU run states.

A fundamental question remains: how tolerant can West German democracy, built on the experiences of political chaos and of Nazi extremism, be toward its dissenters and still survive in a climate of political polarization between the SPD and the CDU, and between East and West? A further question was raised by Heinrich Böll in an essay entitled "Radicality and Hope":

> What would have become of the Federal Republic if there had been no radicals and extremists intent not on their personal enrichment but upon changing existing relationships? Let us think the student movement did not occur in our history and imagine it never took place—how crippled would our educational system be today?

*(42, 223)*

## Reorganizing the Educational System

It was natural for German students to march against those institutions that denied access and equal opportunity to many. With the number of school children on the rise, the conventional elitist school system was bursting at the seams. It needed to be replaced by a more flexible and democratic system. Three steps were taken to achieve this aim: first, school fees were abolished in 1959, textbooks became free in 1966 (in 1982, however, parents were asked to defray part of the state's costs), scholarships were made available for the needy, and school libraries were instituted. These financial changes increased educational opportunities for working-class children. Secondly, the former hierarchical system, which discouraged transfers from one type of school to another, was recast into a horizontal one with more crossover opportunities to further individual talents. This greater flexibility has been achieved by several measures:

a. The elimination of the early (fourth-grade) decision on pupils' educational fate, which frequently involved erroneous and discriminatory judgments which generally could never be corrected once pupils were fixed in a certain type of school. Instead, an *Orientierungsstufe* (orientation stage) was introduced for the fifth and sixth graders in *Hauptschulen, Realschulen,* and *Gymnasien,* which postpones by two years the age when final tracking is decided upon.

b. *Gesamtschulen* (comprehensive schools), somewhat akin to the integrated American high school, were introduced.

c. A *zweiter Bildungsweg* (second educational route) provides "late bloomers" or socially disadvantaged youths a chance to qualify for university admission through evening and correspondence courses after completing a vocational training school.

Thirdly, the traditional curriculum at the upper level of the *Gymnasium* has been replaced by subjects chosen by the pupil according to his abilities and interests. In contrast to the eleven or thirteen subjects pupils had to prepare for the *Abitur* before 1976, they are now permitted to elect written examinations in three courses (two major subjects and one elective), and one elective for oral examination. Consequently, the former division of the *Gymnasium* into two branches, one emphasizing classical and modern languages and the other, mathematics and science, no longer exists.

Other steps have made *Gymnasium* life easier for the pupil: a customary six-day week is slowly giving way to five days with no homework over the weekend. Teenagers eighteen years and older in grades twelve and thirteen excuse their own absences. Instruction is coeducational, it permits a measure of self-government, and it puts less stress on authority than in the past.

These reforms have reduced elitism and made the educational system more egalitarian and flexible. Consequently, the number of *Gymnasium* graduates has risen dramatically—from 27,000 in 1952 to 204,000 in 1978—an increase of from 7 percent of an age group to about 35 percent. This means that the *Gymnasium* "is no longer a class school, even though the number of working-class children is still comparatively small" (*17*, 92f.). Only about 16 percent of university students came from working class homes in 1982.

Despite much progress, many problems remain unsolved. Controversies have arisen among parents and politicians as to the significance and the desirability of certain reforms. The curriculum of the comprehensives and the upper-level *Gymnasium* have been influenced in some respects by the American high school, leading sometimes to a decline in the quality of education. Grades have been replaced by a computerized credit-point system, and students' attitudes, and behavior have become more relaxed.

The *Oberstufe,* which formerly provided a general humanistic education, has now become a training track for admittance to the university; this has narrowed the general education of the matriculating students. For some time they were even allowed to pass the *Abitur* without examination in German, mathematics, natural science or foreign languages. They may possess excellent competence in their favorite subjects, but they are often deficient in basic educational disciplines, so that German universities have been forced to institute courses in elementary core subjects. The loss in quality seems to be the inevitable result of opening the rigid system to the masses of baby-boom adolescents who demanded equal educational opportunities. Masses of students flooding the universities endanger their newly won right to study because they force the universities to restrict admittance to the regular courses, several popular fields, such as dentistry, pharmacy, and medicine, have introduced strict enrollment limits *(numerus clausus)*. Generous government grants free many students from the need to enter the job market, thus adding to the general enrollment pressure.

In spite of the many difficulties, a second educational overhaul would be as difficult as the first attempt was, since the federal educational system, which places the responsibility for school matters on the eleven state governments, operates in a very cumbersome manner through a joint federal-state Commission on Educational Planning, established in 1973. Moreover, these *Länder* are ideologically polarized according to the party that happens to be in power. The states governed by conservative Christian parties (i.e., Schleswig-Holstein, Bavaria, Baden-Württemberg) returned to compulsory core subjects (German, mathematics, science, languages, history), which every *Gymnasium* graduate must pass. In this context, the arguments for or against the controversial *Gesamtschule* derive from the political views of the parents and the local governments. This type of school is the very antithesis of the traditional hierarchical system in which pupils were segregated after the fourth grade into the prestigious *Gymnasium,* the intermediate *Realschule,* or the "lowly" *Hauptschule.* The *Gesamtschule,* by contrast, equalizes opportunities for children from mixed social backgrounds. But critics of this democratic approach link the decline of academic excellence with the demise of elitism.

After 1945 German universities reverted to the rigid ideals and curricula that existed before the Nazi years. At the time of the student rebellion in the 1960s, the West German university had hardly changed in its authoritarian curriculum, professorial privileges, and elitist norms. "The challenge of adapting the Federal Republic to mass higher education was a source of difficulty for the German university" (66,, 68). The students now demanded far-reaching curricular reforms, the most central of which was a restructuring of the educational content to include social issues not only as they affected West Germany but also Europe and the Third World (e.g., racism and imperalism in Vietnam, Greece, Iran, and Latin America).

The obstacles to university reform were formidable. For one thing, each state had its own universities, which in turn had their own statutes, structures, and policies. Ideological polarization between SPD and CDU-ruled state governments made it even more difficult to achieve generally acceptable university laws. Even where the states were ready for reforms, the governing bodies of the "professorial universities" *(Professorenuniversitäten),* deeply entrenched as autonomous entities since Humboldt's time, did not always go along with them—for example, in the conservative universities of Bonn, Cologne, and Aachen.

As it turned out, the German university was restructured, more often than not against the will of its own faculty and administration by reform-oriented *Länder* laws. To coordinate structural reforms, first the constitution was amended in 1969 so that federal authorities were accorded responsibility for the regulation of the entire university system. Then a permanent commission consisting of states and university representatives (professors and students) was established—the Joint Commission on Educational Planning). After six years of difficult negotitions, Parliament ratified the *Hochschulrahmengesetz* (Comprehensive University Law) in 1976, which laid down general guidelines for a reform which had to be implemented by the states by 1979. This law deals with university functions, organization and administration, admissions, curricula, order, and student time spent there *(Regelstudienzeit).*

To what degree the University Outline has actually changed the "professorial university" is debatable (*66,* 90–96). For one thing, the professorial hierarchy which had invested all power in one chairholder has been replaced by a departmental structure or *"Gruppenuniversität."* Parallel chairs have been introduced (since the early 1960s) to replace the *Ordinarius,* who until the reform was the only full professor in each discipline; also all university employees (professors, assistants, staff) and students are involved in the decisions concerning the curriculum, the direction of seminars, appointment of professors, and the like. Such codetermination made it possible to solve conflicts, at least theoretically, on the basis of democratic procedures built into the *Gruppenuniversität.*

Unlike the "departmental university," restricted in the range of disciplines taught, the "comprehensive university" *(Gesamthochschule),* brought about by the Comprehensive University Law, unites the curricula of various universities, technical institutions (TH, TU = TI), art colleges and teacher-training colleges (PH, PA).

Ten West German comprehensive universities now enable students to transfer among different institutions across *Länder* lines.

A more open exchange of opinions in seminars put an end to the idolization of professors and has further democratized the German university. Registration and tuition fees were discontinued in 1970, and up to 60 percent of graduate students received government subsidies of up to DM 750 per month (in 1982) for three to four years of study. Transforming these grants into repayable government loans took place in 1982.

Various measures have been implemented to cope with the mass influx of students into higher education:

1. The number of traditional universities (seventeen in 1966) has been increased significantly by the expansion of technical universities (seven), the establishment of new universities (nineteen), comprehensive institutions (ten), and the upgrading of Polytechnics (ninety-seven) to the rank of universities. Now the FRG has about 260 institutions of higher learning, of which 102 are full universities.

2. An attempt was made by the Comprehensive University Law to introduce *Regelstudienzeit,* that is, to limit study time to three or four years, but this effort had to be abandoned for legal reasons. In practice, presently "more than 28 percent of students are older than 25. Each spends an average of eleven semesters, that is, five years, at university, which is decidedly too long" (*65, 348*). Prior to the reforms, study time used to be even longer when virtually no tests or exams were given until graduation.

3. Admission used to be the legal privilege of any *Abiturient* (student with a *Gymnasium* diploma), and while this still may be true in principle, in practice overpopulation necessitated limiting admissions to certain disciplines. Consequently, a large number of *Abitur* holders may enroll, but not always at the university of their first choice or in their desired discipline, especially if it happens to be medicine, pharmacology, psychology, biology, or architecture.

Understandably, restriction of enrollment has been an explosive issue. Out of 200,000 applications for the summer semester of 1976, Dortmund's ZVS (a student placement agency) rejected 70,000 (*Die Zeit,* October 8, 1976). As a result, since then the Permanent Conference of the State Ministers of Education eased restrictions somewhat.

Despite difficulties and controversies surrounding university reforms, the number of students in higher education has increased fivefold, from around 290,000 in 1960 to more than a million in 1980, and 1.3 million are expected by 1985. During the same time span, the number of university teachers has increased sixfold. Whereas only about seven percent of an age group obtained the *Abitur* and between one and 2 percent completed university studies before 1960, in 1980 23 percent attained the *Abitur,* and approximately 12 percent completed an academic degree. 36 percent were female students as compared to 20 percent in 1955.

The result of this rapid expansion is that the German university has become relatively more egalitarian and accessible to all social classes. As in the case of the *Gymnasium* reform, a considerable degree of "Americanization" has taken place on the university level, not only in structural terms, but also in a levelling downward of standards along with an emphasis on a more secondary school-like nature of studies. German higher education now resembles its American counterpart more closely, in both its strengths and weaknesses.

The educational reforms were originally designed to provide all strata of the population with equal access to universities. In 1952–53 4 percent of the freshmen came from working-class parents, by 1982 the figure had increased to 16 percent (*67, 84*). Thus, expansion of university access has been limited largely to the middle class. But with unemployment and overtraining, fewer students continued on to the university in the early 1980s: 90 percent of *Abiturienten* entered the university ten years ago, in 1981 only 70 percent did so, according to the Federal Statistics Bureau. Nevertheless, an academically trained proletariat is beginning to appear. 20 percent of university graduates were unemployed in 1980, including one third of trained teachers. Only one third of all graduates found positions commensurate with their qualifications—45,000 out of 120,000 graduates. In other words, a university diploma does not guarantee upward mobility as it did in the past. Thus, lack of motivation among students is not really surprising. Many take part-time jobs while they study, and after exams often earn their livelihoods driving taxis (there are about 400 such taxi drivers in West Berlin alone, 1981). Due to the general economic down-turn and a relaxing of standards in the universities, the enthusiasm of the early 1970s has turned into resignation among professors and students alike. Both groups are disaffected, the first resenting teaching the frequently unmotivated, the second feeling like factory workers without a future (see *"Angepaßt, betrogen, verzagt,"* i.e., "adapted, deceived, discouraged," *Die Zeit,* March 30, 1979; also see *Der Spiegel,* May 13, 1985 and *Newsweek,* April 22, 1985).

Many believe the current situation justifies "reforming" or dismantling the reforms altogether. The political pendulum seems to have swung back to the right, and some speak of a "big roll-back." Symptomatic of this change in the temper of university life is the fact that caps and colors are worn once again in public by fraternity members, and that medieval gowns, so despised by the radical Left in the 1960s, are donned again at commencement exercises. The

Marxist Left sees a backlash in the Comprehensive University Law
that revoked the right of student rebels, who interfere with professorial or administrative duties through use of or call to violence, to
study at a university (*77*, 84f.). State governments have either dissolved student governments or tightened their purse strings to prevent politically motivated unrest. Even at the highly "progressive"
University of Bremen, responsibility for deciding academic issues
has been returned to the professorial body in order to prevent
"Marburgization" (Marburg University was controlled by Marxists;
*Der Spiegel,* 29 March 1982).

Despite the reforms and counterreforms, West German "academic freedom" is still preferable to higher education in the GDR
where a commission of political functionaries decides on admissions. Workers' children who have been indoctrinated in
Marxist-Leninism from early on—in the Young Pioneers at age six,
and the Free German Youth (FDJ) at age fourteen—have an easy
time gaining admission to the university. They need only a pro
forma affidavit which attests to their political trustworthiness. 80
percent of the student population stems from the FDJ. Children
from the former middle class and the academic intelligentsia have a
harder time entering the university unless their fathers are party
members.

Strict party discipline determines university life in the GDR;
there is political indoctrination, and work and study periods are
synchronized; reading matter is controlled (e.g., students need the
dean's permission to read Plato and Albert Camus). If a student has
three or more unexcused absences from a seminar or dares to
voice political dissent, he or she is expelled. As a rule, vacations are
planned by the state, and jobs are given only after completion of
examinations. Despite restrictions of individual freedom in the
"worker and farmer" universities, considerably more progress has
been made in the GDR than in the FRG in integrating socially disadvantaged groups. 45 percent of women study in the GDR as opposed to 36 percent in West Germany (in 1981), 45 percent of
workers' children versus 13 percent of middle- and upper-class students (in 1977), and more grants are available in the GDR (for 90
percent of students) as against 60 percent in the FRG.

## The Problem of Violence

Doubts, frustration, and anger at the slow pace and failures of
the university reforms to bring about political changes were at the
root of some students' decisions to resort to violence (*108*, 109f.)
in the 1970s. While most resignedly returned to the lecture halls,
some of them dropped out of sight and went underground. In
1970 the infamous Baader-Meinhof terrorist gang received guerrilla

training from Palestinian radicals, preparing the way for terrorist acts against the West German establishment, which they saw as rigid and repressive. German terrorism remained an important issue in the FRG until 1977. In that year the Baader-Meinhof trial evoked a new wave of student unrest and rebellion before it finally subsided. Although small in number—209 were convicted between 1971 and 1980—the terrorists galvanized the Republic for almost a decade; they had a major impact on the political climate and invited legal countermeasures which jeopardized the rule of law.

Who were these terrorists, where did they come from, what were their aims and ideology, and who sympathized with them? Three groups were active in the underground: The Baader-Meinhof gang, later renamed the Red Army Faction (RAF); the Second of June Movement was named after the date on which student Benno Ohnesorg died in Berlin in 1967 (after 1977 it united with the RAF). Thirdly, the Revolutionary Cells, active since 1973 and modelled on the theories of urban guerrilla leaders such as "Carlos."

The first terrorist generation consisted largely of academically trained students in their early twenties (Andreas Baader, Ulrike Meinhof, Gudrun Ensslin and Horst Mahler) who hoped violence would effect the structural changes which peaceful means through the APO and SDS had failed to achieve. Jillian Becker named this first cell "Hitler's Children" because their fathers had either fallen in WWII or they had forfeited their legitimacy as parental models because of Nazi crimes *(11)*. They wanted to compensate with violence for their parents' failure to resist fascism. They drew parallels between the war in Vietnam and Hitler's empire, and justified their own violent methods with the ethical premise that capitalistic societies were on the verge of reverting to imperialism. Through the use of violence the Baader-Meinhof organization aimed at the overthrow of a "fascist" system by provoking the state to blatant repressive measures, which would reveal its sinister character to the population.

After the capture and suicide of the ringleaders (except Mahler) in the Stuttgart-Stammheim prison in 1977, a second generation reorganized the RAF. Its members apparently did not continue their armed struggle out of political conviction; they did so rather because they could not extricate themselves from the web of terrorist activities; they merely concentrated on strategies designed to insure their own physical survival. Their acts of extortion and murder were meant to avenge for the "state murders' at Stammheim, although a regional parliamentary commission monitored by Amnesty International concluded that the three terrorists had in fact committed suicide in prison.

The RAF's unfocused extremism demonstrates a rapid decline

from ethically motivated political rebellion to the callous murder of innocent persons. Initially the RAF had attacked symbolic "objects" of consumerism (e.g., department store arson in Frankfurt in 1968); then it stepped up its campaign to include bank robberies and kidnappings (Albert Lorenz, of the Berlin CDU in 1975), and bombings of prisons, prosecutors' offices, and publishing houses. Finally, its violence escalated to the shooting of prison guards and police and other "symbolic figures" of West German and U.S. "imperialism." After the raid on the West German embassy in Stockholm in 1975 and the unsuccessful attempt to hijack a Lufthansa plane in Mogadishu, Somalia, violence culminated in 1977 with the murders of two prominent officials of government and industry— Federal Attorney General Siegfried Buback in Karlsruhe, and the President of the Employers' Union, Martin Schleyer.

The terrorists began with idealistic motives and utopian visions, and they ended in despair—flight, prison, or suicide. Only a few emerged from the underground to explain what had motivated them, having belatedly realized the contradictions between their struggle for working-class interests and human rights on the one hand and the actual bombing and killing of innocent workers and others (e.g., at the Springer Publishing House, Berlin 1970) on the other. Sociologists and psychologists developed profiles of wanted terrorists: they came from well-to-do families who had sent their sons and daughters to college (64 percent of 209 convincted). During the student rebellion they were disillusioned by the futility of peaceful resistance and the failure to consolidate with the workers. They withdrew into their small cells fanatacized by an ideology of a radicalizing violence. Their most profound experience was close-knit communal life and the practice of violence against a materialistic society.

Unable to identify with a state that emphasized material wealth and kept itself in power through institutional repression, which Theodor Adorno calls "structural violence," these disillusioned young people found ideological justification in some contemporary social theorists of the Frankfurt School of Thought. Herbert Marcuse analyzed the strategies of the capitalist state (e.g., consumerism and the media), which kept its citizens from thinking critically and acting politically; he defined "emancipating tolerance" as intolerance of the Right and tolerance of the Left (*100,* 13; 257). Adorno asserted that social institutions in a capitalist society were inherently repressive and therefore "violent." Student leaders probably failed to understand all the implications of critical Frankfurt theory, which represents a humane Marxism opposed to terrorism; they later turned to revolutionary theories of Latin America (Tupamaros), Palestine (various terrorist groups), Japan (Red Army), Italy (Red Brigade), and the practice-oriented teachings on guerrilla warfare of Che Guevara and Mao Tse-Tung. Domestically, a Mc-Carthy-type reaction to the terroists led to some striking curtailments of civil liberties. The federal government demanded that a number of leftist professors take a special loyalty oath after having published what they considered a dispassionate and rational statement about the Buback murder and a Göttingen student's reaction to it.

The theoreticians among the first generation of terrorists (e.g., Ulrike Meinhof), mixed Marxist and Maoist ideas, creating an amalgam of utopian extremism that rejected the inertia of the democratic process, which is based on compromise and evolution. This is probably why they turned against Brandt's *Ostpolitik,* his SPD government (1969–1974), and also against him personally, although he had been a part of the resistance himself. For them, all his reforms amounted to stagnation at best, if not to regression. This was especially the case after 1972 when, with the approaching recession, the years of social and political experimentation were coming to an end.

Much has been made of women's participation in terrorist activities. It has been blamed on an excessive emancipation drive, on lesbianism, and on male rejection. A casual remark by a female guerilla may have contributed to this view: "What really impressed me at the time was that women were truly emancipated. There were things they were simply better at than men. We simply felt stronger" (*Rheinische Post,* 9 July 1981). Women played a major role in terrorist activities by providing not only theoreticians but also activists. Ten of the 14 most-wanted terrorists in 1980 were women, but of the 209 convicted only 26 percent were female (*108,* 119).

It is impossible to distinguish between men's and women's motivations for participation in terrorist activities. Ulrike Meinhof, Gudrun Ensslin, and other women came from largely pacifist, Protestant, upper-middle-class families. They had their *Abiturs* and had studied at the university, and they were enraged about Ohnesorg's death in 1967 and the Dutschke assassination attempt in 1968. They opposed nuclear armament and the Federal Emergency Laws of 1968, and they felt completely frustrated by their consumer society. Under their intellectual leadership, initial acts of nonviolent sabotage later escalated into violent terrorism. The second generation of women guerillas seems to have joined the underground movement not for political reasons, but either on account of personal problems or because they wanted to help others (i.e., the RAF prisoners). "Almost all young women terrorists came from the caritative milieu. . . . or they studied sociology and psychology" (*Der Spiegel,* May 11, 1981). In semilegal groups such as the "Socialist Patient-Collective" in Heidelberg or "Red Help," they experienced the police shooting one of their members. Such events radicalized their thinking and convinced them of the state's brutality and the righteousness of their own cause.

Terrorism polarized West Germans and caused strong reactions in neighboring countries, in particular in Italy and France, where the left wing viewed the FRG as a reemerging fascist police state. The screening of public-service applicants was perceived as a witch hunt against dissenting intellectuals, the suicides at Stammheim prison were believed to be murders committed by the state, and solitary confinement was presumed to constitute torture. Different standards were applied to judge West Germany with its Nazi past than to judge human-rights violations in Northern Ireland or in Central America. Some East Bloc countries, including the GDR and Yugoslavia, sympathized with West German terrorists and released those they had jailed.

The terrorists began as moralists, and West German observers dubbed their activities the "rebellion of romantics." But their extreme utopianism brought about their own demise as they tried to exempt themselves from the state's rule of law and became killers. The writer Heinrich Böll (see *The Lost Honor of Katharina Blum,* 1975, modeled on Ulrike Meinhof), the theologian Helmut Gollwitzer, and others approved of their idealism and even their criminal acts. But the state asserted itself in the manner the terrorist theoreticians had predicted (i.e., its attempts to control terrorism would reveal the fascist police nature of the state). Indeed, in coping with the "enemy within," the government took a turn to the right. It passed laws forbidding the verbal advocacy of violence in 1976. It temporarily suspended a suspect's access to his or her lawyer ("contact ban" and surveillance). Two lawyers were sentenced for smuggling weapons, and ten more charged with exploiting their legal position to promote terrorism.

"Defaming the state" and membership in or support of a criminal organization hostile to the democratic order became punishable in 1977. In addition, the right to demonstrate was restricted and imprisoned guerrillas were isolated from other prisoners. By the same token, police search powers were expanded. As the wave of terrorism receded and passions cooled in 1981, the SPD/FDP coalition repealed some of these draconian laws.

What did the student rebellion and subsequent terrorism achieve? Many West Germans realized that not everything had gone well in the young republic since the debacle of the Nazi regime. Materialistic values had been emphasized at the expense of moral values and democratic convictions. Thus, the younger generation tried to bring about changes, but by and large their attempts failed to influence the institutions and the authority of the state. One thing is certain: the student rebellion managed to bring explicit ideological arguments into the center of political life for the first time since the founding of the FRG in 1949.

# 3. Equal Opportunities at the Work Place

## The Factory Worker (Codetermination)

During the Adenauer years (1949–1963) social peace had largely been preserved by the generally good relations between labor and management and between the chancellor and the trade union leadership specifically, and also because the German worker could be mobilized to rebuild the economy. Although social legislation lagged and the progress to "social democracy" was slow, this did not hamper West Germany's economic performance. The FRG's economic power was still formidable at the end of the 1970s: "Unemployment and inflation are low, gross national product per capita is extremely high. . . . For the moment they [the West Germans] are the world's most 'successful' society, the industralized Western nation least scathed by the 1970s" (*Business Week,* March 3, 1980, p. 68).

However, not everything kept on going well. As unemployment and government debts rose, German competitiveness abroad was eroded, and the struggle for equal opportunity in the work place emerged. It has been the traditional domain of the trade-union movement, best represented by the DGB (*Deutscher Gewerkschaftsbund*), which serves as an umbrella organization for sixteen individual unions with a membership of close to eight million. When the SPD, the workers' party, gained power in 1969, the DGB could push for new legislation through the majority party— sometimes against opposition from the FDP (representing management interests) and the CDU/CSU.

The DGB stands for worker democracy within a capitalist system, including equal treatment of minorities, and also of guest workers and women. In times of recession it concentrates on the expansion of the social safety net, a shortening of the work week, extension of vacations, job security, and retraining of workers. The central feature of "industrial democracy" is codetermination at various levels: on the job through collective trade union or labor agreements (between the works council and management), in the factory through workers' councils or shop-floor codetermination, in the business through participation in the supervisory bodies, and finally, on the national "macroeconomic" level, through "concerted action" (*149,* 19).

Codetermination has been an issue since 1848 when the Frankfurt Parliament debated the creation of factory committees, but the first step toward its realization was not taken until 1905 with the Prussian Mining Law. It provided for worker committees in firms with more than 100 employees and in 1916 in plants with more than 50 workers. The Weimar Republic passed a Works Councils Law for factories with more than 20 employees in 1920. Parity codetermination came to heavy industry in 1951 and workers' participation on supervisory boards in 1952. According to this legislation, workers represent one third of the votes in firms that employ more than five people.

Under the chancellorship of Willy Brandt, the *Betriebsverfassungsgesetz* (Labor Management Act) was updated, which gives workers' councils extensive rights of codetermination on working hours, salaries, holidays, work environment, social benefits, and personnel questions. Brandt regarded the development of codetermination as one of his "main tasks" (Government Declaration, January 1973), although the Codetermination Act of 1976 did not go into effect until two years after his resignation. It applies to 500 firms with more than 2,000 employees and stipulates that its supervisory board must be equally represented by shareholders and workers. Giving "full parity" to the workers was, however, considered an infringement on the guarantee of private property, and therefore a second vote was allotted to the tie-breaking chairman of the board, thereby giving management an edge in important decisions. Althouth employers challenged codetermination, in 1979 the Constitutional Court upheld its legality, maintaining that a narrow majority was sufficient to protect owners' rights. Thus, economic democracy, which is especially important in keeping peace in times of crisis, has been preserved. Workers' representatives not only speak for the interests of the workers, but they inform themselves about the other factors that affect the economic health of the entire enterprise upon which workers depend for their livelihood. For example, the chairman of the Workers' Council is also on the firm's board of supervisors which oversees the board of management. This enables him to see what will have to be done to protect jobs and how much money is needed to modernize and to curtail pollution.

The strongest protests against the Codetermination Act of 1976 came from the German-American Chamber of Commerce which, fearing a decline in German competitiveness, anticipated a withdrawal of U.S. enterprises from the FRG. In the U.S. labor unions leave management decisions to employers and only demand their share in profits, although they do insist on humane working conditions. American labor believes there is more to be lost than gained by being on both sides of a bargaining table. Therefore, the AFL/

CIO thinks that codetermination is not transplantable to the U.S. (*The Monitor,* July 8, 1976). Yet the West German model, recognized as the most advanced in Europe, is slowly gaining attention, if not favor, in the U.S. West German workers do not have to be unionized—only every third employee is. There is no "closed shop" system in hiring and firing either. When former Chancellor Helmuth Schmidt visited Washington in 1981, some Senators discussed the feasibility of codetermination in the U.S. But so far only one labor representative has been elected to one board of supervisors—at Chrysler.

Despite conservative political resistance and difficult economic times, codetermination has helped maintain the peace on the German labor front. Until 1977 this was also the case on the national level where a system known as *konzertierte Aktion* (concerted action) brought government leaders together with key business, banking, farming, and trade-union representatives to discuss the German economy and the issue of collective bargaining. Yet the unions, keen on their independence from government interference, have come to insist on their own priorities concerning social legislation and wage inequalities.

Since the oil crisis in the second half of 1973, the FRG has been faced with mounting unemployment, a delicate problem for Germany ever since the figure of 6 million unemployed in the early 1930s was exploited by extremist parties to radicalize the country. By 1976, 5 percent or about 1.4 million workers were out of work. By 1983 about 9 percent or more than 2 million were jobless. In order to take care of these people, the social safety net had to be strengthened. Government social expenditures have risen from 18 percent of the GNP in 1960 to 25 percent in 1970 and to 32 percent in 1976, including payments to the jobless, to social-security recipients, to war victims, to mothers on welfare, to immigrants from the former East German territories, and to ethnic Germans from the Eastern bloc nations. Unemployment benefits are paid from the first day and amount to 63 percent of the person's net earnings for up to a year, or an average of 24,000 DM per year. Some people take advantage of these generous welfare provisions, as they do in the U.S., by enjoying paid leisure time (see *"Auch ohne Fleiß ein Preis,"* Die Welt, October 30, 1977). To some extent the achievement society *(Leistungsgesellschaft)* of the economic boom years has been replaced by a society of expectations (and demands—*Anspruchsgesellschaft*).

Increasingly West German labor leaders and SPD politicians talk about "humanization of work." Their goal is to make work more pleasurable, satisfying, and safe. Beside codetermination and social legislation, this entails shortening the work week and lengthening vacation periods. The steel workers' contract of 1979, which stipulated a 40-hour work week and an unprecedented six-week vacation, was trend-setting. Nowadays 73 percent of the labor force gets at least five weeks off, and everyone receives extra vacation pay. Since 1960 work-free days increased from 121 to 165 per year (by 1979) including weekends, vacation, and sick days. Compared to two or three weeks of vacation in the U.S., West Germany is, along with France and Belgium, indeed a workers' paradise where workers have merged with the middle class in material possessions, security, a share in management, and also in some corporate profits. For social and legal reasons, it is more difficult for German firms to lay off workers. A labor-court system, independent of civil law, resolves labor disputes.

At first glance, the wage situation is bright. West German wages (at 21 DM per hour) nosed ahead of U.S. wages (the equivalent of 17 DM per hour) in 1979, to rank among the top four (Institute of German Economy). A decade earlier, the United States had paid the highest wages in the industrial world (15.80 DM versus 9.42 DM in Germany, 1970). The highest West German earnings are reported in oil and energy industries, followed by automobile manufacturing and mining. Purchasing power grew by 70 percent from 1960 to 1970, thereby revolutionizing the German income pyramid: most of the lower income groups moved into the upper bracket; 52 percent earned 1,200 DM or more per month in 1970, as compared to 19 percent in 1960, according to government statistics. In 1949 it took more than four hours to earn one kilogram of butter, in 1978 only 46 minutes (*151,* 143). This comparison illustrates the increased purchasing power of the worker, who on the average earned about 3,000 DM net a month, of which a fifth went into food, and 400 DM each into transportation and rent (*Die Zeit,* April 23, 1982). Simultaneously, the number of factory workers declined from 37 to 34 percent between 1960 and 1980, that of farm hands dropped from 14 to about 5 percent, whereas white collar and service jobs constitute more than half of all job positions filled, signifying a major change in occupations compared with twenty years ago. Similar developments have taken place in the U.S. and other industrialized Western countries.

But all is not well. The chances for upward mobility are still very slim for children of unskilled workers. According to a recent university study, grave deficiencies continue to exist in the wage system. "The amount earned is still largely determined by factors that have nothing to do with work achievement—such as sex and the position at work and in society" (*Deutsche Forschungsgesellschaft,* German Research Organization, DFG, 1977). For example, gross monthly white-collar salaries amounted to 3,264 DM for men and to 2,106 DM for women in 1979 (Federal Office of Statistics), and managers with an *Abitur* or university diploma can earn up to 50,000 DM more per year than graduates of a *Hauptschule.*

## Women at Work

A German diplomat was recently quoted as saying: "The greatest problem we have is the treatment of minorities, whether dangerous minorities like terrorists, or foreign minorities like guest workers . . ." (*The Monitor,* May 23, 1979). Although women are, strictly speaking, not a minority, the diplomat's failure to mention them is telling. The problem of women's domestic and work status is a large one in German society. Of course, the emancipation of women is not a problem unique to Germany but common to the entire Western world where the Judeo-Christian tradition has placed women in the role of the inferior and weaker sex, as helpmates to men.

Religious restraints imposed on the female sex were reinforced by the rise of commercial capitalism, which relegated women to domestic work and perpetuated centuries-old patriarchal privileges. These conditions brought about a division of labor in which "the woman belongs in the home and the man in the hostile world" (*209,* 162). Traditionally, once girls finished ninth grade, they married and became housewives. Accordingly, women had played only a secondary role in German society, distinguishing themselves neither in politics nor in cultural activities. Apart from a few mystics—Hildegard von Bingen, Mechthild von Magdeburg—German history does not recognize many female writers, composers, scholars, or painters.

Upper-class women's plight was, however, not always entirely bleak as they served as patrons of the arts and had certain social functions in the medieval, renaissance, and baroque courts. Still men—fathers, husbands or male relatives—exercized legal rights over women (see e.g., the *Nibelungen* saga where Siegfried is responsible for Kriemhild's words and actions). Unfortunately, outside the court women's role in society was often limited to "the power behind the throne" or the housewife—a figure largely ignored unless as a target of ribald jest in Shrovetide plays and comedies.

Since the late medieval and early modern periods, the male view and treatment of women has been deeply ambiguous. Their image has been split into "bad" and "good" types. Those "bad" women who failed to conform to patriarchal expectations or could not be readily integrated into society were labeled witches, persecuted, and burned at the stake in genocidal fury (see Sprenger and Institoris' *Malleus Maleficarum,* 1486) by the hundreds of thousands (some estimates range into the millions; the last witch was burned in Switzerland in 1782). "Good" women, on the other hand, were idealized, aestheticized (and often de-sexualized) in poetry and song *(Minnesang* and *Marienlyrik).* Theologians, including Thomas Aquinas, went so far as to debate whether women possessed souls or whether they belonged rather to the soul-less animal kingdom. In modern times women continue to be dichotomized in the male psyche as madonnas or whores. By perpetuating this division, men have retained power and privileges for themselves and have prevented women's attainment of equality.

German women have fought a long uphill battle for their civil rights. Aside from the activities of a few well-educated and creative women (see their literary salons during the romantic period, e.g., Henriette Herz, Rahel Levin-Varnhagen, Caroline Schlegel-Schelling, Bettina von Arnim), their emancipation failed to become a political issue until the latter half of the nineteenth century *(42,* 159). Not until 1893 could girls attend the *Gymnasium,* and only from 1900 on could they enroll in universities, as compared to Oberlin College which admitted women as early as 1837. The first women's trade union was formed in 1899 and only in 1908 women were allowed to join political parties (in Switzerland, 1971). In 1918 they were enfranchised and accorded their civil rights by the Weimar Constitution. Although equal educational opportunities were made broadly available, Sigmund Freud "assigned them a culture-given role of childbearing and nurturing" *(150,* 116)—a role expanded to a duty by the Third Reich, which again relegated women to the children, kitchen, and church, or "KKK" *(Kinder, Küche, Kirche).*

The West German Basic Law of 1949 granted women equality before the law (Article 3), but discrimination continued in practice. Not until 1957 were most of the extant legal drawbacks removed by the Equality of Status Act. Up to that time the Civil Code (Article 1356) stipulated that a woman needed the approval of her husband to take a job. But if her husband felt that his income was insufficient, she had to seek employment, which however, was not to interfere with her household and family duties (Article 1360).

During the last three decades, women in East and West Germany have made great progress in emancipating themselves from their subservient roles at home, at the work place, and in society at large—despite the persistence of patriarchal dinosaurs of the type who compare women with "caviar, useless but *wunderbar"* in an advertisement of the Wiener Wald magazine *Gut speisen and reisen* (1981).

A major turning point came with the student rebellion of 1968. This movement had been strengthened by militant women for some time, until the cry for reforms in higher learning subsided and left women to stand up alone for their rights. During this period, female activists founded an Action Council for Women's Emancipation that declared war on men, called for the legalization of abortion, and demanded an end to sexism at home, on the job, and in society. The Action Council circulated slogans such as: *"Das Weib sei willig, dumm und stumm—diese Zeiten sind jetzt um"* (let women be compliant, dumb and mute—these times are over now), and *"Frauen erhebt euch, Männer ergebt euch"* (Women arise, men surrender).

What was the situation for German women around 1970? There were 32 million women as against 29 million men in the FRG; more than four million women were widows. Women held about one third of the total ten million jobs, but they received only 70 percent of men's wages (compared to 59 percent of men's wages in the US in 1980), only 6 to 7 percent filled high positions, less than 1 percent held professorial jobs. The reasons for this situation are varied: one set of explanations is cultural and psychological, brought about by centuries of prejudice and conditioning that have weakened women's self-esteem and produced in them the so-called Cinderella Complex *(53)*. Despite their greater longevity, women have been indoctrinated into believing they are the weaker sex and should play a secondary role. Other reasons have to do with economics, where discrimination in training, employment, promotion, and wages help maintain powerful patriarchal interests along with the status quo. A crucial prerequisite for major changes rests in women's own hands: "they will have to become less self-discriminating. . . . people are defeated not so much by their opponents as by themselves" *(209,* 167).

In the job market, discrimination has been considerable. Only a few professions in the past have been deemed suitable for women, among them, elementary school teacher, hairdresser, saleswoman, doctor's or dentist's assistant, pharmacist, nurse, telephone operator, accountant or bank clerk, secretary, waitress, and factory worker. Whereas boys plan careers in engineering, management, and trades, girls aspire to teaching, nursing, and sales:

> Thus in 1970 there were only 8,300 master craftswomen compared with 545,700 men, and only 46,800 woman managers compared with 359,000 male managers. . . . In 1980 11.4 percent of all federal permanent civil servants were women. But in the top positions there were only about 3.4 percent women.

> *(65,* 292)

These disproportions in vocational representation are compounded by unequal wage scales.

So far women's constitutional right to equality has not been achieved in practice. Women still form a minority in higher-paid positions, and until the late 1950s their wages were standardized by a specific scale for women at 80 percent of men's wages. This discriminatory wage scale was later replaced by a "lighter work" scale that continued to pay women less relative to men. For example, a male worker in electrotechnology, one of the prime jobs, remains ahead of his female colleagues, regardless of his performance group (I, II, III) (*225,* 46):

|                | I | II | III |
|----------------|---------|---------|---------|
| Male (hourly)  | 15.54 DM | 10.99 DM | 10.55 DM |
| Female         | 10.55 | 9.28 | 9.29 |

Men are also paid more by means of the so-called job-market bonus for night work and changing shifts. Moreover, women have been excluded from better paying jobs by laws that go back to the Nazi period; for example, they cannot become bakers because of night work, nor are they allowed to do a "man's job" on construction sites because of the *Mutterschutzgesetz* (Law for the Protection of Mothers, 1938). This explains why more than 50 percent of working women earn no more than 1,000 DM per month, as compared with only 15 percent of their male counterparts (*225,* 45). Even skilled women earn less than untrained men, taking home 1,000 DM less per month on the average than men (*Statistical Yearbook,* 1979).

The EEC-Treaty of Rome with its article 119 outlawing discrimination in industry has been invoked to bring the FRG and other countries in line with legal requirements. First came a directive in 1975 from the European Commission in Brussels requiring employers to pay men and women equally for equal work. A year later, a second directive guaranteed women the right to equitable working conditions and equal access to jobs, vocational training, and promotions. A third directive, of 1978, gave women equal social security benefits. These EEC directives became law in West Germany in 1980, establishing an "affirmative action" policy. But legislation is one matter, and reality another. In the 1980s women still get paid 25 percent less than men. They hold only 3 percent of professional jobs, 5 percent of higher government positions, and not quite 7 percent of executive jobs. In 1982 only 8.6 percent of the *Bundestag* members were women.

Sex discrimination is hard to eradicate in the face of opposition from employers, unions, the Catholic Church, and from the traditional educational and social power structures. Battles must be waged "in Parliament and on the streets, in the office and in bed" (Alice Schwarzer). Only in public-service jobs has the principle of equal pay for equal work become a reality. Outside of this safe haven, women have only been able to cope successfully with wage discrimination by taking their employers to the Federal Labor Court. Since 1982 the burden of proof in discrimination cases has rested on the employer.

During the 1970s women's attitudes toward their roles in society began to change, in particular among young intellectuals with leftist leanings. A new consciousness regarding marriage and motherhood has been engendered by a number of campaigns in support of abortion (*Nationaler Frauenkongreß*, 1971), against male violence, and against discrimination toward working women—struggles led by women's organizations and leaders such as Alice Schwarzer.

Although a national German Council of Women (*Deutscher Frauenrat*, Bonn) has become an umbrella organization for numerous regional and local splinter groups, the women's movement seems to have been most successful in consciousness-raising at the local level with the establishment, especially in Berlin and Munich, of women's centers *(Frauenzentren)*, segregationalist radical self-help communes for women and children, and a *Frauenforum* for the formation of a feminist party, which tries to influence politicians. The *Forum* admits nonchauvinist men and has about 300 members. These groups are responsible for a women's health spa, a discotheque, a shelter for battered women (*Frauenhaus*, in Berlin since 1976), a publishing house, an art gallery, and a bookstore.

With her feminist magazine *Emma,* highly praised and muchmaligned Alice Schwarzer represents "the autonomous feminist movement" which differs from the Cologne-based "Socialist Feminist Action Group." Schwarzer has crusaded against sexism in weekly magazines; she advocates military service for women. All these organizations express women's disenchantment with the low social status afforded to reproduction and child rearing and with women's traditional sexual, financial, and psychological dependence on men.

Although "84 percent of men and 87 percent of women between 35 and 40 are married" (*Mannheimer Morgen,* January 9, 1982), divorce rates and single households have risen along with feminist consciousness. 70 percent of West German divorce cases are now instituted by women, 35 percent of all households are led by singles, and every third woman between 18 and 65 is single. The social implications of this trend are controversial. Germans wonder who will work for the social security of the present adult work force a generation from now if the severe drop in the birthrate continues. And what will the future of Germany be in the year 2,100 if the present population of 60 million West Germans drops as expected by some 20 million?

Many feminists have rejected the traditional notions of female beauty. They wear unisex clothes to deemphasize their gender and to stress instead their intelligence and achievements (see Ulrich Greiner, "Jede Frau ist schön," Die Zeit, February 12, 1982). As in the United States, a backlash at certain radical feminist theories has sprung up, which reasserts the positive values of motherhood and housework. Even some older feminist activists opt for motherhood after twenty years in a career ("Gebärschlußpanik," Der Spiegel, No. 21, 1981, p. 198). As societal attitudes became more conservative in the eighties, the birthrate crept up, and many women favored domestic work and the freedom from employment once again. Yet even these women do not want to relinquish the advantages gained in recent years.

Full legal equality came in 1977. Women may now keep their maiden names after marriage and make their own decisions about employment. Illegitimate children now have the same rights as children born in wedlock; as of 1979, working mothers receive up to five months maternity leave at full pay while retaining job security. Divorce law has replaced the principle of guilt with the concept of the "breakdown of a marriage," and it protects the material security of the economically weaker partner. Thus, a divorced woman has a right to part of her ex-husband's pension if he happens to be the economically stronger partner, and to his support for her education if she has no profession or trade.

After a divorce, children are awarded to the parent best able to care for them and who has their greater affection. Men have not been slow in turning a divorce from an economically stronger woman to their own advantage by making the ex-wife pay for their upkeep and further training.

Along with women's legal equality,

> There has been a marked improvement in the vocational training of girls and women. For example, the proportion of female students at all universities increased notably during the sixties and seventies (in 1980–81 it was 35.7 percent compared with 22.7 percent in the 1957–58 winter semester).

(65, 290)

Also, the strict division between male and female jobs is slowly disappearing. It is no longer unheard of to encounter women entrepreneurs, crane drivers, truckers, police, engineers, chemists, precision instrument mechanics, fire fighters, and pilots. Women have gained some influence on the works councils (a share of 19 percent of the available seats in 1981, and more in certain industries, such as textiles, where they held 55 percent). A German poll has reported a sex-role reversal in the making (Allensbach Institut, 1979): In the last 25 years German women have shown themselves to be the stronger sex. They out-perform men, hold up better under stress, and are generally more efficient. While women become more dynamic, active, self-confident, financially independent, and shed domination (of men and church, for example), many men with traditional values become demoralized and less active. Young couples, on the other hand, try increasingly to share responsibilities at home and at work, acknowledging women's equal rights in these areas *(72)*.

Despite progress, West German women are not fully emancipated in the early 1980s. 40 percent of married women hold jobs, many of them part-time and therefore dispensable in times of recession. Approximately 60 percent of the unemployed are women, including many who trained for "unconventional" male jobs in government-sponsored pilot projects since 1978. As in the case of the university reforms, a reaction set in that has in practice rescinded some of the legal gains of the women's movement of the 1970s; for instance, the right to terminate an unwanted pregnancy (Article 218 of the Penal Code). As early as 1975, the Constitutional Court rejected this reform, reinstating punishment for termination, with few exceptions. Finally, although the number of female students has increased considerably, and women's studies courses have been instituted (forty-seven such courses at the *Freie Universität* in Berlin, Winter 1981/82), paternalism among professors and employers still discriminates against women.

The situation of West German women is similar in some ways to that of the United States. In both countries women have their legal rights, many of them work, but usually not in high positions; they are less well paid than men and frequently suffer from a conflict between motherhood (family) and career. They have to combat deeply entrenched social prejudices and they read some of the same literature—books by Germaine Greer, Gloria Steinem, and Kate Millet, for example. But there are also differences.

There is no real women's movement in West Germany that could rally around an issue like ERA. Instead of a mass movement or a party, German women have founded small groups and communes on the local level, because they are less mobile than their American counterparts and more rooted in families and neighborhoods. Furthermore, American feminists gained their political experience in the Civil Rights Movement, whereas German feminists reacted against the male-dominated student rebellion, and a few joined the terrorist underground.

How does the situation of East German women compare to that of West German women? In the GDR, women also share equal legal rights with men. Since 1945 nonsexist education has been practiced in primary and secondary schools. From 1949 on, women have received superior vocational training compared with the FRG and have made considerable inroads as butchers (35 percent of all trainees as compared with 0.4 percent in the FRG), as physicians (46 versus 20 percent), as dentists (46 to 17 percent), as lawyers (30 to 5 percent), in the chemical industry (76 to 22 percent), and in data processing (82 to 38 percent; *209,* 75). A fulltime housewife "is an almost nonexistent phenomenon in the GDR" (*209,* 163). Working women get a year's maternity leave and a 1,000 Mark bonus for a baby. Still the gender division of jobs has not been overcome. "Bricklayers, auto mechanics, and carpenters are virtually all men, and textile workers and typists virtually all women" (*209,* 73). Upward mobility is rare, and employers hesitate to hire young women in essential positions. In the GDR women are also paid less than men for equal work and are considerably underrepresented in leading governmental positions (e.g., one woman member among thirty-nine men on the Council of Ministers). Signs of "outer domination" have increased while they have been weakening in the FRG. Generally, the GDR has been a pioneer on the legal front, combatting sexual discrimination from above. Yet no women's movement has developed because, according to Marx, the revolution would end the oppression of women (along with all other kinds of oppression). Discrepancies between theory and practice, however, which remain in the GDR can be explained by the communist party's refusal to recognize the power and persistence of patriarchal, e.g., Prussian paternalism, beyond the economic revolution.

## THE GUEST-WORKER ISSUE

To provide equal treatment and opportunities for millions of guest workers *(Gastarbeiter)* is the most urgent social problem facing the FRG in the early 1980s. The continuing influx of newcomers and a confused government policy make this problem ever more intractable. It has been compared to a social time bomb on the scale of America's ethnic minority question, but so far there has been little progress toward a solution in any of the West European or Scandinavian countries that have large numbers of aliens. The migrant labor problem is European in scope and arose mainly because of a severe economic lag between industrialized Northern Europe and the poor underdeveloped Mediterranean South. The number of workers, their ethnic backgrounds, and local circumstances, vary from one European country to the other, making a unified approach difficult. England has many immigrants from the Commonwealth (mainly India, Pakistan, and Africa), who live in heavily industralized areas such as Bristol, Manchester, Birmingham, and London and total 7.4 percent of its work force (1981). In France 11 percent of the work force (or four million people) are immigrants from its former colonies, including Algeria; 4.5 percent of the Netherlands' work force comes from Indonesia; in Switzerland foreigners account for about one third of the work force or 2.7 million out of 8.3 million; almost one in eight Swedish residents is an immigrant; 36 percent of Luxembourg's labor force consists of aliens; and finally, Austria's industry has many workers from its former East European Empire.

Most of the migrant workers were recruited during the industrial boom of the 1950s and 1960s; their flow from southern Europe to the industrial north peaked at the beginning of the 1970s and started to decline slightly with the ensuing economic recession. The immigrants hold the least desirable menial jobs, they live in the poorest areas, sometimes illegally, and increasingly they are victims of xenophobia and racism. Immigrants have become convenient scapegoats for all social and economic woes.

Foreign workers totalled about eight million in 1973, or 28 to 30 million if their family members are included, accounting for 10 percent of the Common Market's total population. Some countries have tried to reduce their numbers as unemployment worsened. Switzerland expelled 200,000 foreign workers in the mid-1970s as the country's construction industry nearly collapsed. A movement is under way to restrict foreigners to 12 percent of the Swiss population. The French government offered 2,500 dollars to each immigrant who would leave the country. Less than 5,700 took advantage of the offer. Unless there is an economic upsurge soon, coupled with long-range policies of integrating the "seasonal workers," the future for social peace in Western Europe looks bleak as one third of its children will be "foreign" by the end of the century.

Compared with the racial clashes in Britain and the tension between North Africans and the native French, the situation in West Germany is still relatively peaceful. During the period of the "economic miracle," in the 1950s and 1960s, German companies brought in cheap labor from Southern Europe. Recruiting efforts increased in Turkey after the Berlin Wall was built in 1961, cutting off East German labor from the booming economy in the West. In 1960, 650,000 resident aliens were registered in the Federal Republic; in 1963, 1.1 million; in 1969, 2.4 million; and despite a recruiting freeze in 1973 due to the oil crisis, the number had swelled to 4.1 million foreigners in 1975; in 1982 there were about 4.7 million, not counting illegal aliens, or about 7.5 percent of the total population. One in thirteen West German residents is a foreigner. The percentage of working immigrants jumped from 1 to 10 percent between 1960 and 1982, or about two million, 12 percent of them unemployed. Thus the traditionally homogeneous West German society faces massive social and economic problems. Some big cities are already reeling under the avalanche of migrants, who have gravitated toward certain areas, such as Berlin-Kreuzberg, Hamburg-Altona, and Frankfurt-Bockenheim.

Who are West Germany's underprivileged, what are their problems, what solutions are proposed? The label *Gastarbeiter* suggests both the original purpose of recruiting outside the country, and it continues to point to the problems that have evolved. "Guest workers" originally referred to a temporary, seasonal work force that would fill in the gaps in the German labor market and then return home "based on a policy of rotation" (*128,* 75), without social consequences to anyone. But Germany's intention to exploit this work force proved to be at odds with the guest workers' expectation of equal treatment and their desire to settle or at least remain in West Germany an average of eight to ten years. In practice, if guest workers returned at all to their native country, they often left grown-up children behind in Germany. Those who became permanent German residents often had children who lived in their native countries join them in Germany.

For about two decades (1954–1973), West German industry welcomed this low-cost labor which enabled it to continue its rapid expansion without causing a wage explosion. And with German jobs, migrants escaped unemployment, minimal wages and social misery in their underdeveloped native countries. The "seasonal worker" took the menial and arduous jobs that no skilled German worker wanted—garbage collecting, grave digging, street cleaning, construction labor, car assembly (Ford-Opel in Cologne, VW Wolfsburg, Mercedes Stuttgart), and also in mining, catering, health services, and the heavy work in textiles, shipbuilding, and the electronics industry. Some started businesses of their own, such as small tailoring shops, laundries, groceries, and pizzerias since as unskilled laborers they were deprived of better career opportunities. The guest worker now plays such an important role in the labor force that any large-scale loss would result in a breakdown of municipal services and a paralysis of entire industries. Moreover, the work performed by foreigners enabled German workers to shorten their hours and to move into white-collar jobs.

The influx of about a quarter (1.2 million) of its migrant workers to prosperous West Germany from Common Market countries reflects the EEC's principle of the free movement of labor. For example, in 1981 280,000 Italians were employed in the FRG, half of the 300,000 Greek residents were employed, 100,000 of 177,000 Spaniards had jobs, and 637,000 Yugoslavs, 60,000 Portuguese, and 242,000 Asians lived in West Germany in 1982. But more than a third of all migrant workers (1.5 million including family members, 1982) come from Turkey. Many circumvented the hiring freeze of 1973 by claiming political asylum from such countries as Sri Lanka, Poland, Pakistan, Afghanistan, Arabian countries, and Vietnam.

How well were these divergent ethnic groups received in West Germany? Employers took care of their basic needs for a long time by providing collective housing (i.e., barracks or trailers on or near factories and construction sites). Trade unions asked the new arrivals to join them and thus become equals with their German colleagues. Municipal governments were happy to recruit new sanitation crews from among their ranks. But as soon as certain minorities crowded into specific city areas, turning them into ethnic ghettos, overwhelming problems arose in housing, schooling, employment, legal status, asylum, and social integration for which neither city and state governments nor federal agencies had solutions.

Housing has been a major problem for foreign workers. When workers (usually men) want to leave their barrack-type housing, they can generally only find overpriced, overcrowded, dilapidated living quarters for their families and themselves, frequently without heating and washing facilities, often managed by absentee landlords. Many migrants subdivide their apartments illegally to reduce their rents. It may take up to a decade, if at all, for a worker to move into decent lodgings. As in the early stages when guest workers were often housed in factory barracks, the recent housing shortage has been so severe that asylum seekers have been put into transit camps, third-rate hotels, and collective housing.

Until 1973 there were plenty of jobs in West Germany, and all recruited workers automatically received work permits. But as economic growth slowed, it became harder for migrant workers to renew their permits. However, as of 1978, five years' residence in Germany along with sufficient knowledge of the language, adequate accomodations, and proof of school attendance by their children usually insures permanent residence and work permits to foreigners. As the West German unemployment rate rose to over 10 percent in 1983, resentment against foreign workers also increased despite the fact that employers are convinced that the unemployment of German workers is generally unrelated to the employment of nearly two million migrants. Unless they are single and willing to return home, unemployment for guest workers can mean disaster for large families in ghetto areas, who are without welfare protection. Since they pay taxes, union dues, and social security, it is only fair that they also receive welfare benefits. Out of half a million Turkish workers, two thirds have lost their jobs (*Die Zeit,* January 8, 1982). But as long as employment and income prospects remain substantially worse in southern and eastern Europe, only one out of ten recruited workers is willing to leave, particularly since the West German cradle-to-grave welfare system pays more than they could earn in the home country Endemic unemployment for the second and third generation of foreign children seems to be unavoidable unless they are successfully integrated.

Statistics show that the integration task is formidable. There are more than a million migrant children in West Germany and Berlin—400,000 in preschool, 630,000 in schools and vocational training centers, and 300,000 have finished or dropped out. Each year, according to 1980 statistics, an additional 100,000 children are born to foreigners. The arrival of dependents from the homeland adds to their numbers. Thousands are waiting to join their parents. Almost one in ten elementary-school pupils is of foreign parentage, mostly Moslem. In some places this percentage is much higher (e.g., in Berlin 27% percent), with some elementary schools almost completely "ethnic."

Most of these children have never been to kindergarten, and 50 percent fail to earn school-graduation certificates, which would entitle them to vocational training and apprenticeship. Only 25 percent continue this route, 4 percent go on to *Realschule,* and only 2 percent attend *Gymnasium.* Many foreign children have difficulties with German, and because of the lack of social integration, their truancy rate is high. As a result, roughly three out of four employed foreign juveniles are unskilled. And others never held jobs or they were denied them because of legal complications.

The difficulties of these adolescents vary according to when and where they were born or brought into the country, and how early they attended German schools. Those born in West Germany and who attended kindergarten (30 percent of all foreign children do so, but only 15 percent of Turks) have no real problems with the language. They speak the local dialect and often act as interpreters for their parents or for the other less fortunate pupils who never went to nursery school. Real difficulties arise with second-generation children who came to Germany when they were already ten or so, in many cases having graduated from their native schools without a foreign language or vocational instruction. The immigrant children worry educators most because they are illiterate in both languages and caught in a culture conflict that causes emotional and learning problems. The so-called third generation, youngsters born of parents raised in Germany, hardly differ from German children, unless they grow up in segregated ghetto areas.

The clash between two cultures is most extreme at home when foreign parents would rather allow their children to grow up illiterate than to expose them to a different language, lifestyle, and religion. Identity problems, insecurity, alienation, and rebellion are often experienced by these students.

The split in languages, values, and mentality cannot be solved by "returning" to a country where they were neither born nor raised. Frequently these adolescents are rejected by Germans as well as by their parents' nation.

Although Italians, Yugoslavs, and Spaniards have relatively few difficulties integrating, cultural conflicts for Greek and Turkish children at home, at school, and on the job are great. They are not made easier by their attendance in German schools in the morning and Greek or Moslem schools in the afternoon. It remains to be seen whether a middle ground can be found between social integration and preservation of ethnic identity.

Should these children go to mixed or ethnic schools? Since schools differ among states and sometimes even within cities, the actual situation is chaotic. In ghetto areas it seemed natural to leave the children in *Nationalklassen* taught in their own language on a bilingual basis; depending on the proportion of ethnic minorities attending, schoolchildren are instructed in regular German classes outside of the ghetto. Sometimes extra language courses prepare pupils for entry into the normal track. Interestingly enough, not only German but also many foreign parents favor divisions along national lines, because they want to maintain their religious and cultural identity at all costs. In Wuppertal, Greek fathers went on a hunger strike to protest the transformation of *Nationalklassen* into regular German grades (*Der Stern,* December 17, 1980). While they actively desired segregation, some German school officials imposed a *numerus clausus* on integration by inner-city schools to prevent German children from becoming a minority. In Baden-Württemberg foreign children may not exceed 30 percent in a mixed class, in Berlin no more than 20 percent. Because there is sometimes a shortage of German children, many of them attend classes made up exclusively of foreigners.

Since 1965 working parents have been permitted to send for their offspring left in their homeland, provided they had jobs and adequate accomodations. This opened the floodgates, until 1977 when a new regulation denied work permits to youths who had not attended German schools and had not spent five years with a working parent. This policy has been undercut, however, by a liberal child-support provision *(Kindergeld)* in effect since 1975, which allows each migrant parent a fixed amount for each child. The Alien Law of 1965 *(Ausländergesetz)*, which denied citizenship to foreign workers and their children, compounded legal problems. To alleviate this outright discrimination, eighteen-year olds who have lived in the country for at least eight years may now obtain German citizenship, compared to ten years of residence for adults.

The Right of Asylum in West Germany, guaranteed by the Basic Law (Article 16), causes another problem. West Germany is the first choice of asylum seekers among European countries, because it is the only one to have written such a law into its constitution in gratitude to the many states which gave asylum to Germans abroad during the Hitler years and in memory of the innumerable victims of racism during the Nazi regime. East Germans and ethnic Germans automatically qualify for West German citizenship; East Europeans, especially Poles and Soviet Jews, as well as refugees according to certain quotas (such as 20,000 Vietnamese) have no problem obtaining political sanctuary. But other minorities, from Turkey and Ethiopia to Bangladesh, are less successful: 80 percent are refused, but they have the right to a time-consuming court review and to monthly subsistence payments of up to 330 DM per person (1981–1982), free living quarters, and a clothing allowance—an approximate total of 650 DM per month—until their case is settled. As a result, severe housing, job, and welfare coffer shortages have surfaced in some cities along with a rise in German resentment of these minority groups who seem to take advantage of their tax money. A rapid screening procedure was ruled out on constitutional grounds in 1981, and court cases may drag on for three to four years.

Over the last decade the guest-worker issue has become more and more a Turkish issue. Turkish communities exist in most German cities, and Islam has become the second largest religion in the Federal Republic. Prohibited in Turkey, fundamentalists strive to keep their sway over all Moslems by creating a national identity in a foreign environment. They also insist on segregation and preach intolerance of other denominations. Afternoon Koran schools teach children values and moral codes at odds with German customs, fostering paranoia and prejudice. Pupils are pressured not to attend senior school, and indeed half of them become truant and fail to find jobs. Unmarried adolescent girls suffer most from the feudal-patriarchal structure of traditional Turkish life. Since their virginity must be protected at all costs in order to increase their bridal value, girls are "grounded" at home and thus forego schooling, youth clubs, and friendships. Most don headscarfs and long-sleeved dresses even in summer. Outings on their own to discotheques or movie theaters, for example, are unthinkable. Unable to speak German, sexually and culturally discriminated against, their plight does not change after marriage when they are reduced to complete subservience to their husband. Mixed marriages (between Turkish women and German men), which might offer a way out of their isolation, are extremely rare. (Turkish males frequently obtain illiterate brides from their native villages.)

The Turks and their German hosts seem to be caught in a vicious circle. Legally, these migrants are Turks, but their children are, at least in social terms, Germans. Although most Turks have a residence permit for only a year or two, 40 percent want to stay indefinitely. The more Turks there are, the more they are blamed for what goes wrong in the Federal Republic on the labor front and in society, especially for the rise in crime. Indeed, many ethnic teenagers, lacking work, education, and recreational facilities, drop out, join gangs, and push drugs. They often develop criminal records between the ages of fourteen and twenty-one. Although some are deported, they return illegally, having failed to fit into the strange environment of their "homeland" due to their mixed languages and customs. "What to do with the Turks" has become a major political issue (see Nina Grunenberg, *Die Zeit,* February 5 and 12, 1982).

The sheer numbers of foreigners are bringing the welfare system close to bankruptcy (costs have increased fourfold within a decade to a total of 27 billion DM as of 1980). "it was a mistake to allow so many foreigners into the country. But now we must beware of making them pay for our mistakes." (Helmut Schmidt, *Der Spiegel,* December 7, 1981). Yet German resentment spreads and nourishes frustration, insecurity, and rebellion among alien residents. "Foreigners test the mettle and the limits of German tolerance"—such statements made the headlines of the Western press in the early 1980s.

The government has offered 10,500 DM per worker and 1,500 DM per child for guest workers to return home, and 300,000 workers have consequently left West Germany as of 1984. But this decrease has not been enough for rightwing German extremists of the NPD who have called for the expulsion of unemployed migrants and have waged a campaign *(Bürgerinitiative Ausländerstopp)* against ethnic minorities who do not want to integrate, especially Turks, Greeks, and North Africans.

The government has imposed some effective immigration curbs on guest workers, their spouses, children, and asylum seekers. In 1981 no teenagers over sixteen years of age could enter the country since the language barrier precluded their chances of getting an apprenticeship. Now efforts are under way to lower this age to twelve. In addition, asylum laws have been amended to restrict residence permits to a two- or three-year period, during which grantees cannot get a work permit. On welfare, they receive goods rather than cash to support themselves. The prospect of Turkey's entry into the EEC in 1987 and with it a new influx of Turks raises xenophobia in the FRG. Attempts are being made to renegotiate the terms of the 1982 Association Treaty to rule out automatic freedom of residence. By supporting the formation of workers' companies in Turkey, the Federal Republic is trying to reverse the immigration trend (so far 100 factories have been built with West German development aid, providing jobs for 34,000 workers, *Die Zeit,* March 26, 1982).

The most important response to the problems of guest workers involves the economic and social integration of those who have lived and worked in the FRG for many years. The integration effort is most successful when geared primarily to children from kindergarten through secondary schools, and in clubs and vocational training. Language and job-training classes have been instituted, but more needs to be done.

Pilot projects to train foreign adolescents for skilled jobs are under way. At present there exist about eleven such projects in 110 companies such as Audi-NSU in Ingolstadt, but only a small number of trainees (700) are involved (*Die Zeit,* April 16, 1982). German initiatives by churches, by social welfare agencies, employers, trade unions, political parties, and the courts need to be met with equal determination by those migrants willing to integrate if true assimilation is to be realized.

Over the last decade foreign workers have been slowly but steadily emerging as a political force. This has only been possible since 1973 when they joined German unions in increasing numbers to protect their own interests: equality in labor legislation, pay, vacation time, fringe benefits, and protection against unlawful firings. They have run for office, they sit on the works councils, they have become shop stewards ("By 1967, IG-Metall already had some 642 foreign shop stewards," *158,* 157), and they have organized strikes (e.g., the Ford strike in Cologne, 1973). Although they are not entitled to vote (unless they have become citizens), they may participate in advisory councils *(Ausländerbeirat)* and coordinating circles *(Koordinierungskreis)* to express their views on municipal government issues. On the local level *(Bezirk und Gemeinde)* voting rights for foreigners are under discussion or are being implemented. Their recommendations concerning public policies on foreign workers are sometimes influential. Current evidence suggests that West Germany is well on its way to becoming a multinational pluralistic state *(Vielvölkerstaat)* similar to the US. It is even evolving its own "Gastarbeiter Literatur" (*Die Zeit,* April 13, 1984).

# 4. The Cultural Scene

## Culture and Politics

The period of political and social experimentation in the sixties and early seventies was short-lived. The Germans did not heed the students' call for a complete transformation of society. The German worker, whose support the radicals sought, resisted all efforts to forge a revolutionary link between students and the labor movement. In the international field, Russian intervention in Czechoslovakia during the summer of 1968 snuffed out a significant attempt at liberalizing the Soviet socialist system. This reaction against change behind the Iron Curtain also had a dampening effect on progressive political developments in the West. Another impediment to social change in West Germany can be found in the internationalization of conflicts, not only in the political sphere (with the Berkeley-Berlin-Paris student revolt) but also in the economic sphere where the ever greater interdependence of nations and national economies became obvious. In this atmosphere of increasing interdependence it was impossible for a national movement of radical social change to be successful. Willy Brandt, a social democrat who belongs to the left wing of his party, declared in 1972: "We need the dialogue with industry" (*FAZ* 1972), and thus prepared the ground for Helmut Schmidt's economic management approach to all spheres of the society. In 1973 the international oil crisis illustrated in graphic terms the limits of economic growth on a global scale. The Social Democrats were sympathetic to the student revolt in 1968. Some of the leading party members praised their political goals, if not their methods. By 1974, however, Schmidt declared that the students were "obscuring the picture" (*Verunklärung des Bildes; FAZ,* 1976). The trend towards global interdependence and economic limits as well as the politically unrealistic expectations of the students (a blueprint for a new society without a major social class in support of it) contributed in bringing about a period of restoration in German culture and society.

No single event activated political restoration more quickly than the debacle of the Olympic Games at Munich in 1972. These Games were to present modern West Germany to the world as an open society, critical of itself, yet sure of its internal and external strength. The official government publication, *Deutsches Mosaik,* 1972, exudes optimism about the future and a sense of pride in economic accomplishments and political stability. But there in Munich before the entire world to see, Israelis were held hostage and murdered by Palestinian terrorists. The inept reaction of the German security forces shocked Germans to the core. The country was simply not prepared for this kind of massive terrorist activity within its borders. The notorious Baader-Meinhof gang already had caused alarm. The exposure of ineptness at Munich prompted the West German government to mobilize its security apparatus not only against terrorists but, as time went on, and with the aquiescense of the general populace, also against real and imagined sympathizers of terrorists as well as of all left-wing spokesmen. The political reaction developed a specific mode of operation: the control of the Left through political discrimination in hiring policies *(Berufsverbot)* was coupled with a well orchestrated media mobilization against radical students and left-of-center Germans to the point of undermining the fragile roots of civil liberties that had just barely taken hold in the country.

Politically active writers decried what they considered the demise of German parliamentary democracy. Foremost among these writers was Heinrich Böll who saw the nation-wide hysterical search for members of the Baader-Meinhof gang as an attempt by the state to practice totalitarianism. He was immediately denounced as a sympathizer. For the first time in postwar society an explicitly conservative point of view with considerable support emerged in literature. The poet Hans Egon Holthusen was one of its leading spokesmen, and the historian Golo Mann, another. Mann had once supported Willy Brandt and the SPD, but by the mid-seventies was moving into a political alliance with the right-wing politician Franz Joseph Strauß, the Minister President of Bavaria and the CDU/CSU's unsuccessful party candidate in the 1976 elections. The Right argued that West Germany was falling prey to a *Volksfront,* a left-wing alliance between the bomb-throwing terrorists, the left-wing politicians in parliament and Marxist theoreticians in the lecture halls. The fifties under Adenauer were held up as a model of an economically stable and politically healthy Germany.

In spite of the revolutionary fervor for a new literature based on a heightened social consciousness, "the generation that rebelled in 1968 turned out to be silent . . ." (*186,* 108). German film, however, gained international stature in the seventies and jumped into the breach. New films became a significant expression of contemporary German culture both in the complexity of their visual messages as well as in their eloquent defense of civil liberties. Although the subject matter and style of the various filmmakers varied greatly, two themes predominated: (1) the trauma of the years following the war and the moral decadence inherent in the pursuit of material wealth during the period of economic recovery under Adenauer (particularly well portrayed in Rainer Maria Fassbinder's film, *Die Ehe der Maria Braun (The Marriage of Maria Braun)*; and (2) the defense of civil liberties against political reaction, i.e., the portrayal of a "democracy in crisis." Foremost among these films is *Die verlorene Ehre der Katharina Blum* (1977; *The Lost Honor of Katharina Blum,* 1979), a Fassbinder film based on a novel by Herinrich Böll. Böll, who had gained an international stature with his 1972 Nobel Prize for Literature, expressed in this work his deep political and moral concerns about the political reaction spreading in West Germany. Katharina Blum, a simple working girl, falls in love with an army deserter. She takes him home for a night and helps him elude the police. *Die Zeitung (The Newspaper),* an influential paper that thrives on sensationalism, denounces her as a member of a radical conspiracy and calls her "sexually promiscuous." The immense pressure of publicity and her own intense shyness and sense of shame drive her to despair. Emotionally cornered, she shoots a reporter of the *Die Zeitung* who has come to interview her. What Böll had singled out for criticism was the widely read tabloid *Bild-Zeitung* and its sensational reporting of events surrounding the radical Baader-Meinhof gang. This "well-organized conservative campaign against civil and intellectual freedom under the guise of concern for state security" (*42,* 223) moved many political observers both inside and outside of the Federal Republic to question the stability of West Germany's parliamentary democracy. The Germans' commitment to civil liberties appeared in doubt.

One troubling aspect of German political conflict-solving has been the tendency to explicate each disagreement, conflict, or contradiction in terms of fundamental principles. This is both an expression of a traditional cultural pattern that some have traced back to Martin Luther's fundamentalism and a result of postwar political developments. In the divided country political issues of general significance quickly bring to the surface questions of national identity. The political right saw the terrorist problem as the first step towards a revolution; the political left saw the state's overreaction to terrorism as the first sign of the end of democracy.

Many writers, critics, and filmmakers rallied to document the deteriorating political atmosphere in the mid-seventies. Fassbinder, Böll, and others collaborated to make the film *Deutschland im Herbst (Germany in the Autumn),* an indictment of political reaction. This somewhat diffuse film documents two funerals, one of an industrialist killed by the Baader-Meinhof gang and the other of three members of the Baader-Meinhof gang, who ostensibly committed suicide in prison. The film puts into sharp relief the two funerals. One is attended by the leading dignitaries of industry and government and projects an aura of glitter and wealth. The other is attended by a straggling group of sympathizers and friends under the ever-present, watchful eye of the state security apparatus.

The defense of civil liberties against totalitarian methods of deal-

ing with political dissent was expressed not only in films and nov-
els, but also in poems. Erich Fried's *Deutsche Volksfahndung (German Search Warrant,* 1972) attacks as totalitarian the state's call to
the populace to hunt down political radicals.

> An entire people
> Is asked to do police duty
> Unpaid
> But not without reward
> The President of the Federal Bureau of Crime
> Dr. Horst Herold
> Calls this "a
> People's search warrant"
> What is he announcing
> With such a sonorous
> Word?

> *(231,* 287)

In manifestoes, letters, and speeches the writers rallied against
what was perceived as a new totalitarianism, bent on destroying
the still fragile political culture of parliamentary democracy. A letter sent to the President of the *Bundestag* and signed by many of
the leading writers of the seventies states the issue succinctly:

> The cooperation between the executive power of the state and rightist
> conspirators against our first democracy brought Hitler to power. . . .
> Just as in our country today the state is taken to mean the executive
> branch of government and thus the division of powers is ignored"

> (June 14, 1972; *231,* 287–288)

The concerns about Nazism and its significance are still one of
the most potent elements shaping contemporary political life. This
explains to some degree the German allergic reaction to all political
conflicts. Towards the end of the decade, however, the political
conflicts surrounding civil liberties and totalitarianism shifted to
problems of the ecology and issues of disarmament.

## NEOSUBJECTIVISM

While many writers and filmmakers continued the sixties' legacy
of direct political involvement, a general trend away from activism
towards individual and private concerns also developed. This
trend has been described as neosubjectivism (*Neo-Subjektivismus;*
*57,* 77ff.), a term that is adequate in a general way but fails to explain fully this reaction against political solutions. Even more important than neosubjectivism itself are several cultural trends

related to it: 1) the rejection of "system explanations" of society *(Systemanalysen);* the ideological collapse of the Left reflected this sceptical attitude towards system explanations; 2) the emergence of feminist consciousness based above all on the principle that all people should control their own lives and bodies; 3) the ecological movement, which more than the other trends, points beyond the seventies to a zero-growth postindustrial society.

New subjectivism in the literary sphere has not merely been a restatement of postwar existentialism with its claim of the radical uniqueness and isolation of the individual. Neosubjectivism in the seventies has not excluded political, social, and cultural considerations. In other words, the political experience of the sixties has not been discarded. This change away from answers derived from ideological systems to questions about individuals and their lives is all-pervasive. Günter Grass, the committed writer of the sixties, states it concisely: "It is quite all right to start with myself again and to ask where I stand, where is my place" (*57,* 79). Even a writer such as Erika Runge, who had made a name for herself with *Bottroper Protokolle* (a prime example of realistic documentary literature), rediscovered the central role of fantasy in fiction, and she concluded that the sphere of politics and the sphere of literature are separate after all (*57,* 80). Peter Schneider in his novel *Lenz* (1973) graphically caught the change in attitude. The protagonist of his novel, a left intellectual, has a picture of Karl Marx over his bed "that he cannot stand anymore. He hangs it upside down in order to let the rational content flow out of it . . ." (*57,* 83). The feminist Karin Struck put her criticism of a ready-made Marxism most bluntly: "Without fantasy socialism is nothing" (*220,* 118). Hans Magnus Enzensberger, whose writings in the early sixties had pointed the way towards political and cultural experimentation, made the failed Cuban revolution the theme of his *Der Untergang der Titanic,* 1978 *(The Sinking of the Titanic).*

Sociologists have provided a whole range of explanations for the changing political climate in the cultural sphere. Helmut Schelsky, a conservative, stated with some glee (in the *FAZ, Frankfurter Allgemeine Zeitung* April 16, 1977) that *Das Prinzip Hoffnung* (Principle Hope), a major work by the Marxist philosopher Ernst Bloch outlining utopian thinking, had to be changed to *Das Prinzip Erfahrung* (Principle Experience).

> The high esteem and defense of the private sphere has become characteristic for this generation; it is neither the introverted bourgeois exclusiveness of the family nor an unbridled privatistic life style but the decisive political fact of the person . . .

> (*FAZ,* April 16, 1977)

Likewise, unorthodox Marxists have come to the conclusion that socialist theory and social practice should place greater emphasis on the subjective needs of individuals in an overall reassessment of Marxist dogma *(64).*

No one has been more articulate in his attacks on all-inclusive "system answers" than the Austrian writer Peter Handke. His play *Kaspar Hauser* (1968; English translation, 1969) written during the heyday of political and cultural experimentation, points in some respects towards the new subjectivism of the seventies. In a broader sense, however, Handke puts into words the essential problem of an entire generation born and raised in Central Europe during the Nazi and postwar reconstruction years. The drama is based on a nineteenth-century documentary report of a person who was said to have been without language, without a name, and without a known past. The play deals with the slow process of acquiring speech, identity, and a social context. Kaspar Hauser stumbles onto the stage with one sentence that he repeats over and over again: "I want to become such a one as once another was." Hidden prompters introduce him to the mysteries of conceptualization, memory, and language manipulation. The highly complex educational process emphasizes indoctrination and control, both of which Kaspar Hauser accepts: "Since I can speak, I can bring order to everything" *(99,* 30). Yet that same learning process traps him in an identity that he finds oppressing: "I cannot get rid of myself anymore" *(99,* 100), and finally he becomes a "Kaspar" (a proper name in German, but also a designation for a puppet: *Kasperl-Theater* = puppet play). Kaspar Hauser is both a victim and a beneficiary of this unusual introduction to himself and the world around him. Handke's man without a past or a present is more than a fictionalized case study. He captures the modern psychological phenomenon of utter isolation, which Alexander Mitscherlich called the "Kaspar Hauser" complex *(86,* 33). This psychological complex has nothing to do with either existential exposure or romantic inner-directed loneliness. It is rather an

> absolute isolation that renders a person without culture as far as the world is concerned and asocial as far as other human beings are concerned—it makes him asocial and negative towards culture. Modern mass man in his complexity is meant here. He . . . no longer knows himself as a historical being, but as a creature of impulse bound to the moment.
>
> *(86,* 33)

The "Kaspar Hauser" complex as Mitscherlich described it in 1950 and Handke captured it in his drama in 1968 attests to that specific postwar sensitivity towards fundamental questions of individual

worth. Beyond that, however, it describes the modern psychological phenomenon of total individual isolation as well as the lack of a
personal identity due to the influence of mass culture *(141)*. The
technological society of the United States is not specifically criticized, but this psychological analysis has the unmistakable ring of a
European defense of history and culture against the onslaught of
American modernization.

With its specific focus on questions of memory, identity, and
human communication, Handke's play *Kaspar Hauser* set the tone
for neosubjectivism. Autobiographical themes, personal diaries,
and historical biographies—themes which allow for heightened
introspection—became the appropriate literary vehicle for neosubjectivism. Handke traced in his later novel, *Die Angst des Tor-
manns beim Elfmeter* (1970; *The Goalie's Anxiety at the Penalty
Kick,* 1972), the psychological disintegration of a murderer by
chronicling in detail his increasing alienation from his surround-
ings. While the plot is not unique, the evocation of a character
from within, through shifting perceptions, is innovative. In another novel *Wunschloses Unglück* (1972: *A Sorrow Beyond
Dreams,* 1974) traumatized by the suicide of his mother, Handke
traces her life story with fine introspection.

A turn toward subjective interests as a reaction against the collapse of political utopias and collective creeds is found both in East
and West Germany. One of the leading German writers on both
sides of the divide, the East German novelist and essayist Christa
Wolf, pays exclusive attention in her first major work, *Nachdenken über Christa T* (1968; *The Quest for Christa T.,* 1970) to
the individual, posing the individual life as the subject of history.
After the death of her close friend Christa T, the narrator seeks to
understand the reality of her friend's life. The conscientious re-
cording of recollections and unraveling of assumptions about her
make this *Nachdenken* (tracing of a person's life by means of
thought and language) a significant statement about the importance of the individual as an idea yet to be discovered and fully appreciated. What gives this novel as well as two other novels
*Kindheitsmuster* (1976; *A Model Childhood,* 1980) and *Kein Ort
Nirgends* (1979; *No Place on Earth,* 1982) their impact is that
Christa Wolf, as a writer living in the GDR, sees individualism as a
dream still to be realized in the socialist system.

In her *Kindheitsmuster* Wolf examines the "maturation of her
own generation" and the "impediments to this maturation." It is a
painstaking look at individual childhood experiences in the Nazi
period and adult life in a socialist state after the war. No contemporary German author is more convincing than Christa Wolf in probing the significance of the individual human life and its potential.
When Wolf traces in thought *(nachdenken)* the life of an individual

human being, it is an eminently political act, with different implications for East and West Germany. In the East, the search for the individual is a plea for a new view of human possibilities. In the
West, it is a reminder that individualism is in danger of being sub-
merged in a consumer-oriented mass culture.

Unlike her West German contemporaries, Christa Wolf's focus
on the individual is never divorced from its political context, and
whatever her personal concern with writing and self-identity, the
issue of language and individualism remains fundamentally a political one:

> A host of words by which we lived, such as "freedom," "equality,"
> "brotherhood," "humanity," "justice," have been taken from us, con-
> fiscated by newspapers, and have become nothing—no faith corre-
> sponds to them anymore.
>
> (Georg Büchner Prize Speech, October 16, 1980)

Peter Handke and Christa Wolf provide neosubjectivist literature with intellectual and cultural substance. In both cases we have
a radical rejection of established conventions of speech, personality, and memory. While the Austrian writer stresses the psychological aspect of his revolt, Christa Wolf never discards political
considerations in her evocation of the fullness of individual existence.

Peter Härtling's novel *Das Familienfest* (1969), typical of the
neosubjective trend in literature, tells the story of a history professor on the basis of the memory fragments of family members and
citizens of his home town. Heinrich Böll was always interested in
drawing intimate portraits of individuals even though moral issues
dominate his writings to the point of allegorizing his fictional heroes. His novel *Gruppenbild mit Dame* (1971; *Group Portrait
with Lady,* 1973) investigates the personality and intimate life of a
woman in her forties, Leni Gruyten, who is having an affair with a
Turkish guest worker. As her life is unraveled, it becomes evident
that she had been in love during WWII with a Russian prisoner of
war. What emerges out of a web of uncertainty is the heroine's effort to pit her intimate love for the Russian prisoner against the all-
encompassing destruction of the war. Again, as in many of Böll's
other novels, the moral concern of the author condenses the plot
into an allegorical configuration: a German girl and a Russian prisoner of war as main figures. The details of an individual's life are
central in the work, marking it as a novel of the seventies.

Günter Grass, in his compendious novel *Der Butt* (1977; *The
Flounder,* 1978), combines broad epic description with contemporary feminist issues and mythology. The prose epic is based on one
of Grimm's fairy tales, *Vom Vischer und siner Fru* (1830) in

which a flounder bargains for his release by promising to fulfill all of the wishes of the fisherman who had caught him. The insatiable fisherman's wife in turn manipulates the contract between her husband and the flounder to demand ever more wealth and fame for himself. Günter Grass gives the plot of this traditional fairy tale a contemporary twist: in return for its release, the flouder promises to defend the interests of men by advising them how to deal successfully with women. But the flounder is finally caught by three modern feminists and put to trial. Around this simple narrative Grass weaves various stories, myths, and events from the stone age to the present. The male appears in many historical guises—as fisherman, monk, bishop—while the female, who always appears in the role of a cook, undergoes eleven metamorphoses ranging from Aua, the stone-age goddess, to the cook who serves the rebelling Polish workers in the Gdansk shipyards in 1970. Grass's ribald humor, vibrant imagination, numerous narrative and descriptive details, and sense for the picaresque are linked with his "private mythology" about women.

Another writer of renown, Martin Walser, also turns from political and social concerns to the problem of human relationships in his novel *Ein fliehendes Pferd* (1978; *A Horse in Flight,* 1980), in which he describes the meeting of two married couples on vacation. The husbands had not met since their school days twenty-three years before. One is an intellectual, forever caught in unfinished research projects, and the other a healthy freelance writer trapped in a limiting macho image of himself. The presumed death of the writer in a boating accident on Lake Constance brings about subtle changes in the relationships of those left behind.

## FEMINISM

Contemporary feminist writings represent among other things a significant influence on neosubjective literature in West Germany. Birth, childrearing, work, disease, death, abortion, and rape become themes in feminist literature. The quality of daily life replaces generalizations about values in the abstract. Feminist literature in West Germany is not merely an extension of radical political consciousness but rather a reaction to "systems explanations" which ignore the history, experience, and needs of women. The first stirrings of a contemporary independent feminist movement can be found in the women who reacted to the patriarchal behavior of the radical student leaders: "comrades, your meetings are insufferable" (57, 336). The main concern of the feminist movement and feminist writing is to make women the subject and not the victims of history. In 1971 various women's groups rallied around a woman's right to an abortion. The controversy over Paragraph 218 for-

bidding abortion highlights one of the central themes of feminist
writing, namely control over one's own body. Verena Stefan's
widely read book *Häutungen* (1975; Shedding) pits the experience
of herself and her body against the established social order. Her
novel attacks the limits set for women's perceptions of themselves,
bound as they are by home, children, limited professional opportunities, and a web of obvious and hidden cultural restrictions, one
of the most important of which are language patterns that camouflage prejudices against women and repress feminist consciousness. The feminist movement is international. Anja Meulenbelt of
the Netherlands, Simone de Beauvoir of France, and Kate Millet of
the United States were translated into German and avidly discussed
in German feminist circles. Next to Verena Stefan's novel, Karin
Struck's *Klassenliebe* (1973; Class Love) is one of the most notable
feminist works of the seventies. She describes her own social rise
to the middle class. The central character, however, is a victim
rather than a person shaping her own life. In this sense Struck's
protagonist is more like an updated heroine of a nineteenth-
century novel in which the suffering of women under the established social norms is portrayed:

> I live between two classes and I have to deal with men from both
> classes, and get involved with them. I have no other choice but to have
> children from both classes, suffer in both classes, be made pregnant by
> men in both classes."

(*220,* 124)

Diaries, letters, and documentaries are the preferred media of
feminist writers because they are most apt to capture the immediacy of personal experiences. Also film, particularly in the second
half of the seventies, became an important medium of feminist culture (e.g., Margarethe von Trotta). A major work by Ernest Bornemann, *Das Patriarchat* (1975; 23) presents a comprehensive
historical analysis of the "origins and the future of our social system." This work is dedicated to all women: "It should serve the
feminist movement just as [Marx's] *Das Kapital* has served the
labor movement." Bornemann outlines with innumerable historical details the appearance of patriarchal, male-dominated hierarchical structures out of the "pre-patriarchal classless societies" in
which collective behavior was not yet characterized by the rule of
men over women.

Both the feminist movement of the seventies and the radical student movement of the sixties suffered from internal conflicts between those who stressed political activism and emancipation
(e.g., Herbert Marcuse) and others who concentrated on personal
awareness, failing to link their intimate experience with a larger

social context (e.g., Norman O. Brown). Disagreements also existed between the academic feminists whose activism consisted largely of research into women's history, and the more community-oriented feminists who concentrated their efforts on social reforms such as abortion rights, jobs, wages, pensions, child care, and the like.

Certain feminist writing is closely related to neosubjective literature, which deals with reality by ignoring comprehensive system explanations. In these works, specific fragments of daily experience and eloquently presented details that characterize authentic human communication, often take the place of theoretical abstractions. Such contemporary cultural trends towards decentralization have fed into the most significant social, political, and economic movement to emerge in West Germany in the course of the seventies, the ecological movement. It is local and single-issue oriented on the one hand (e.g., preventing the building of nuclear reactors at specific sites or the expansion of an airport), and on the other hand it relates to global concerns about disarmament and peace. While the peace and ecological movement is an important factor in contemporary West Germany, it has also made its modest appearance in the GDR, particularly within the Protestant Church.

## GERMAN LITERATURE: EAST AND WEST

At the beginning of the eighties we are witnessing the emergence of a vital concern shared by the populations and governments of both German states. Both states are determined to keep confrontations between the superpowers to a minimum. Furthermore, as the superpowers lose some of their control over Europe, there is more room for flexibility on both sides of the divide. Erich Honecker continues to watch over the purity of the socialist state but retains his ability to maneuver on his own; Helmut Kohl modifies Reagan's anticommunist stance with a pragmatic attitude toward economic cooperation. This rapprochement between East and West Germany was anticipated in the sphere of culture. East German writers paid heed to the writers of West Germany, while West German writers noted with some envy that the writer in the East is taken very seriously and consequently "has a function that can never be obtained in the West" (57, 93). The cultural, political and economic cooperation of the two German states is limited of course by the superpowers' domination of Central Europe.

Also important is the impact of the *emigré* writers from the GDR now living in the FRG. Most of these writers remain socialists at heart in spite of their disillusion with East Germany, and they tend to ally themselves with the politically radical wing of West German culture. One of the most interesting among these *emigrés* is Wolf

Biermann, poet, lyricist, and singer, who was forced into exile when the GDR took away his citizenship for having publicized his politically critical songs. His *Drahtharfe* (1965; *The Wire Harp*), "probably the most successful collection of lyric poetry since 1945" (*186,* 278), is a powerful indictment of the xenophobic East German state:

> The barbed wire slowly grows
> Deep into the skin, chest, and leg
> Into the brain and the grey cells
> Wrapped in a wire gauze
> Our land is an island
> Surrounded by leaden waves
>
> (Ballad about the Prussian Icarus,
> written in the West; *186,* 286)

A rebel in his country now in exile in the West, this German Bob Dylan had the courage to criticize the GDR sharply in his songs. His art had a cutting edge honed by feuding with a political system that strongly objected to him. Once in the West, Biermann was free to criticize and express himself as he wished, but it was a freedom with consequences: he became the pampered virtuoso of the West German entertainment industry, and his political impact was neutralized by his compliance with mass consumer culture. His role in the West German political film *Deutschland im Herbst (Germany in Autumn)*, in which he uttered only a few nondescript remarks, was a telling one.

Hand in hand with this cultural rapprochement between East and West Germany, there is a widespread interest in dealing on both sides of the national divide with German cultural history. Great German authors, literary masterpieces, and significant events in Germany's cultural past have become increasingly important subjects for today's writers. Härtling's *Hölderlin,* Hans Gunther Heym's *Wilhelm Tell,* Peter Kühn's *Ich—Wolkenstein,* Wolfgang Hildesheimer's *Mozart* (1963; Engl. 1982), Adolf Muschg's *Gottfried Keller,* Ulrich Plenzdorf's *Die neuen Leiden des jungen W.* (1973; *The New Sufferings of Young W.,* 1979), Peter Rühmkorf's *Walther von der Vogelweide,* Peter Stein's *Tasso,* and Christa Wolf's *Kein Ort Nirgends,* give contemporary relevance to historical subjects. This novel way of taking the culture of the past out of its traditional setting and giving it contemporary meaning has far-reaching implications.

During the era of the *Bildungsbürger* (the educated middle class who supported German culture from the eighteenth to the middle of the twentieth century), the cultural past had its fixed place in the schools, universities, theaters, and museums. This past with its inflexible canon of significant literary works formed the basis for a continuing cultural elite.

But established historical reference points such as "Enlightenment," "Storm and Stress," "Romanticism," or "Classical Antiquity," eventually lost their significance. This development freed writers from established traditions and enabled them to seek in the past new ways of interpreting the present. This is not the first time a fresh approach to the past has been discovered. Greek antiquity's classical art was once the interest solely of the aristocracy, but the Weimar classicism of Goethe and Schiller along with Johann Joachim Winckelmann's work made its moral and aesthetic aspects accessible to the emerging bourgeoisie.

Christa Wolf's *Kassandra,* published in 1983, is a reinterpretation of classical mythology that has a broad significance for contemporary German culture. The plot of her story is simple enough: the city of Troy has fallen to the Greeks. They return to their native Greece with the spoils of their victory, which includes the visionary Kassandra, daughter of the Trojan king, Priamos. She prophesies that the Greek king who is bringing her to Greece will die the day he arrives and that she will also die at the hands of the king's wife, Klytemnestra. Wolf concentrates on one moment in the mythic tale: Kassandra in the carriage just before she enters the gate of the Greek city. This moment provides us with the memories, feelings, and fears of Kassandra and opens up to the heroine and to the reader the rich cultural texture of myth. Glimpses into a matriarchal consciousness that predates patriarchal society, the life of the woman (Kassandra), who refuses to be an object of history, and the warning and insistent plea of a contemporary author who fears the ultimate fateful consequence of the thirst to dominate, namely nuclear obliteration, are all interwoven. The work is not only central to contemporary feminist consciousness (although Wolf cannot be called a feminist in Western political terms), it also makes an important contribution to the neosubjective trend in literature by expanding its scope to include mythological and political elements. Last, but not least, *Kassandra* is a German's plea against making the continent a victim in the global struggle of the superpowers.

## EXCURSION: THE PROBLEM OF NATIONAL IDENTITY

One of West Germany's principal preoccupations in the late seventies was the question of a national identity. The thirtieth anniversary in 1979 of the two German states and the television series "Holocaust" in 1978–1979 triggered in Germany an extensive and soul-searching national debate over its Nazi past. Writers, cultural critics, political scientists, and sociologists on radio and TV, in newspapers, journals, and books, dealt with many key issues that touched the core of West Germany's postwar democracy. Several factors gave the discussion of national identity an added poignancy. First of all, West Germany as an export nation is immediately exposed to any downturns in the global economy. Secondly, a divided country with young democratic institutions sees all political strife and social conflicts as a threat to the fundamental principles of democracy. Furthermore, West Germany is culturally not a pluralistic society and thus particularly averse to cultural and political diversity in spite of the fact that its constitution is progressive and supportive of diversity. Finally, West Germany is gradually drifting away from the influence of the United States. This emergence of a "German way," vague as it is, may have far-reaching consequences not yet fully apparent.

Two general trends have characterized the debate over national identity: 1) The Germans display a remarkable impatience and intolerance when assessing their democratic institutions. The political right argues that radical criticism of the system will undermine it, while the left believes that the democratic institutions have failed to provide protection for civil liberties. As proof the right points to the activities of the extreme left, not just left liberals but left-wing terrorists. The left points to the persecution of dissidents and the extensive data bank at Wiesbaden that records the social, political, and economic behavior of West Germans as thoroughly as any totalitarian state; 2) Both on the political right and left, the Germans show an increasing interest in issues of nationalism. The right reaffirms the reunification goal set down in West Germany's federal constitution, while the left, which includes groups stressing issues of peace and ecology, advocates a *Nationalneutralismus* (a reunification based on neutrality and nationalism). This national neutralism advocated by the left touches the German population as a whole because of the widespread awareness that a nuclear war would make "Germany a shooting gallery of the superpowers" (*Die Zeit,* November 17, 1981), and end civilized life in the center of Europe. While both sides of the political spectrum are articulate about what went wrong and what ought to be done about it, both reveal considerable uncertainty as to their own ideological premises. The left recognizes that, "There is no orientation anymore. There is not one single revolutionary movement, even more, there is not one single socialist country upon which we could build . . ." (*96,* 516).

There is a similar uncertainty on the right about individualism and its role in a democratic society:

As to the question of a new principle of individualism, which would not discard the achievements of bourgeois political culture but expand

and increase them . . . from where should the forces come that would show the way to a quasi-postbourgeois individualism no longer based on the repression of others?

(96, 537)

One feature common to many of the comprehensive specula-tions concerning national identity is an insistence on local and re-gional issues and the conditions that affect everyday life. At first glance, the quest for a national identity seems to reinforce broad "systems explanations." This is not at all the case. The new subjec-tivist trend is linked with the larger political and cultural context: the ecological movement and the fear of nuclear war provide the connection between personal and global realities. Thus, contem-porary neosubjectivism and collective interests directed against both major military blocks in Europe merge in Germany to provide the first outlines of a major shift in Central Europe; it may eventu-ally affect all spheres of society—cultural, economic, and political.

Günter Grass, 1927-
(Courtesy of the German Information Center)

Hans Magnus Enzensberger, 1929-
(Courtesy of the German Information Center)

WEST GERMAN CULTURE

Heinrich Böll, 1917-1985.
(Courtesy of the German
Information Center)

Peter Weiss, 1916-1982.
(Courtesy of the German Information Center)

Rolf Hochhuth, 1931-
(Courtesy of the German Information Center)

Uwe Johnson, 1934-1984.
(Courtesy of the German Information Center)

Margarethe von Trotta, filmmaker. (Courtesy of the filmmaker)

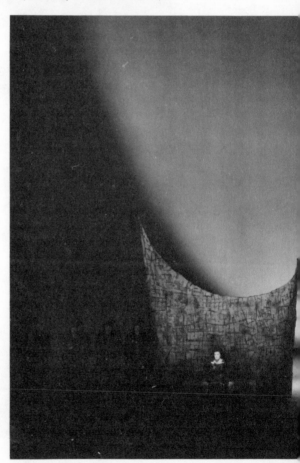

Rainer Werner Fassbinder, filmmaker. (Courtesy of Film-verlag der Autoren)

Wieland Wagner's staging of *Tristan und Isolde* in Bayreuth. (Courtesy of the German Information Center)

Christa Wolf, 1929-
(Courtesy of the German
Information Center)

Heiner Müller, 1929-
(Courtesy of the German Information Center)

1958 West German Poster:
  No Tests
  No Nuclear Weapons
  We protest against nu-
  clear arms buildup
  *[Undersigned]*
  Committee Against Nu-
  clear Arms

Politicians of all parties made an effort to carry on a dialogue with critical and rebellious students in the late sixties and early seventies. Professor Ralf Dahrendorf (FDP) during a discussion with student leader Rudi Dutschke in 1968. (Courtesy of the German Information Center)

The largest Bonn demonstration took place on June 10, 1982, as 350,000 people protested against further arms escalation during the NATO Summit Meeting. (Courtesy of the German Information Center)

# GUEST WORKERS

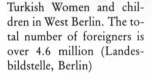

Turkish Women and children in West Berlin. The total number of foreigners is over 4.6 million (Landesbildstelle, Berlin)

Turkish shops in the Kreuzberg district of West Berlin. (Courtesy of the German Information Center)

Map of the Federal Republic of Germany (West Germany), German Democratic Republic (East Germany), and Berlin.

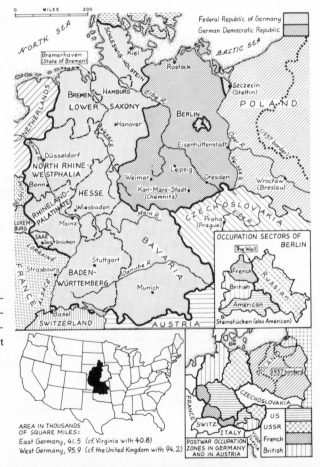

AREA IN THOUSANDS
OF SQUARE MILES:
East Germany, 41.5 (cf. Virginia with 40.8)
West Germany, 95.9 (cf. the United Kingdom with 94.2)

# Chapter V

# THE EARLY EIGHTIES

## 1. Problems in West Germany

### THE ECONOMY

In 1979 the Federal Republic celebrated its thirtieth anniversary with reason to be proud. Out of the rubble the older generation had rebuilt a country of great material wealth while laying the foundation for a stable democracy. Today West Germany plays an increasingly assertive role among the superpowers. For three decades progress meant growth in the GNP and an ever higher standard of living. But at the same time the economic boom began to show signs of ending, the younger generation raised doubts about the value of economic achievement and the legitimacy of democratic institutions.

*Der Spiegel* devoted three issues to the West German mood of uncertainty, depression, and *Angst* in January and February of 1982. It related personal anxieties to larger sociopolitical concerns: first, a general cultural malaise became apparent in the increasingly sharp criticism of technological progress as a road to humanity's destruction. Second, an economic crisis engendered by two oil price explosions and "Reaganomics," made itself felt with a rapid rise in interest rates, unemployment, the national debt, and a deficit federal budget. (Reaganomics influences West Germany because three quarters of the European Money Market transactions are in dollars). Third, West Germans suffered a crisis of collective identity, centered around the question: what kind of state is the Federal Republic and what does it want to be (*Der Spiegel,* Nov. 3, 1982, p. 70).

The three crises are interdependent; they find expression in a mixture of contradictory feelings and attitudes. Whereas some call for more intervention by the state, others demand less state inter-

215

ference. While some, afraid of losing everything, strive to keep what they have gained, others call for sweeping changes and a transformation of society (restoration versus reforms).

Are West Germans really less well off than they used to be? Is the German reputation as an economic giant no longer deserved (*The New York Times,* March 1981)? On the surface, things have never been better. In 1979 two-thirds of the work force earned at least $750.00 a month, more than their American counterparts. Most West German workers have six weeks of paid vacation, "thirteen-month" salaries, and they share with the Belgians, French, and Austrians the shortest work week in Europe. Comprehensive social security laws protect workers from unemployment, illness, and deprivations in old age. West Germany continues as one of the major contributors to international trade with an 8.8 percent share of the world's total exports in 1984.

But the period of high growth in Europe seems to have come to an end. The 1970s clearly belonged to the Japanese, who outperformed all other industrial nations. With a decline in population growth, zero economic growth, low returns on investments, aging industries such as steel and shipbuilding, and a precarious foreign trade balance, West Germans may have to become accustomed to a lower standard of living. Unemployment and inflation are only two symptoms of a recession that has burdened the state with debts. The estimated cost of unemployment compensation for the two million unemployed in 1982 alone was DM 18 billion.

Unemployment, caused by the downturn of the economy, the entrance into the job market of the baby-boom generation (including for the first time many women job seekers), and automation, threatens to become the chief economic problem of the 1980s. Many West German firms (about 12,000 in 1981) have gone bankrupt as a result of the severe recession. AEG-Telefunken, the second largest electronics enterprise, hovered on the brink of financial disaster, with 100,000 jobs at stake, and was purchased by a French firm. Less mobile than their American counterparts because of a traditional preference for working close to their homes and neighborhoods, West Germans resist being transferred. A survey in Bonn in 1981 found only one out of sixty-five unemployed workers willing to ride a factory bus to a new work place an hour away.

Of major concern are the many thousands of overtrained jobless academics (115,000 were on record at the Federal Labor Office in Frankfurt in 1985), as well as the technical-school graduates *(Berufsschüler)* who frequently search in vain for jobs. Statistics revealed that in 1983 some 30,000 young people were looking with little hope for apprenticeships. Even well-trained and certified job applicants are administered qualifying examinations that test education and aptitude before prospective employers will consider their applications. Admission to job-training programs has become fiercely competitive (for example, out of four hundred applicants for nursing school in Essen, only twenty-five were accepted for further consideration in 1981).

Particularly for young job seekers, employment prospects will decline even further because of labor-saving technologies, over-crowding in certain fields, and finally, because of overqualification brought about by the educational reforms of the 1970s. In the lat-ter development those with more education tend to displace those with less education from positions that once were open to them—for example, *Abiturienten* dislodge *Realschul*-graduates from pro-spective apprenticeships, while the latter fill the slots formerly reserved for *Hauptschüler.*

Economic as well as political uncertainties are all-pervasive while answers are few. The realization that everyone has to work harder and earn less has been extremely slow in coming. Personal sacrifices are unpopular among West Germans, who tend to expect solutions from their government. A comprehensive program of economic incentives and restructuring has been proposed. To meet growing competition from Third World countries with their lower labor costs, old industries (e.g., steel and shipbuilding) have to be phased out or retooled. The future is said to rest in high-technology goods and organizational know-how. The FRG is attempting to regain its edge in international competition by pro-moting mechanical engineering (machine tooling is the most im-portant pillar of West Germany's industry) and by stimulating automobile production and sales (in per capita terms, car exports are still three times higher than Japan's). West Germans also look to their chemical industries for a needed upturn. Finally, both indus-try and state encourage capital-equipment investment, subsidize research, and seek new export opportunities abroad.

Labor has had to make sizeable concessions (IG-Chemie, a major trade union, is doing without a pay raise), raises for civil servants were postponed in 1982, and a curtailed work week has been in-troduced in some industries. Recipients of unemployment benefits are now required to accept either retraining or lesser jobs; chil-dren's allowances, student grants, and pensions are all being cut back; and the government has established a job-generating pro-gram. With unemployment at an all-time high of 10 percent in Jan-uary 1984—higher than it had been for a quarter century—the specter of Germany's economic depression and Nazi past gave rise to concern at home and abroad.

Yet hopeful signs have emerged as well. As an international cur-rency, the DM is in second place behind the dollar and accounts for 14 percent of world trade (invoicing). Politically and financially, West Germany is still the safest place in the world for U.S. investments. This is especially true since exports pulled the economy out of its malaise, contributing to a reduction in the balance-of-payments deficit and putting West Germany ahead of the U.S. in the export of industrial goods (1982). As exports, which produced about a quarter of the GNP, recovered, merchants benefited from the appreciation of the dollar, and the return to a relatively low inflation rate (2 percent in 1984), the quality and reputation of German goods, reliable contracts, and an excellent service network. Last, but not least, in the early 1980s West Germany paid its oil bills on the spot because of surpluses in its exports to the OPEC countries.

## THE QUEST FOR PEACE

The most striking phenomenon of the early eighties is undoubtedly the antinuclear movement, which has not only caught on in West Germany but has become the most crucial peace movement in Europe. Nuclear anxiety arose from fear of Washington's bellicose rhetoric about the Soviet Union at a time when Chancellor Schmidt urged NATO to redress the imbalance that gave the Warsaw Pact a two-to-one advantage over the Western alliance in European-theater long- and medium-range nuclear warheads. This is not the first time that antinuclear protests have swept the country, nor are they limited to West Germany, to one single issue, or to one protest group. Nuclear anxiety seems also to be the catalyst for many uncertainties of modern life with which a new generation is faced: alienation between young and old, the gap between political theory and reality, disappointment with democratic institutions, fear that technology and materialism will destroy nature, and frustrations with massive unemployment. But above all, this *Angst* is felt most strongly by the first generation to grow up with the possibility of global annihilation through a nuclear holocaust. Behind young people's protests against the social structure lies "a deep instinctive insistence . . . on sheer survival—on survival as individuals, as parents, and as members of a civilization" (George Kennan, *The Monitor,* December 7, 1981). U.S. talk about a nuclear warning shot in Central Europe, the deployment of neutron bombs, and a limited and winnable nuclear war threatens the Germans with annihilation, since they live on the ideological and military boundary between East and West. Although the peace movement is especially important to West Germans, it has assumed European dimensions and has spread to the U.S. and Japan, as well as to the East-bloc countries.

In this century the tradition of pacifism goes back to disarmament parades by youths in Holland, Denmark, Belgium, and France in the late 1930s—parades incidentally that proved to the

Nazis that the Western democracies were decadent and unwilling to defend themselves, as some conservative thinkers had predicted in the nineteenth century (e.g., Heinrich von Treitschke). Germany's tradition goes back before WWI to the SPD's futile efforts under Karl Liebknecht to control the military establishment. After 1945, the international framework for peace between the major powers through the United Nations was generally successful only because both sides maintained nuclear forces in balance. As early as in the 1950s, the issues of nuclear arms for the *Bundeswehr* and atomic-weapons research (at Aldermaston, near London) gave rise to very strong protests. "Ban the Bomb" marches were first organized by Bertrand Russell and the left wing of the British Labour Party. They spread to the SPD and the churches in West Germany (e.g., the protest of eighteen German nuclear scientists in 1957, the committee "Death to the Atom Bomb," a mass rally in Hamburg in 1958). These German pacifist demonstrations against Adenauer's policies came to an end as a result of the Berlin crisis of 1958, the Godesberg platform of the SPD (1959) which supported Adenauer's rearmament policy, and the election of John F. Kennedy in 1960, who was popular with the Germans. The plan for a nuclear free zone, advanced by Adam Rapacki, the Polish Foreign Minister in 1957, was unacceptable to the West because it would have neutralized Germany. And neutralization was interpreted as selling out to the Soviets. During the early 1960s, Easter marches continued, but without SPD participation. Later in the decade the *Ostpolitik* of the SPD's Willy Brandt attracted and absorbed many pacifist sentiments. It won him a Nobel Peace Prize and renewed hope for peace.

In the late 1970s the peace movement reemerged first in Holland, then in England with Michael Foot's Labour Party, and in West Germany. This time the movement in West Germany was directed against the SPD-led government, with national demonstrations by a "post-materialistic" youth generation born in the 1950s and 1960s. The catalyst was American foreign and defense policy and the concurrent NATO decision to deploy a new generation of nuclear weapons in Europe. But beyond this specific issue, young pacifists question the basic structure of society and its political institutions, traditional values, as well as Europe's dependence on the U.S. Like the student rebellion of 1968, this is also a generational conflict, only this time with minimal interest in Marxist theory. In spite of the hostility between the generations, the peace movement includes both young and old, the political left (SPD, communists, trade unions), the churches, the "alternatives" (various counterculture groups), the unemployed university graduates, as well as some terrorists, who have attacked U.S. installations in the hopes of exploiting the new pacifist movement for their own ends.

Most important is the leadership provided by Lutheran ministers. Church groups have increasingly called attention to the Fifth Commandment and the Sermon on the Mount and have rallied many nonpolitical youths to their cause, for example, at the Protestant Church Meeting in Hamburg in 1981. Leaders of the Reformed Church and of the Roman Catholic group *Pax Christi* work together with Lutherans (Peace Corps of Atonement—*Aktion Sühnezeichen*) in order to promote peace policy. The Lutheran Heinrich Albertz, former SPD mayor of West Berlin, is now a major spokesman of FRG pacifism. Nobel laureate Heinrich Böll has become the peace movement's literary conscience.

Antinuclear demonstrations grew nationwide in 1981, spreading from Hamburg to Berlin and Bonn. The Krefeld Appeal, although communist-backed (DKP), was supported by an entire spectrum of churches, trade unions, and pacifists. It collected over five million signatures in support of peace. A quarter of a million demonstrators rallied in Bonn. Although the demonstration included hundreds of disparate antinuclear groups, its unifying element was the initial call for unilateral disarmament of the West. Demands included total abolition of the *Bundeswehr,* resignation from NATO, and a rejection of new U.S. medium-range missiles in Central Europe.

Some pacifists have gone so far as to view the stalemate between the superpowers as an opportunity to work for a new German state, a reunited neutral Germany, after both Soviet and U.S. forces have withdrawn from German soil. Their aim is national neutralism *(Nationalneutralismus)* to be achieved by the withdrawal of the two Germanys from their respective pact systems, by political and economic confederation, and finally by a peace treaty ("Berliner Plan," 1981).

When Willy Brandt inaugurated his *Ostpolitik* he claimed: "A good German cannot be a nationalist." Now Peter Brandt, his son, leader of one faction of national neutralism, asserts in a manner reminiscent of the immediate postwar years that the road to a united and peaceful Europe must be built on a reunited neutral Germany *(226)*. Many representatives of the establishment parties, however, believe that neutralism would amount to Soviet supremacy in the long run, and might possibly invite aggression. Therefore, church-backed segments of the peace movement have publicly denied any connection with a new German nationalism.

The controversy is intense. Pacifists call those who oppose them warmongers, and the supporters of a nuclear military see in the pacifists "Moscow's fifth column." One side cannot accept the paradox inherent in the "balance of terror" (Churchill, 1947), the other side fails to appreciate fully the dangers of an accidental nuclear war, given the complexities of modern electronically guided defense systems. Nuclear physicist Carl Friedrich von Weizsäcker thinks it likely that unilateral disarmament and the resulting dissolution of NATO ("Berliner Plan") would destabilize the chances for peace (*Die Zeit,* April 2, 1982). Yet while peace is the only hope of the young generation for survival, immediate solutions are not in sight. This very real dilemma contributes toward increasing political polarization in West German society in the eighties.

Despite their organizational weakness (no president, no national committee, but a multi-faceted grass-roots movement), the pacifist groups have been successful in forcing Western governments to negotiate with the Soviets. They have made people aware that immediate measures must be taken to prevent the "unthinkable." At the same time, the imposition of martial law in Poland in 1981 made the pacifists more aware of Soviet military power. It undercut the argument that the peace campaign is a pan-European movement only against the hawks in Washington, who have stationed new US missiles on the continent. After Polish martial law, writers from both Western and Eastern European nations have supported the peace movement. This fact seems to validate Weizsäcker's statement "that the European peace movement is neither essentially anti-American nor in any way pro-Soviet" (ibid.).

The fear of nuclear war has spelled the collapse of a foreign policy consensus in effect since the Adenauer era. Although the *Bundestag* voted to accept the installation of new US missiles, the SPD opposition turned against deployment. A common West German security policy has come to an end because the SPD, with an altered political platform (Cologne, December 1983), is again, as in the early 1950s, in search of a solution to the division of Germany that relies less on the US and NATO and emphasizes rather detente and a broadening of East-West German contacts.

The peace movement has not been restricted to the West but has surfaced also in Romania, Hungary, Poland, Czechoslovakia, the Soviet Union, and the GDR. Although the Lutheran Church in East Germany is not as strong as is the Catholic Church in Poland, compulsory military training for ninth and tenth grades in 1978, and for eleventh graders in 1981 sparked a peace initiative within the East German Lutheran Church that called for alternative social service for conscientious objectors. Soon afterwards the "Berlin Appeal" initiated by an East German pastor advocated that peace instruction replace military instruction in schools, that the production and sale of military hardware cease, and that all foreign troops and weapons be removed. The Rostock Appeal of 100 GDR citizens to their government to reject the stationing of new Soviet nuclear missiles followed in 1983.

Public peace rallies were permitted at Potsdam and in Dresden, and at the December 1981 meeting of German writers in Berlin,

GDR author Stefan Hermlin defended East Berlin demonstrations against the nuclear arms race of the superpowers. About 5,000 people took to the streets in Dresden and participated in peace discussions organized by the Lutheran Church. Ironically, the GDR authorities who had previously praised the international peace movement finally became targets of their own propaganda. As in the West, the government argues that peace must be maintained by a military machine. Accordingly, antiwar demonstrations have been deemed unnecessary since the party and the government are the "real" guardians of peace. A plea of the East German churches to the government not to criminalize pacifism has gone unheeded. Young people who persisted in wearing the Soviet peace badge "Swords into Ploughshares" have lost their jobs or have been suspended from the university. Some leaders of the pacifist movement were even exiled from the GDR in 1983.

## THE ECOLOGY AND THE SEARCH
## FOR ALTERNATIVES

West German pacifism is only one current in a larger political and cultural movement that embraces other ecological issues including peacetime use of nuclear energy, housing, the preservation of woodlands, and, alternative personal life styles and values. These diffuse, antiestablishment causes have found partial expression in a new grass-roots party, "the Greens" *(die Grünen)*.

While the first stirrings of "green" sentiments were voiced in simple requests, such as for youth centers, they have deepened and broadened with time to embrace alternative lifestyles that acknowledge the importance of the ecological system *(Öko-System")* to the sustaining of human life. Many West German youths are hostile to science and technology; they are also opposed to the entire "system"—its parties, its parliament, its capitalist economy, its militarism, and its often brutal overreactions to protest demonstrations. There are some discernible links between the heterogeneous alternative movement and the German Youth Movement *(Jugendbewegung)* of 1900–1933 as well as to the American counterculture generations of the beats in the 1950s and the hippies in the 1960s. They scorn materialism; perferring to *be* rather than to *have*. They withdraw emotionally from the traditional ideals of achievement, consumerism, and technology, and instead emphasize self-expression, creativity, and self-help in a community spirit. They drop out from the economic rat race and reject the entire bourgeois system of rewards and entitlements.

All this constitutes a powerful reaction to the consumerism that since WWII galvanized West German society into working for a higher standard of living, based on performance and material benefits but at the expense of "postmaterialistic" values such as self-determination, community spirit, codetermination, and interpersonal communication. These highly emotional altruistic ideals, rediscovered by alternative groups, stress communal and anticapitalist notions of living and working together—solidarity, equality, equal pay for equal work, a minimal concern with profit, reduction of labor specialisation, and concern for the environment. On the one hand, these new values serve as a critical mirror held up to capitalist society; on the other, they express the desire to make the world more livable, more humane, embracing Ernst Bloch's philosophy of hope: "The human being is the creature who has a promising future ahead" (*108, 181*).

Central to the understanding of the alternative movement are the concepts of self-help and independent initiative as counterweights to consumerism and materialism. The Berlin "scene" contains a myriad of "alternative" enterprises such as dairies, farms, organic food stores, restaurants, communes, publishing companies (e.g., the *Tageszeitung,* TAZ, with a circulation of 33,000, health services, schools, environmental initiatives, women's rights' way stations, taxi collectives, and moving companies. The Berlin catalogue of alternative projects *(Alternativkatalog)* contains about 2,000 addresses of self-help initiatives loosely held together by an umbrella organization called "Network Self-Help" *(Netzwerk Selbsthilfe),* which serves about 100,000 people.

Although the alternative movement is extremely heterogeneous, consisting of environmental protesters and civil-rights leaders, Marxists, pacifists, feminists, gays, and squatters, they all rally to any cause that challenges the state. In many cases, members of the alternative scene have simply dropped out of society, turned their backs on jobs and studies in order to live according to their hearts' desire and on whatever the countereconomy can provide. They "squat," or set up commune-style housekeeping in abandoned empty quarters of the inner city (Berlin, 1979) as a means of focusing attention on inadequate housing and exorbitant rents. Violent confrontations between police and squatters have occurred all over Europe, in Amsterdam, Zurich, Nuremberg (1980), and West Berlin (1982). Not all participants are political activists, but once a local issue emerges, such as over airport-runway expansion at Frankfurt, destruction of forests for highway construction between Berlin and Hamburg, or over nuclear-waste disposal at Gorleben in Lower Saxony, many respond militantly to prevent a "crime" against the environment, attracting in many cases the support of the local populace.

To make a living in the alternative scene is usually not possible without subsidies from the despised state. For instance, *TAZ* receives financial support from the Berlin Senate as do informative video-tape projects, way stations for women, alternative clinics, and other efforts (in 1982 the Berlin Senate earmarked DM 52 million for self-help projects). The counterculture is in a dilemma: it has broken away from the system and militantly confronts the state wherever it sees its new work ethic ("do what you like without profiting") and its communal relations in harmony with nature endangered. Yet on the other hand, its projects cannot survive without state protection and subsidies. Alternative people in West Germany as well as in the U.S. reject and ridicule the formal aspects of institutionalized, representative democracy in the British tradition (e.g., of Edmund Burke), and instead practice a "direct democracy" according to Jean-Jacques Rousseau's model of a *contrat social.* Accordingly, everyone should have the same rights and duties in communal politics.

It would seem that parliamentary party politics should be anathema to the counterculture and its economy. But the surprising fact is that out of citizens' initiatives and ecological concerns the new Green party has emerged. It is practicing Rousseau's ideal of a "basic democracy" by binding elected representatives closely to the will of the electorate and by rotating its members of parliament every two instead of every four years.

This *"Antipartei-Partei"* has become the voice of the ecological movement, the peace movement, the women's movement, and of many alternative church and socialist groups. Its party platform advocates foremost: civil disobedience, and resistance to the established parties and their policies of military and civilian use of nuclear power. As Petra Kelly states: "The more civil disobedience . . . is employed and the more citizens' initiatives and self-help projects are founded, the closer we come to a genuinely democratic society" (*Der Spiegel,* No. 24, 1982, p. 49). True, a party organized as if it were no party seems contradictory, but its antiestablishment, anti-SPD program has been so successful since 1980 that its elected representatives are seated in six state parliaments. In 1983 it cleared the 5 percent hurdle (5.6 percent) in the national elections. It remains to be seen, however, whether the Greens with such a diverse and volatile group of supporters will stand the test of time. So far, their party has failed to establish a firm political identity.

For the government as well as the alternative scene, energy supplies and environmental protection have become crucial issues over the last decade. With stringent conservation efforts in force, oil consumption in 1983 was below the 1973 level (only 9 percent of electricity was generated by oil in 1978) whereas coal production has been on the rise again and natural-gas supply contracts have been made with Algeria, the Netherlands, and the USSR. With the opening of a coal liquefaction plant at Bottrop in the Ruhr region, the Federal Republic has reduced its dependence on imported oil. Significant advances have also been made in developing wind and solar energy. But atomic energy, which provids 30 percent of the FRG's electricity from more than a dozen reactors (in 1985), causes the greatest controversy between those who want to increase the number of nuclear power stations and others who are concerned about safety and environmental impact. Radioactive waste has been termed Europe's number one nuclear-energy worry, at least through the eighties, a problem put into sharp focus in West Germany by massive demonstrations not only against the building of new plants (at Brokdorf, near Hamburg) but also against nuclear waste reprocessing plants and underground storage facilities (at Gorleben, near Lüneburg).

West German waterways have deteriorated significantly because of detergent dumping and industrial waste. The Rhine and Elbe rivers have become "open drains" so severely polluted by chemicals that fish are hardly able to survive in them. Automobile exhaust, oil heating, and factories pollute the air. The North Sea's ecosystem is threatened with irreversible damage, and elsewhere plants and animals are becoming extinct at an alarming rate. Above all, the German forests are suffering and dying rapidly as a result of acid rain and exhausted soil, for example, in Bavaria, Baden-Württemberg, and Lower Saxony.

Environmentalists have successfully lobbied for a number of environmental protection laws: a Waste Removal Law, 1972; (Federal Environmental Agency founded, Berlin 1974); Smog Emission Law, 1974; Detergents Law, 1975; Effluency Levies Act, 1978. Since 1981 environmental crimes (including water pollution and construction of faulty nuclear plants) have been incorporated into the West German criminal code. As a result, there have been considerable improvements in combatting smog (e.g., in the Ruhr district), in waste disposal, and in water-quality control. For the first time in twenty-five years, salmon are being caught again in the upper Rhine region.

Peace, the economy, and a change in values are the overriding concerns on the minds of most West Germans in the eighties. The alternative movement believes the future is at stake, but, if the environmentalists have their way, West Germany's performance as an exporting country may suffer.

Former Chancellor Schmidt issued a warning to the advocates of the counterculture:

I think it is a good idea that young citizens turn against an overemphasis on material values. I think it is right when young people search for new alternative lifestyles. But: a total rejection of society, a total withdrawal into the private sphere is questionable, particularly when they want a share in society's institutions when these are advantageous to them.

(Scala No. 9, 1981, p. 15)

# THE END OF AN ERA

The social-liberal coalition of the SPD-FDP with its expensive reform programs dissolved in 1982 when a "constructive" vote of no confidence (one in which the replacement has already been selected) forced Helmut Schmidt of the SPD to yield the chancellorship to Helmut Kohl of the CDU. The dismal state of the economy together with basic disagreements over remedies brought down the coalition that had been in power since 1969. Social and political reforms, which overextended the welfare system, had depleted the coffers of the state and incurred huge debts.

The era of SPD rule had consisted of two phases, the Brandt-coalition between 1969 and 1974 and the Schmidt-coalition of 1974 to 1982. The FDP had joined Brandt's government in 1969 because it was, like the Chancellor himself, convinced of the necessity for the West Germans to come to terms with the results of WWII and to establish a constructive relationship with their eastern neighbors. This reconciliatory trend initiated by the SPD found expression not only in *Ostpolitik* but also in a policy of reexamining the "suppressed part of German history, the Weimar Left, the emigrants, the sufferings of all those persecuted by the Nazis" (Ralf Dahrendorf, *Die Zeit,* October 1, 1982). However, this reform-minded spirit of conciliation was short-lived. The turning point came as early as 1973 with the oil-price explosion, with strikes, and with a spy case, the Guillaume affair. While the world economy retrenched to cope with the global recession, the left wing of the SPD, buoyed by its success in the federal elections of 1972, rushed ahead with its reform programs.

When the moderate Helmut Schmidt became Chancellor, he used his coalition partner the FDP (which was in control of key federal departments such as Justice and Interior) to slow down radical reforms, but only with limited success, to the dismay of the conservative and liberal middle class. Historians have resurrected the term "cultural revolution" (*Kulturkampf,* from the Bismarck era) to describe the Social Democratic years in government as an attempt to "turn bourgeois Germany inside out" (Hans-Peter Schwarz, *Die Zeit,* October 29, 1982) in schools and universities, in literature and theater, and in the mass media. The "struggle for equal opportunities" appears in retrospect as a

venture onto thin ice. Instead of quantity, people clamored for quality; instead of the individual, for the collective; instead of the materialistic, for the humane; instead of the free market economy, for political arrangements, instead of spontaneity, for regulated provisions.

(H. Gierisch, *Wirtschaftswoche,* July 30, 1982)

When Helmut Schmidt stepped down in 1982, his government was replaced by a "coalition of the fifties" (Hans-Dietrich Genscher, i.e., CDU/FDP) which wanted to strengthen the FRG's Western ties and roll back reforms by cutting costs. Although Schmidt's removal from office, brought about by a parliamentary switch in allegiance by the FDP, left a considerable political vacuum in West Germany, his place in history is secure (Henry Kissinger, *Der Spiegel,* October 11, 1982). After Adenauer and Brandt, he was the third greatest chancellor of the Federal Republic. He held power twice as long as Brandt. Having served as senator in Hamburg, as SPD party leader, and as secretary of the Treasury and Economics before he rose to the chancellorship made Schmidt the best equipped politician in the West to deal with the economic recession. Because of his undisputed international stature he has been referred to as "sometime deputy leader of the Western world" (Elizabeth Pond, *The Monitor,* September 20, 1982). Schmidt did not shy away from expressing the West German views on Reaganomics and detente in a climate of increasing East-West polarization. One of his major achievements was to prod Washington and Moscow into a dialogue on nuclear disarmament. Unlike Adenauer or Brandt, however, Schmidt lacked a mandate to bring about major changes in the Federal Republic. With the Eastern treaties ratified, the last phase of the reconstruction period was completed. The FRG, a mid-size power, was securely anchored to the Western alliance; at the same time, it was able to play a mediating role between East and West. Schmidt succeeded in balancing the Adenauer *(Westpolitik)* and the Brandt *(Ostpolitik)* legacies without sacrificing either one as his special relationships with Giscard d'Estaing and Leonid Brezhnev proved. It was largely due to Schmidt that inflation and unemployment were kept relatively low, giving the FRG considerably more economic stability compared to the other industrialized democracies. As Theo Sommer (*Die Zeit,* November 5, 1982) pointed out, Schmidt was neither authoritarian like Adenauer, nor confident of a better future like Brandt. Instead, his achievements derived from his insistence on common sense, on continuity, and on politics as the art of the possible. Above all, he showed West Germans how, after decades of extraordinary successes, to adapt to more moderate expectations.

West Germany's fourth postwar era has begun with Helmut Kohl at the helm, elected as a majority chancellor of the CDU/CSU-FDP coalition in March of 1983. According to some conservative circles he has taken up the Adenauer legacy while adopting some of President Reagan's remedies to solve the economic crisis that brought him to power: less state and more emphasis on long-term budgetary restraint, on job-creating programs, as well as on the adjustment of social welfare benefits to the limits of the federal and state budgets. These economic policies have had a certain measure of success in bringing the inflation rate down from about 6 percent in 1982 to below 3 percent in 1984, unemployment down from over 10 percent to just over 8 percent.

A severe challenge to Kohl's government came from the metal workers' union when it went on strike in June of 1984 in favor of a 35-hour work week. However, a compromise average work week of 38.5 hours was finally decided on. Despite the prolonged strike, West Germany still managed to produce a large trade surplus in 1984. Among all Western nations, the FRG exported the most to the Eastern Bloc, including East Germany, which is virtually a tacit member of the EEC tariff-free zone. As a result of the favorable dollar-Deutschmark exchange rate the United States jumped (in West German exports) from sixth position to second place behind France for the first time since the early sixties. In addition, an economic as well as technological opening to China is promising a new market abroad.

In national European and international politics Helmut Kohl has stood his own ground. He carried out the NATO missile deployment in December of 1983 without polarizing the country. So far, he has been able to neutralize the rightwing Bavarian CSU led by Franz Josef Strauss with the center liberal FDP which, however, is rapidly loosing support among the voters in favor of the Greens.

Surprisingly enough, "the end of an era" has not led to a complete break with previously pursued policies. On the contrary, Chancellor Kohl has continued with West Germany's *Ostpolitik* begun more than a decade ago under SPD-leadership. Recognizing its responsibility for peace, the conservative Bonn government entered into a prolonged dialogue with the GDR Minister President and party chief Erich Honecker, who in turn stressed the need for "limiting the damage" in East-West relations and for a security partnership. Although Soviet pressure made his projected visit to West Germany impossible, the positive results of this dialogue are tangible; among them is East Germany's transfer of the West Berlin *S-Bahn* (surface rapid transit system), which it had controlled since 1945, to West Berlin administration; the sharp increase in family-visit approvals for trips to West Germany (more than a million retired East Germans were allowed to visit relatives in the FRG in 1983); a record number of over 25,000 emigrants permitted to leave the GDR in 1984; the gradual dismantling of the automatic shooting devices along the "wall"; and Lufthansa's opening of direct airline flights to the Leipzig industrial fair for the first time. Such concessions were motivated largely by economic, rather than political, considerations. Through huge credits, Bonn helps to maintain the GDR's high standard of living as well as its technological edge vis-à-vis the rest of the Soviet bloc. In the late 1970s those dissidents who applied for exit visas were often discriminated against in employment, put under surveillance, imprisoned, or found their children put up for forced adoption. Now, through these huge credits, West Germany is paying for their release as well as for those East German squatters in the West German mission in East Berlin (July, 1984) and the 140 refugees from the GDR who crowded into the embassy of the Federal Republic in Prague (fall, 1984).

There is a second area where Kohl has continued Adenauer's and Helmut Schmidt's policies; that is, in his cooperation with France. Initially, some problems developed between the conservative Kohl and the socialist François Mitterand over economic differences in the EEC and divergent reactions to martial law in Poland (1981–83). West Germany, with its precarious existence at the ideological and military frontier between East and West, reacted more cautiously than France or the United States to the Polish crisis in order to preserve some benefits from the previous decade of detente. But to everybody's surprise, the two leaders have gotten on better with each other than expected. During his six month's presidency of the European Council of Ministers (1984), Mitterand "relaunched Europe" not only by negotiating a compromise over British contributions to the EEC-budget but also by strenghtening the French-West German cooperation, which had flourished under Giscard d'Estaing and Helmut Schmidt. Their revived tandem approach is particularly visible in close defense coordination (e.g., helicopter and airbus production, joint military exercises, formation of a French rapid deployment force for friendly intervention in Germany) within the context of the resurrected Western-European Union (WEU) of 1954 with its seven members coordinating their defense; beyond this, cordial ties between the French and the Germans have been symbolized by their two leaders' linking hands at Verdun, on the anniversary of the major battle of WWI (1984). This has been the second of two great symbolic events in postwar ties between the former arch enemies; the first one was the joint attendance of a Mass in Reims Cathedral by Charles de Gaulle and Konrad Adenauer 25 years ago.

# 2.  Society and Culture: East Germany

## ECONOMIC GROWTH

The Stalinist phase of the GDR under the Walter Ulbricht regime roughly corresponded in time with the period of restoration in West Germany under Adenauer. It was gradually replaced during the sixties by the post-Stalinist era of massive economic growth, technological modernization, and considerable cultural activity as well as a heightened national self-confidence. Due to an effective use of human and material resources, the GDR emerged in the seventies and early eighties as one of the ten most technologically advanced societies in the world. The traditional German ability to mobilize under pressure, the efficiency of a Prussian civil service, a centralized political authority that muzzled dissent in the cultural sphere and encouraged productivity in the economic sphere— these were the factors that made the GDR the most advanced socialist country. In 1981 its per capita GNP stood at $9,750 (based on CIA estimates, *208*), roughly equivalent with Japan's of $9,780, and twice that of Italy's at $5,220. In 1981 the industrial output increased by 2.9 percent and the increase in agricultural production stood at 1.6 percent, generally surpassing the performance of western European countries. This robust economic performance is all the more remarkable because it was achieved with no unemployment (the GDR constitution guarantees the "right to a job") and no inflation. In addition, social services are comprehensive and include medical insurance, day-care centers, generous maternity leaves, and legally guaranteed sick leaves for all workers.

In 1963 the SED developed a modern plan for restructuring the economy (NÖS = *neues ökonomisches System*) that combined the centralized planning known in all socialist economies with elements of free enterprise at the local level, developed by the Soviet economist Yvey Liberman. The GDR used the most advanced technological theories in liberalizing their economic decision-making processes. While central control in all spheres of the society is still paramount, today the society no longer functions exclusively as a unified whole but rather as a constellation of various subsystems, each with its own intrinsic mode of operation. Together with encouraging local initiatives in the economic sphere, some degree of liberalization in the cultural sphere has also been possible. In effect, two decades later than the FRG, the GDR has had its own "economic miracle." It is less spectacular, to be sure, being more limited in scope, but also because its primary emphasis has been less on conspicuous consumption and more on other areas of economic productivity. Whether this period of sustained economic growth can be maintained depends to some degree on factors beyond the GDR's direct control, for example, rising raw-material prices and an oil dependency on the USSR.

Whereas the GDR can point toward great strides in the economic sphere since the early sixties, in the sphere of culture the problems inherent in state socialism remain acute, particularly the controversy about the function of writers and artists in a socialist state.

Several factors characterize the literary culture in the GDR that are not applicable to West Germany. First of all, writers are given an important role in shaping the values of society. The manifesto of one of the leading literary figures of the GDR, Johannes Becher, called literature "the most developed instrument people have to achieve insights into themselves" (61, 20)—a sentiment often echoed by leading political leaders at SED party congresses. There are three reasons for the state's interest in writers: (1) Marxism emphasizes the written text, foremost, of course, the writings of Karl Marx himself; (2) most socialist states lack Western-style mass culture with its emphasis on the visual and aural, and thus these states still find relevant the "older" form of social communication, namely writing and reading; (3) the culturally conservative SED regime encourages the preservation of the German literary heritage of the nineteenth century and its main genre, the novel. Although writers occupy a central place in socialist society, all social and literary communication is closely monitored by party functionaries and thus remains under state surveillance. On the one hand, writers are encouraged to "name conflicts, contradictions, things forgotten and repressed" (61, 26), on the other hand, they run the risk of being arrested or being stripped of their citizenship and deported if they cross the threshold of tolerance. The full ambiguity of the writer's role vis-à-vis the state is obvious in Erich Honecker's 1971 statement in which he advocated more artistic freedom: "If one starts from the firm position of socialism, there can be no taboos in the field of the arts and literature as far as I'm concerned" (61, 181). Thus the issue seems to involve less the notion of artistic liberty than the definition of socialism.

Secondly, the cultural scene closely reflects the political, social, and economic developments of the GDR from the end of WWII into the eighties. During this period the role of literature has ranged from nearly complete instrumentalization within the state to relative flexibility beyond the political context.

Thirdly, the utopian element central to Marxist theory sustains many GDR writers, even those who are critical of the reality of the state-run society. This explains the generally optimistic and affirmative tenor of much of East German writing in contrast to literature in the West. Beyond the positive hero of socialist realism, who is merely a set of norms dictated by the state, authentic and relatively independent writers such as the novelist Christa Wolf and the dramatist Heiner Müller never close out the possibility of a qualitative change for the better as one of the moving impulses in their works.

To view the literature of the GDR merely as a complement to the shifting cultural policies of the state ignores the variety and complexity of the creative work being done and obscures the tensions that do exist between a state bent on having its status quo affirmed and the writers who see their society as a promise yet to be kept.

# LITERATURE

Three major trends shape the literary culture of the GDR: antifascist literature, literature of socialist realism, and literature as personal calling.

1. Antifascist literature deals with the Nazi years, their political, personal, and moral significance and impact. The immediate postwar period provided the most supportive context for antifascist literature to flourish. This literature is broad and open-ended in its definition of what constitutes progressive writing, and it is pragmatic as to the role of literature in society. Not necessarily committed to a socialist future, it is strongly optimistic and utopian, and not restrictive in its choice of themes and literary forms. Finally, it counts bourgeois writers, such as Thomas Mann and Ricarda Huch within its ranks. The *Kulturbund zur demokratischen Erneuerung Deutschlands* (Cultural Association for the Democratic Renewal of Germany) founded in Allied occupied Germany in 1945 provided a focus for antifascist literature. Along with its political stance, this association advocated a turn to the German cultural past and the literary treasures of Germany in order ". . . to reawaken great German culture, the pride of our fatherland . . ." (Johannes Becher, *61, 39*). Cultural conservatism remained one of the hallmarks of East German literature in the decades to come. Political restoration under Adenauer in West Germany added fuel to the antifascist tone of East German literature: "In the shadow of the gallows of Nuremberg, the Krupps and cohorts got their billions back" (Stefan Hermlin, in "In diesem Mai 1955;" *230,* I, 126).

A significant example of antifascist literature in its early phase is Anna Seghers' work, *Das siebte Kreuz* (1942; *The Seventh Cross,* 1942), which deals with the flight of a concentration-camp inmate. Decried as propaganda in the West ("tear-jerking story, with a schoolbook didacticism;" *61, 93*), Bruno Apitz's controversial novel of 1958, *Nackt unter Wölfen* (1960, *Naked Among Wolves),* is based on the true story of a three-year-old Jewish girl who was smuggled into Buchenwald from Auschwitz in a suitcase and kept hidden by the inmates. A conflict arises when several communist inmates involved in saving the little girl also plan an uprising. American soldiers free the inmates towards the end of the war, and for the first time in her life the girl dares to cry out loud.

The later phase of antifascist literature that appeared in the sixties and seventies is best characterized by Christa Wolf's *Nachdenken über Christa T.* For Wolf and her generation it is no longer a matter of placing real or fictional events within a moral context of antifascism. Rather, the author shows how the fascist experience shaped individual consciousness and distorted individual behavior and speech in her own generation, which came of age in the postwar years. Unlike the Freudian unconscious—a universal paradigm in the West for revealing hidden elements in the individual human psyche—Christa Wolf's "patterns" (see *Kindheitsmuster,* 1965), interrelate private individual experience and the collective traumas of an entire generation.

2. The literature of socialist realism is the cultural expression of the building of the socialist state from 1949 onward. The general economic and political mobilization of the German lands east of the border under Walter Ulbricht's SED put a characteristic stamp on literature for more than two decades. Literature was assigned a specific political goal, namely motivation of the workers in the "development of enthusiasm for work on . . . all levels of the society" (Alexander Abusch, Minister of Culture during the first party congress of the SED held in 1948). This cultural policy remained intact (in spite of a short period of flexibility prior to the Hungarian uprising in 1956) to the end of the decade when the Fifth Congress of the SED told the writers in 1958, "to overcome the alienation between artists and people" (*61,* 87). This trend culminated in the *Bitterfelder Konferenz* (1959) in which writers were given the primary function of "clarifying ideological positions" (*184,* 61). Workers in turn told the writers in 1960: "Write as we are." One of the earliest victims of the *Bitterfelder Konferenz* was Bertolt Brecht himself. He had collaborated with the composer Paul Dessau in writing an opera, *Das Verhör des Lukullus* (1939; *The Trial of Lucullus,* 1943). After the premiere it was forbidden as too formalistic and not conforming to the party guidelines (*231,* 303). A number of writers and philosophers fled the GDR at the time, prominent among them was Ernst Bloch, the philosopher of hope. Some were incarcerated for a time by Ulbricht for their stated objections to the regime. It was not so much that the writers had launched a frontal attack on socialism but rather they had focused their criticism on the entrenched party bureaucracy's narrow views of "acceptable" literature.

The problems of workers and the worker's state were to be the exclusive themes for the writers to follow. The Hungarian Georg

Lukács had provided the theoretical base for socialist realism (although he fell into disgrace for his role during the Hungarian uprisings of 1956) by insisting that general values could be made more immediately relevant. His plea for the harmonizing of general principles and specific situations may be called the gentle or aesthetic side of totalitarianism. For the novel, it meant the appearance of the positive hero of socialist labor, and a search was on for individual paradigms of character and action appropriate to the building of a socialist society. Not only SED spokesmen were dedicated to the new task defined for them, also well-known writers such as Hermann Kant and Erwin Strittmatter set the patterns for the less gifted in writing novels of socialist realism.

The party congresses and the *Bitterfelder Konferenz* did not bring the literature of socialist realism into being. After all, Anna Seghers in her novel *Die Toten bleiben jung (The Dead Remain Young)*, written between 1945 and 1948, in part during her exile in Mexico, had set the pattern much earlier. In her novel Seghers places the story of three generations of fighters for the socialist cause against fascism and political reaction within an epic chronicle that traces the history of Germany from 1918 to 1945. Despite the stark realism pervading the novel, it is imbued with an indestructible optimism about the German socialist future.

By contrast, Erwin Strittmatter's novel *Ole Bienkopp* (1963; *Ole Bienkopp*, 1966) no longer projects the unbroken optimism of Seghers' postwar work. Written after the final consolidation of the GDR as a socialist state (1960: completion of agricultural collectivization; 1961: "closing of the open border," that is, the building of the Berlin Wall and border fortifications; 1963: new centralized economic planning), Strittmatter's novel depicts the dilemma of an active and imaginative party member and worker who runs up against the party apparatus, which resists him at every step either by design or by sheer bureaucratic inertia. The protagonist literally works himself to death without having been able to enjoy the results of his efforts.

3. A literature of socialist realism that embodies the theory and practice of the state along ideologically pure lines was bound to bring reactions from the writers themselves. The third major trend in GDR literature therefore, may be called "literature as personal calling" because it implies a belief in literature as literature without giving up the collective utopia inherent in Marxist thinking.

As early as 1950, Arnold Zweig, a writer with socialist loyalties, had insisted that "the human imagination is the only channel for finding a place in the innermost being of your fellow man" (*231*, 95). These sentiments were echoed by many GDR writers who became increasingly restive as the party leadership began to redefine the function of literature in ever more orthodox terms. In reaction to the manifesto of the *Bitterfelder Konferenz,* a hallmark of party control over the cultural scene, Franz Fühmann declared in an essay provocatively entitled "Nicht alle Wege führen nach Bitterfeld" ("Not all Roads lead to Bitterfeld," 1964): "The social task has frequently been defined and passionately discussed in recent years. It is what we describe with the formula 'the Bitterfeld Road.' But what about the personal calling?" (*231,* 212).

This reaction against the narrow path assigned to literature continued into the seventies when Heiner Müller saw the problem of the socialist state "not in the great literature of socialism but in the grimace of its cultural policy: the desperate falling back to the nineteenth century by unqualified functionaries" (19 September 1977; *231,* 308). The same author articulated the problem of his generation most revealingly: "The generation of those who are thirty today in the GDR has experienced socialism not as a hope for something else but as a deformed reality" (statement made in 1977; *61,* 15). Instead of sharing the utopian optimism of the older generation, who had developed a solidarity during the traumatic years of fascism, this younger generation was no longer satisfied with writing literature extolling the virtue of a state which had decreed that its promise was already fulfilled. The lyric poet Volker Braun pleaded: "Don't come to us with finished products. We need half-finished material. Away with cooked venison—give us the forest and the knife" (*61,* 170). Wolf Biermann turned to the authorities that were to oust him as an anarchical individualist:

> The Present, for you
> Sweet goal of all those bitter years,
> Is for me only a bitter beginning, and I scream
> For change.—
>
> (*61,*174)

Accordingly, the literature of socialist realism underwent a fundamental change by a generation that could no longer accept the political and cultural status quo as satisfactory. Central to this change was the "self-realization of the individual beyond an integration into the society" (Christa Wolf). The adjustment to the socialist state or the complete solidarity with it as expressed in the positive hero of the novels was replaced by a search for the "authentic self," in the lives of the authors, and also in the characters of their novels and dramas. Formerly forbidden themes such as suicide and personal failure of the protagonist were introduced. Christa Wolf was one of the first to introduce the theme of *Republikflucht (*flight from the GDR*)* in her *Der geteilte Himmel* (1963; *Divided Heaven,* 1976)—the love story of an East German couple. He flees to the West and she stays and tries to commit suicide.

There is no ideological typing of characters, and the complexity of human feelings is brought to the surface. A decade later Ulrich Plenzdorf's *Die neuen Leiden des jungen W.* (1973: *The New Sufferings of Young W.,* 1979) pits his hero, Edgar, as Goethe had done with Werther in the eighteenth century, against the rationalistic authorities. Against the grain of an unfeeling bureaucracy at his place of work, the hero unfolds his own ingenuity and creativity. However, in the end he electrocutes himself with a new kind of spray gun he invented, and the author leaves it up to the reader to decide whether it was an accident or a suicide.

Lyric poets even more than dramatists and novelists could not as easily be integrated into socialist realism because the subjective element remains an indispensable part of the lyric craft. Unlike Western lyric poetry, which remains largely a private matter, poetry in the socialist countries is a public act. Therefore, state control is often administered not through actions against the poets themselves but by restricting or forbidding their public appearance. Stefan Hermlin had brought a number of young poets together in Berlin in December 1962 at the *Akademie der Künste* (Academy of the Arts). The public display of these poets' solidarity, even more than their real or imagined political deviancy, brought them into disfavor. Many of them fled the country. Finally on November 7, 1976, Wolf Biermann was stripped of his citizenship. Yet the poets continued to speak out in the name of their authentic self:

> Installed in the stars
> of our pain
> like a barrack. But firmer than any fortress
> and more lasting. Exposed
> to the most bitter weather. Eternally tentative:
> I.

("Verkündigung," "Annunciation," Gunther Kunert, born 1929; *71, 88*)

Poets and writers of the GDR are engaged in the search for the immeasurable wealth of an authentic self, rooted in private and cultural memory and moving towards spontaneous and responsible social communication. This search remains a challenge to the socialist state. Yet these authors put before the West a challenge as well: namely to rescue the notion of the authentic self from our own consumerism and political fictions.

This plea for the self goes hand in hand with the recognition of a self-perpetuating machinery that guides modern states not only in the East but also in the West:

> Sober to the bone, we stand aghast before the reified dreams of instrumental thought that still calls itself reason but has long since lost the en-

lightenment impulse towards emancipation and responsibility and has entered the industrial age and the empty delusion of useful efficiency.

(Christa Wolf, Büchner Prize Speech, 1980)

In sum, the contemporary writers of the GDR are moving out of the introverted confines of their own national literature to draw up paradigms of universal value and concern.

# 3. Germany and Europe

In 1973 the original six-member Common Market or "European Economic Community" (EEC) admitted England, Ireland, and Denmark in the hopes of further strengthening the European economy. Since that time, however, a degree of stagnation, pessimism, and disintegration has set in. First of all, unemployment is widespread. 40 percent of the ten million jobless are under age twenty-five, with women outnumbering men two to one. Nearly one quarter of Europe's unemployed are in France, but figures are rising in Britain, Belgium, and West Germany. There is no promising unemployment policy in sight, and only about 4 percent of the total Common Market budget is spent on social welfare. Most of the funds disappear in the "bottomless pit" of agricultural subsidies. In *The Monitor* of March 24, 1981, EEC President Gaston Thorn remarked: "Europe is at the center of a crisis of long duration."

According to some Common Market officials, a redistribution of burdens and benefits among its members is urgently needed. For instance, the farm subsidies favored by France use up two thirds of the strained EEC budget. For this reason Britain, which pays a great deal into the budget but gets very little in return, resisted many of the Common Market's fiscal policies until a compromise was agreed upon in 1984 that satisfied Prime Minister Thatcher as well as the EEC members. In the early eighties Britain and the FRG provide about 90 percent of its budget. Between 1970 and 1981 German contributions to the EEC rose from two to fourteen billion DM, making the Federal Republic the "paymaster of Europe" (Hans Apel, the former FRG Finance Minister). To be sure, about half of the West German funds return to her in the form of allocations. Still, about a fourth of the FRG's balance-of-payment-deficit is apparently the result of paying too large a share of the Community's bill. To alter this situation, however, would endanger the Community's very existence and curtail West Germany's favorable export situation vis-à-vis its member states. In the absence of trade barriers, the FRG achieved a trade surplus of $7 billion with France alone in 1982. As a result, Germany dropped its demand to limit her net payments to the Community.

The decision-making process suffers due to the Common Market's cumbersome bureaucracy in Brussels. Each of the ten members (Greece joined in 1981) defends its national interests, each may veto new proposals, and each speaks its own language at conferences and in Parliament. Many of the regulations issued by the Brussels Eurocrats and the Strasbourg Parliament are not even understood by some of the EEC's own experts. And two more languages will be introduced upon the admissions of Spain and Portugal in 1986.

The Common Market Commission in Brussels tries to harmonize everything from energy policies to currency exchange rates, from the production and composition to the labeling and taxation of goods. But disputes erupt, based on national interests and sharpened by recession. A deadlock developed, for example, over fishing rights. While the British stand firm against a flood of cheap German-caught cod, the West Germans press for the right to fish off Canada. The European Parliament was paralyzed for hours by Britain's and France's insistence on determining their own summer time. Trading across frontiers is supposed to be free, but in practice, 100,000 customs officers collect offset payments to make up for different VAT (value added tax) rates in the Community as well as to enforce EEC standards of safety, packaging and labeling. The Strasbourg Parliament elected by popular vote in 1979 seems to be a great step forward, yet it is hampered in its legislative functions by irregular meetings and by the peripatetic life of its members, who travel between their homes, their constituencies, their national capitals, Strasbourg, and Brussels. Its formal powers are limited to vetoes of the EEC budget, to votes of confidence on the Council of Ministers, and to recommendations.

In spite of its shortcomings, the Common Market has brought together 270 million people who used to fight each other on the battlefield. The Community has helped maintain living standards in the North and increase them in Mediterranean regions by the free flow of goods, people, and community funds. With 36 percent of the world's trade volume in 1980 and 42 percent of development aid, it has become a powerful bloc, more cohesive and influential than the OPEC countries or the Third World.

The creation of several new agencies helped consolidate Community ties during the 1970s. To counter an each-man-for-himself attitude, Western European nations agreed to coordinate their weapons production and procurement by forming the European Program Group (EPG) in 1976. This not only diminished some wasteful duplication in arms production but also increased European bargaining power in arms sales vis-à-vis the U.S.

In their alarm over the unstable dollar, Chancellor Helmut Schmidt and President Giscard d'Estaing initiated the European Monetary System (EMS) in 1979 with fixed exchange rates and a European currency unit (ECU). The purpose was to allow the currencies to fluctuate only marginally in relation to each other. If prices and costs do not keep pace with each other, exchange-rate realignments become necessary (the seventh realignment occurred in March 1983). Britain did not join the EMS because it thought political union should precede monetary union. Its skepticism has been proven right in the light of wild fluctuations in economic policies and in inflation rates among the member states. Still the ECU has become the third most important international currency unit after the dollar and the mark.

Although the EEC has neither been able to reform its farm-subsidy program nor solve unemployment, it has considerable consensus in an area least expected, namely foreign policy. This is remarkable, since concern for European Political Cooperation (EPC, 1970) has ranked low among countries who put their own national interests above the Community's. But in informal EPC meetings, Western European foreign policy has to some extent been coordinated for the past twelve years. The time is not yet ripe to formalize the status quo with a European Union, but already Western Europe has begun to speak with one voice—in the case of the Helsinki Security Conference (1975), in matters of the European-Arab dialogue, in the Falkland Islands crisis of 1982, and against Reagan's Russian Pipeline embargo. Thus, the Soviet Ambassador to the UN once addressed the EEC representatives as a group, quipping: "I am glad to be able to speak in front of the Mighty Nine." The Common Market has had observer status at the UN since 1974. This entitles the Chairman of the Council of Ministers to represent the group in the General Assembly.

For a long time after WWII the President of the U.S. was able to dominate the policies of the alliance by dealing with European statesmen individually. In the early eighties, a more coordinated European stand has emerged since the ten foreign ministers, their government heads, and their ambassadors hold regular and frequent meetings.

Despite occasional confrontations and a number of unresolved issues, the Common Market is still Western Europe's best hope for survival between the superpowers. As one British diplomat put it: "Imagine what it would be like if we were still ten contending nations without the structures of cooperation we have so laboriously devised" (*The Monitor,* December 22, 1981). Although the British Labour Party and the Greek Socialist government would like to withdraw, all other parties and governments are afraid of the political and economic consequences of such a step.

# 4. Germany and the Third World

In 1976 former West German President Walter Scheel proclaimed:

> The continuously widening social gap between the industrialized countries on the one hand and the developing nations on the other is a danger not only to developing countries but also a danger to peace in the world. The real threat, the danger to the existence of the world, lies in our possibly failing gradually to close the gap in the living conditions of the people of the world. If we do not succeed, the increasing tension will inevitably explode at some point or other.

Attempts to cope with this explosive global issue both nationally and internationally have been under way since the end of WWII. The Truman doctrine of 1947 guaranteed American aid to any free nation resisting communist propaganda or sabotage. In contrast to this policy, Ludwig Erhard, Chancellor from 1964 to 1966, introduced the principle of unconditional aid. From its inception, the Federal Republic channelled development funds to the Third World via European or UN organizations. In 1974 the "North-South Dialogue" began in the UN General Assembly when developing countries adopted a program for establishing a new economic world order. This dialogue culminated in the 1980 report of an international commission chaired by Willy Brandt (170) and a conference at Cancún, Mexico, in 1981.

The major problems that face the world community are staggering. They involve not only a politically explosive income gap between rich and poor—currently 800 million live in extreme poverty—but also a population explosion (the present population of four billion could double by the year 2015), the international economic system, arms purchases, a deteriorating ecology, and the survival of humanity itself. Sporadic problems involve oil consumption, the exchange of raw materials, the transfer of technology, and the enormous indebtedness of many countries. Presently, total development aid provided by the Western allies does not even equal the Third World's oil bill. "The annual [world] military bill is now approaching 450 billion dollars while official development aid accounts for less than 5 percent of this figure. For the price of one jet fighter (20 million dollars) one could set up about 40,000 village pharmacies" (170, 14).

The Federal Republic plays a leading role in multilateral UN organizations (such as the Worldbank group, UNESCO, and the UN Development Program), as well as in the EEC. These organizations place a high priority on closing the economic gap between North and South. The FRG is the highest contributor to the EEC budget, and second only to the U.S. for the UN budget. In the seventies, the European Community developed the Lomé Convention to provide free access for finished and semi-finished farm goods of fifty-eight developing African, Caribbean, and Pacific states to the European market. Over time, the FRG has also evolved its own policies and bilateral treaties with the developing world.

In former times developing countries that supplied only raw materials to Germany grew increasingly indebted, since their income from the raw materials was insufficient to pay for finished goods. German aid went to international and national institutions to alleviate need or to "buy" the friendship of rulers or dictators in the South, who usually used the aid for personal gain or spent it on weapons.

As a consequence, West German development policy underwent a number of changes during the last decade. Now it starts from the premise that there is nothing wrong with aid that also promotes German exports and employment at home. Foreign Minister Hans-Dietrich Genscher stated at the UN in August 1980: "Development aid is a humanitarian duty. But it is equally an act designed to protect our own vital interests." Thus, an interdependent "partnership of equals" is believed to be the best safeguard for mutual economic well-being, employment, and growth. For example, about two thirds of the cash that flows from Germany to developing countries returns in the form of export orders. These orders can only be placed and paid for if the trading partner is economically healthy. In the early eighties experts on foreign affairs came to realize that "no strings" financial subsidies and strategies for rapid industrialization of Third World countries do not produce economic health; rather self-help on a country's own terms had to be encouraged. Genscher elaborated on the new policy at the UN wherein a "labor-intensive agricultural system [became] a priority concern, industrialization in interaction with agricultural advancement, and as a basis for the two, the development of national energy resources." The FRG has opted for a "strategy of joint responsibility" which requires both self-reliance and the observance of fundamental human rights. Furthermore, as Konrad Porzner states,

> Social development is no longer subordinate to economic development. . . . Greater emphasis is placed on agricultural development and on the importance of education and vocational training. . . . The aim is to reduce reliance on imported oil . . . and to maintain the ecosystem".

> (*The German Tribune,* October 3, 1982)

In contrast to the gifts and loans of former times which did not enhance a poor people's independence, now the FRG prefers to help a people build their own projects in their traditional ways (e.g., wells instead of pumped-in water; ox-driven plows instead of tractors). The focus of development has been shifted from machines and institutions to people (*170, 23*).

Partnership, as a departure from colonialism (denied to Germany by the Treaty of Versailles in 1919), requires industrialized countries to open their markets to the Third World. On the one hand, this increases competition at home but on the other, it promotes diversification in the developing world. Due to this new policy, the Federal Republic's trade with non-OPEC countries of the Third World has shown an import surplus since 1977 of semi-processed and manufactured goods.

Cooperation with developing countries takes various forms, the most important of which are financial aid and technical assistance; and money is invested in the construction of factories, roads, harbors, dams, and irrigation systems. "Commodity aid" is provided in the form of machinery, equipment, spare parts, and raw materials. Banks in developing nations receive loans, at very favorable terms. Nevertheless, in view of the increased indebtedness of many countries, Bonn canceled the debts of the thirty poorest countries and extended free grants to them instead. In addition, private investment of German firms in the form of securities, credits, and direct investment amounts to 66 percent of the Federal Republic's development program.

Since 1963 a German Development Service modeled on the U.S. Peace Corps has been at work especially in Africa and Latin America. Its aim is to stimulate self-help in schools and universities, in health services, and in agriculture and industry workshops. Further, West Germany has a vocational training program for foreign workers from the Third World as well as southern Europe.

West German aid projects have included bilateral university research plans emphasizing science, engineering, and agriculture; investment schemes for electricity-supply and food production co-financed by the developing countries; technical training programs for unskilled laborers or refugees in Angola, Namibia, and Zimbabwe. In Brazil, Mexico, Malaysia, and Nigeria, German experts help host countries improve food production and industrial bases.

In 1982, the U.S. gave out $8.3 billion in developmental aid, France $4 billion, and West Germany $3.2 billion. As a percentage of GNP, however, FRG aid (at 1.06 percent of the GNP) far surpassed the U.S. (at 0.2 percent of GNP), Japan, and Great Britain. The state-planned economies of the East-bloc contribute only $2 billion total in aid, as compared with $28 billion spent by the West, on the pretext that the former colonial powers alone are responsible for the exploitation and the economic problems of the underdeveloped Third World. West Germany, on the other hand, has in the past supported countries struggling between East and West for the purpose of giving them a chance to become truly independent. For example, at a time when the U.S. suspected that the Marxist Sandinistas of Nicaragua might be tied to Moscow (or Cuba), the Federal Republic, like France, nevertheless maintained its aid level to that country. Similarly, when the U.S. suspected Marxist political leanings of Robert Mugawe, the FRG ran a successful technical training program for his followers in Zimbabwe. Recently the Kohl government has adopted a policy more oriented toward the U.S. which links aid to political loyalty. In general, however, while the Reagan administration stresses private initiative in poor nations, the Federal Republic still prefers a "dovetailed" approach that combines government directives with self-help and private initiative—a combination proved effective in its own dramatic recovery after WWII.

# 5. A Revival of Nationalism?

Much discussed in the foreign and domestic media, one of the most explosive issues of the early 1980s has been a reemergence of nationalistic trends in West Germany, including a renewed interest in Nazism and in Prussia. Some of this interest is due to the media and some is an expression of grass-roots nationalism.

Hitler committed suicide in 1945, but his career and spirit are "still the fundamental trauma of the century, the wound through which our shared humanity leaks" (*Time* Essay, 21 May 1973). In the first decade after the war the problem of coming to terms with the past was completely shunned in West Germany. Cold-war confrontation with the Soviets brought the "de-Nazification" begun by the Western occupation forces to an abrupt halt. The Western powers seemed to fall for Hitler's propaganda ploy that the Nazis were the West's anticommunist allies. Former Nazis were allowed to reassume their positions as civil servants, teachers, judges, and politicians. Persecution for Nazi crimes dwindled. Despite the protests of angry young writers in the 1960s such as Rolf Hochhuth and Günter Grass, who wanted to come to terms with Nazi atrocities, most West Germans repressed or exorcised these events as if nothing had happened. The people were generally unwilling to admit their guilt or to express their grief *(160)*.

This repression of the past lasted until 1972–73 when Chancellor Willy Brandt introduced *Ostpolitik* and knelt on behalf of the German people at the Warsaw Ghetto memorial. At this point, a wave of interest in the past surfaced, which lasted intermittently throughout the next decade. At first it led to a "Hitler boom"—not of adulation or nostalgia—but of healthy critical analysis. Since the late 1950s, school curricula had required courses dealing with the Third Reich. But now adults, at a generation's distance, wanted to understand Nazism. Books, articles, and films began to feed the war generation's great interest in Hitler and his closest collaborators. Fourteen books—biographies, confessions, and documentaries—appeared in 1973 alone, the most prominent of these was Albert Speer's *Inside the Third Reich* (1970). Coming to terms with the past was a slow and painful process. The student rebellion added urgency to this interest in the Nazi period. Hitler was demythologized and transformed from a monstrous demon, a human Antichrist, into a mere criminal, a gifted madman, an insane genius with oratorical skill, magnetism and an indefatigable drive to dominate *(223)*.

The younger generation did not share their parents' fascination. He was their parents' problem. While the older generation felt compelled to admit its guilt, Hitler seemed ridiculous, absurd, or comical to their children. For them he was and still is a mysterious figure about whom they know very little, despite their teachers' efforts. According to a 1977 poll, many teenagers believed Hitler to have been variously a Jew, a communist, a conqueror of East Berlin, someone who quelled the influx of foreigners, or who put a stop to political kidnappings and terrorist attacks *(24; 42,* 77f.).

With this degree of ignorance among *Hauptschüler* and *Berufsschüler* it is not surprising that some of them fall for neo-Nazi recruitment practices. Exploiting political issues, such as the ecological movement, or a proposed limitation on foreigners, the right-wing fringe has been able to hold its own, while leftist terrorism has been checked to a large extent. The neo-Nazi extremists have been imitating the Baader-Meinhof gang in some respects: they gather weapons, ammunition, and explosives, they forge identify cards, rob banks, contact foreign sympathizers, maintain hideaways and training camps, distribute pamphlets and organize hunger strikes in prison. Parallel to the radical left's move to the underground, the extreme right has opted for ever more violent means of putting its "ideology" into practice. Their hard-core militants have moved from harassment and beatings to assassinations and mass terror (e.g., a bomb explosion at the 1980 Munich Oktoberfest).

Since 1952, when the first neo-Nazi youth organization, the Viking Youth, was founded, many similar small groups have come into being. By and large they maintained a low profile until the late 1970s, when they suddenly burst into the open with acts of violence against Jews, foreigners, and police. There are some seventy-five large and small organizations with a total membership of around 20,000. Perhaps as many as 1,200 belong to a hard core of terrorists. The more notorious paramilitary organizations include the *Wehrsportgruppe Hoffmann,* which held mock maneuvers in the Bavarian forests; the Munich-based VSBD *(Volkssozialistische Bewegung Deutschlands,* People's Socialist Movement of Germany*)*, the *Deutsche Aktionsgruppe* (German Action Group), led by a former attorney from Bavaria, and the *Aktionsfront nationaler Sozialisten.* Although it took the Federal Office for the Protection of the Constitution (the German equivalent of the FBI) some years to ferret out these radical cells, they have all been declared illegal (1980–83). Nevertheless, such extremist groups have many sympathizers among the 100,000 readers of the *Deutsche Nationalzeitung,* the *Stahlhelm* (steel helmet), and other right-wing magazines. The Sinus Institute of Heidelberg estimated that 13 percent of the voting population was sympathetic to right-wing causes (*Die Zeit,* 15 May 1981).

So far neo-Nazi groups have failed to form a national organization, although their various ideologies tend to converge in some respects. They all endorse racism, antisemitism, and xenophobia: foreigners, Turks, Jews, Vietnamese should depart, and asylum seekers turn elsewhere. They reject democracy as a "cancer of the people," and the West German constitution and parliament as an incompetent debating club. Instead they idolize Hitler and aim to model society and the state on the *Führer* principle. "Nation, fatherland, and family" are idealized while American and Russian troops have become their terrorist targets. All deny Germany was to blame for WWII; they claim the Jews and the communists destroyed the Reich, and they demand their *Lebensraum* back, saying, "Germany is larger than the Federal Republic." They ridicule the historic fact that the Nazis tried to exterminate the Jews and claim that Auschwitz is a fabrication. To combat such inflammatory propaganda, the FRG's Penal Code makes it an offense to incite racial hatred by alleging, for example, that Jews circulate lies about the Nazi gas chambers in order to win financial compensation from West Germany. In 1985, legislators made it a crime to issue publications that deny or minimize the facts of genocide during WWII.

However, banishment of right-wing extremists tends to drive them underground and sometimes radicalizes them even more, particularly since they are supported by an underground network of international fascists, the "Worldwide Teutonic Unity" (*Der Spiegel,* March 30 1981, p. 75f.). This became obvious in 1980 when neo-Nazi terror struck Bologna's train station, synagogues in Antwerp and Paris, at the Munich Oktoberfest, and in Marseille. Underground connections linking explosives, leaders, and training camps have been established between most Western European capitals and the Near East (e.g., Turkey and Lebanon). Weapons and money flow from France (cf. the illegal Fane group and the neo-fascist Nouvelle Droite) and Belgium (cf. Vlaamse Militanten Orde) to West Germany; training is provided in Austria, Belgium, Spain (Fuerza Joven) and, until recently, in Lebanon. American and Canadian neo-Nazi publishers supply the necessary propaganda material to West German rightists. Although no umbrella organization or common operational plan exists, the differences among the white-supremacist organizations in the U.S., the Flemish fascist organization, and the West German neo-Nazis are insignificant. This does not mean that these groups are harmless; the opposite is true. The less political opportunity and leeway to maneuver in public they have, the more their ideology drives them to acts of violence.

West German right-wing extremists have no official connection to the legal National Democratic Party (NDP), although it is often described as "hostile to democracy." Still, it neither advocates violence nor has it been able to garner the five percent of the votes necessary to qualify for representation in the West German Parliament *(Bundestag)*. Its membership dwindled in 1983 to about 5,000, only 0.2 percent of the popular vote. How unattractive its platform is became apparent in 1982 when the NPD's youth wing called for a demonstration against "guest workers" in Hamburg, and only one supporter showed up, whereas over one hundred counter demonstrators appeared.

Another variant of nationalism in the early 1980s, but emerging from the political left and for very different reasons, is "national neutralism," with a unique mix of ecological, pacifist, and socialistic perspectives. It advocates a reunited demilitarized Germany free from the influence of both superpowers. While under present global realities the movement's utopian ideas are nothing more than that, it is nevertheless fueled by strong sentiments and a broad popular sympathy, as it grows increasingly obvious that Europe, and primarily the two Germanys, could become the first victims in a nuclear war.

The crucial question is whether the Federal Republic's democratic system is firmly enough established to withstand radical onslaughts from the extreme left and right without abusing the power of the state. The evidence is still somewhat inconclusive. Distressing has been a tendency to resort to state force both in combating terrorism and in suppressing dissent and social unrest, for instance during squatter incidents in Berlin, during protests at the Frankfurt airport, during antinuclear demonstrations at Brokdorf and Gorleben, and in the aftermath of a large squatter demonstration in Nuremberg in 1981.

Despite extraordinary cases of backsliding into an authoritarian style of government, there are also healthy signs that the FRG and its citizens are slowly overcoming the last vestiges of the Nazi mentality which advocated "All power to the State." The first judicial condemnation of a Nazi-era court verdict occurred in Berlin in 1981 when a lower court overturned the infamous 1933 Reichstag conviction under which the communist van der Lubbe was executed. There were hundreds of murderers in judges' robes during the Third Reich. Many survivors among the 560 judges who presided over the notorious Nazi People's Courts obtained positions on the bench in the new FRG after WWII. None was ever punished on the rationale that judges only fulfilled their duty to the state in administering Nazi law. In the van der Lubbe case, a miscarriage of justice was admitted for the first time. More Nazi court decisions are being challenged at long last.

Spectacular was the trial of the playwright Rolf Hochhuth versus Hans Karl Filbinger, which unseated the former Governor of Baden-Württemberg because of his part in several death sentences while a Navy judge and zealous prosecutor during WWII.

A similar uproar occurred when two West German generals were dismissed for defending Nazi air ace Rudel in 1976, insisting that he had as much right to free speech as former communist Herbert Wehner—member of parliament. Under democratic rule, the military does not have the right to disparage any member of Parliament.

Also indicative of the health of the FRG's democracy was the *Bundestag's* call in 1978 for a third extension of the Statute of Limitations on Nazi crimes on the fortieth anniversary of the *Kristallnacht* (the "Night of Broken Glass," during which Jewish property was vandalized in 1938). In the same year, the West German TV broadcast of the *Holocaust* was watched by many millions and had a broad social impact, which led to a general and serious national soul-searching.

Resurgent German nationalism may also be the motivating force behind a remarkable renascence of interest in Prussia. The fundamental questions raised in both West and East Germany are: to what extent did Hitler's Reich reflect a continuation of Prussian traditions? and, was Hitler heir to Frederick the Great and Bismarck (*97, 156*)? And further, which features of Prussia have managed to survive in contemporary Germany?

Three decades after the end of the war, Prussia's image has been reexamined and to some degree rehabilitated. During the annual West Berlin Festival Weeks in 1981, Prussia was the subject of dozens of books and movies, as also occurred in East Germany. The question at the root of the striking revival is "Prussian history—our history?" The State of Prussia was liquidated in 1947 by decree of the Allies, who attributed the Third Reich's militarism, authoritarianism, and blind obedience to Prussia. Now it appears that both the Allies and the postwar Germans were too simplistic in ignoring the ambivalent character of Prussian history and in drawing a direct line from Prussia to Hitler. In truth, Prussia was always more than a mere military machine.

From the late seventeenth century until the death of Frederick the Great in 1786, Prussia was a model of the Enlightenment; with its benevolent despotism, it was the most progressive state of the period. Built on a feudal agricultural system, its three main pillars of power and order were the aristocracy, the army, and the civil service. These branches were constantly made more efficient to bring them in line with the mechanistic model of the state: "A well-led state government must have a system as well fitted together as a philosophical system in order to coordinate finances, politics, and military power for a common goal, i.e., the strengthening of the state and its increase in power" (Frederick the Great, *Political Testament* I, 1752). Or as Theodor Fontane put it in his novel *Schach von Wuthenow:* "The world does not rest any more securely on the shoulders of Atlas than the Prussian state on those of its Prussian army."

Paradoxically, it was the well-integrated authoritarian structure of the "classical" Prussian state that made it possible to grant more individual freedoms—e.g., promotion of philosohy, discussion, and support for religious tolerance toward various Christian denominations (Huguenots, Catholics, Jesuits) and Jews (*42,* 129) —than perhaps any other absolute state of the eighteenth century. (In "What is the Enlightenment," 1784, Kant wrote, "Argue as much as you want and about whatever you want, but obey.")

Following the French Revolution, the "mechanical" state became hopelessly outdated, and Prussia reached its nadir when it was defeated in 1806 by Napoleon's victories at Jena and Auerstedt. Despite the reform efforts of Karl Reichsfreiherr von und zum Stein, Karl August Fürst von Hardenberg, Wilhelm von Humboldt, and General G.H.D. von Scharnhorst, promises of revitalization were not fulfilled, neither in 1815 at the Congress of Vienna, nor in 1848 by the Frankfurt Parliament, nor in 1871 when Bismarck founded the Second German Reich. The Prussian state remained a virtual military machine ruled by the aristocracy. A slogan of the Wilhelmian era was telling: "Der Mensch fängt erst beim Leutnant an," one becomes human after achieving the rank of lieutenant.

When Prussia became a constituent state of the Weimar Republic following the debacle of WWI, a new phase of Prussian history was ushered in. A democratic Prussia was born out of the ashes of its military past, but this time it was governed by the former enemies of the Bismarck-Reich, i.e., the Social Democrats and the leftist liberals and Catholics, among them Konrad Adenauer, President of the Parliamentatry Council. "This democratically transformed *Obrigkeitsstaat* gained a stability which was denied to the Reich" (i.e., to the Weimer Republic as a whole, *35,* 277). For example, until 1932 the Prussian State Parliament enjoyed a stable majority of its democratic coalition parties with only nine seats allocated to the Nazi Party, whereas the Diet in Berlin could never muster enough votes to keep its government in power (*18,* 335).

In 1932 the Prussian state brought about its own demise when Reich Chancellor von Papen overthrew the government by his "Prussian *coup d'état*" (*97,* 154). His aim was to undercut the Social Democrats and the National Socialists in order to strengthen the German conservatives. Shortly afterwards, on March 21, 1933 (the infamous "Day of Potsdam"), the alliance between von Papen and Hitler, that had been based on political expediency, was given a symbolic stamp of approval. Thus Nazism and Prussianism were fused for propaganda purposes, despite the fact that Prussia had already ceased to exist. "No separate Prussian role can be detected in Hitler's Reich even with a magnifying glass" (*97,* 156), yet under the influence of Goebbels' propaganda ("National Socialists . . . are Prussians," 1932; *35,* 248), the Allies turned Hitler into a "Prussian." This transformation is ironic since Hitler was an Austrian by birth, in character quite the opposite of Frederick the Great— without tolerance, self-discipline, or altruism—although he claimed to revere the Prussian king and modeled his campaign to the very end on his "predecessor's" Seven Years' War (1756–63). In the process, Hitler perverted venerable Prussian virtues such as duty, obedience, service to the leader, and sacrifice to the state, into submissiveness and blind tenacity to the bitter end. Moreover, Hitler's state was not an authoritarian state based on the rule of law, as Prussia had been under Frederick, but his Nazi party ruled autocraticly. "Hitler's racial and nationality policy was the extreme opposite of Prussia's. So was his political style the extreme opposite of Prussian soberness" (*97,* 156). According to some estimates, the majority of the Nazi leadership stemmed from non-Prussian regions, e.g., from Bavaria. In fact, much of the resistance against the Nazis came from Prussian-trained military, civil service, and church groups.

Under the Allies' liquidation decree, Germans fell understandably silent about Prussia in the postwar years. But under the surface, Prussia remained an important ingredient in postwar political culture in Germany (*18,* 12). Millions of refugees had fled from Prussia to West Germany, so that Prussian civil servants and military personnel provided a bridge between the Weimar Republic and the new beginnings after WWII.

In the Federal Republic fundamental principles of tolerance were incorporated in the Basic Law, e.g., articles 4, 33, and 140, based on the Prussian constitution of 1850 (via Weimar's of 1919). Moreover, the idea of federation was not really of American origin but had roots in German history. The Holy Roman Empire had been a federation of various sovereignties from the Middle Ages to 1806; and Humboldt had drafted the federal system of the *Deutsche Bund* (1815–1868) as a confederation of states bent on preserving peace and a balance of power in Europe (K.D. Erdmann, *Die Zeit,* March 7, 1980). Further, some believe that the Prussian military machine had been progressively transformed into an industrial giant that flourished on its efficiency and discipline. Yet the Federal Republic, which built its economic miracle on the same principles, failed to acknowledge its debt to Prussian ideals. East Germany, on the other hand, which inherited the old Prussian electorate territory, was very conscious of the Prussian past.

GDR party leaders entered history by blowing up the *Junker* manor houses and the Berlin *Stadtschloß*. They removed the equestrian statue of Frederick the Great from Berlin and concentrated on the "progressive" heritage of German history, the peasant rebellion with Thomas Müntzer in 1525, and the class struggle during Prussia's industrialization (e.g., in 1848). Any continuity between Prussia and the GDR was overtly rejected on the basis of Marx's contention that world history had not produced anything more miserable than Prussia. In practice, however, the GDR's Prussian heritage began to assert itself rather early in the military field, namely in the National People's Army, formed in 1952, with its goose-stepping soldiers and Scharnhorst decorations. In other, but related areas, too, the Prussian spirit has been alive for decades; obedience seems to be the first duty of the East German citizen ("Gehorsam ist die erste Bürgerspflicht") in all areas of life—traffic regulations, behavior in schools, restaurants, and public meeting places. ". . . . I have often wondered whether this is not typically German: this insistence on being right, this prohibition of everything that does not represent official opinion" (*Die Zeit,* April 9, 1982). Whoever deviates from the official line is demoted, exiled, or imprisoned.

Since 1976–77 the GDR has viewed its own history as the essence of German history in which the FRG is only an episode. As successor to the Prussian State on Prussian soil, it exploits Prussian history for its own purposes. It consciously lays claim to the heritage of the reformers (Stein, Hardenberg, Humboldt, Scharnhorst), to the famous military theoretician Karl von Clausewitz (*Vom Kriege,* 1832f.; *On War*), whose ashes were transferred from Breslau to Magdeburg in 1971, and to Frederick II whose statue was returned to prominence on Unter den Linden in East Berlin in 1980. Party boss Erich Honecker alludes to Frederick in his speeches, thus furthering an official revisionism of Prussia, which for him embraces the formerly maligned Martin Luther as well as the field Marshall A.G. Neithardt von Gneisenau, the old Museum and Berlin Cathedral, the painter Adolf von Menzel (1815–1905), and the architect Karl Friedrich Schinkel (1781–1841), as well as Bismarck and the *Rote Kapelle,* a political resistance group against Hitler. This cultural emphasis, which has been underestimated by the FRG, serves the GDR's political claim to a separate national identity. "The GDR rebels, as the Hohenzollern once did, against German unity, it steps outside the 'Reich' (as long as it does not have the biggest say in it), it separates itself, it excludes others, bleeds them financially" (K. H. Janssen, *Die Zeit,* 21 August 1981). But with its lack of liberalism, "the GDR is rather Wilhelmian than Prussian with all its *Brimborium* (fussiness) and its *Zackigkeit* (spit and polish), its tightly structured, fossilized hierarchies and chains of command" (*Die Zeit,* February 13 1980; *42,* 299f.).

In neither East nor West Germany has the "Prussian revival" been merely a nostalgic remembrance of a bygone era. Instead it has been a search for roots and for national identity. "Prussia is part of our history, not only Weimar," claimed the East German FDJ *(Freie Deutsche Jugend)* magazine *Forum* in 1978. For West Germans, on the other hand, the central question stresses personal and moral issues: "Only when we really understand why things happened as they did, when we, as a nation, have studied Prussia and its history, will we win the freedom Prussia never knew" *(180).*

# Bibliography

1. Adenauer, Konrad. *Erinnerungen.* 4 vols. Stuttgart: Deutsche Verlagsanstalt, 1965–1968.
2. Aichinger, Ilse. *Meine Sprache und Ich. Erzählungen.* Frankfurt: Fischer, 1978.
3. *Anschläge. Politische Plakate in Deutschland, 1900–1970.* Arnold Friedrich, ed. Frankfurt: Bücher Gilde Gutenberg, 1973.
4. Arad, Yitzhak, et al., eds. *Documents on the Holocaust.* Jerusalem: Yad Vashem, 1981.
5. Arendt, Hannah. *The Origins of Totalitarianism.* New York: Harcourt, Brace and World, 1951.
6. Arnold, Heinz Ludwig, ed. *Text und Kritik. Sonderband. Die Gruppe 47.* Munich: A. Aumaier, 1980.
7. Arp, Hans. *Gesammelte Gedichte.* Vol. III. Zurich: Die Arche, 1974.
8. Bahro, Rudolf. *Elemente einer neuen Politik. Zum Verhältnis von Ökologie und Sozialismus.* Berlin: Olle und Wolter, 1980.
9. Balabkins, Nicholas. *Germany Under Direct Controls: Economic Aspects of Industrial Disarmament, 1945–1948.* New Brunswick, N.J.: Rutgers University Press, 1964.
10. Bauer, Yehuda, and Keren, Nili. *A History of the Holocaust.* New York: Franklin Watts, 1982.
11. Becker, Jillian. *Hitler's Children: The Story of the Baader-Meinhof Terrorist Gang.* Philadelphia: Lippincott, 1977.
12. Benn, Gottfried. *Gesammelte Werke.* Vol. 4: *Autobiographische und Vermischte Schriften.* Dieter Wellerhoff, ed. Wiesbaden: Limes, 1961.
13. Bergsträsser, Ludwig. *Geschichte der Politischen Parteien in Deutschland.* Munich: Isar Verlag, 1955.
14. Bernhard, Thomas. *Verstörung.* Frankfurt: Insel Verlag, 1967.
15. Berthold, Eva, ed. *Kriegsgefangene im Osten.* Königstein: Athenäum, 1981.
16. Bidinian, Larry. *The Combined Allied Bombing Offensive Against the German Civilian 1942–1945.* Lawrence, Kansas: Coronado Press, 1976.

17. *Bildung und Wissenschaft* (Inter Nationes, Bonn), No's 8/9, 1980, pp. 81–105.

18. Blasius, Dirk, ed. *Preußen in der deutschen Geschichte*. Neue Wissenschaftliche Bibliothek 111, Geschichte. Königstein: Athenäum, 1980.

19. Blumenwitz, Dieter et al., eds. *Konrad Adenauer und seine Zeit. Politik und Persönlichkeit des ersten Bundeskanzlers*. Vol. II. Stuttgart: Deutsche Verlags-Anstalt, 1976.

20. Böddeker, Günter. *Die Flüchtlinge. Die Vertreibung der Deutschen aus dem Osten*. Bergisch-Gladbach: Bastei Lübbe, 1982.

21. Boeschenstein, Hermann. *The German Novel, 1939–1944*. Toronto: University of Toronto Press, 1949.

22. Böll, Heinrich. *Billiards at Half Past Nine*. New York: McGraw-Hill, 1962.

23. Borneman, Ernest. *Das Patriarchat. Ursprung und Zukunft unseres Gesellschaftssystems*. Frankfurt: Fischer, 1975.

24. Boßmann, Dieter, ed. *"Was ich über Adolf Hitler gehört habe." Folgen eines Tabus: Auszüge aus Schüler-Aufsätzen von heute*. Frankfurt: Fischer (Nr. 1935), 1977.

25. Bovenschen, Silvia. *Die imaginierte Weiblichkeit*. Frankfurt: Suhrkamp, 1980.

26. Bracher, Karl Dietrich. *Die deutsche Diktatur*. Cologne: Kiepenheuer & Witsch, 1969.

27. Bramsted, Ernest. *Goebbels and National Socialist Propaganda, 1925–1945*. Ann Arbor: Michigan State University Press, 1965.

28. Brandt, Willy. *Friedenspolitik in Europa*. Frankfurt: Fischer, 1968.

29. ———. *Peace. Writings and Speeches of the Nobel Peace Prize Winner 1971*. Bonn-Bad Godesberg: Neue Gesellschaft, 1971.

30. ———. *People and Politics: The Years 1960–1975*. Trans. J. Maxwell Brownjohn. Boston-Toronto: Little, Brown, 1976.

31. Brenner, Hildegard. *Die Kunstpolitik des Nationalsozialismus*. Hamburg: Rowohlt, 1963.

32. *Brockhaus' Enzyklopädie*. Vol. 21. Wiesbaden: Brockhaus, 1974.

33. Broszat, Martin. *German National Socialism 1919–1945*. Santa Barbara: Clio Press, 1966.

34. Bullock, Alan. *Hitler: a Study in Tyranny*. London: Odhams Brooks, 1952.

35. Büsch, Otto, ed. *Das Preussenbild in der Geschichte. Protokoll eines Symposiums*. Veröffentlichungen der historischen Kommission zu Berlin, 50. Berlin and New York: de Gruyter, 1981.

36. Carr, William. *Arms, Autarky and Aggression: A Study in German Foreign Policy, 1933–1939*. London: Edward Arnold, 1972.

37. Catudal, Honoré. *A Balance Sheet of the Quadripartite Agreement on Berlin: Evaluation and Documentation*. Political Studies 13. Berlin: Berlin Verlag, 1978.

38. Cecil, Robert. *The Myth of the Master Race: Alfred Rosenberg and Nazi Ideology*. New York: Dodd Mead, 1972.

39 Claessens, Dieter. *Sozialkunde der Bundesrepublik*. Düsseldorf: Dietrich Verlag, 1979.

40. *Constitutions of the German Länder*. Berlin: Office of the Military Government, United States, 1947.

41. Conway, John. *The Nazi Persecution of the Churches, 1933–1945*. London: Weidenfeld & Nicolson, 1968.

42. Craig, Gordon A. *The Germans*. New York: Putnam's Sons, 1982.

43. Dahrendorf, Ralf. *Bildung ist Bürgerrecht: Plädoyer für eine aktive Bildungspolitik*. Hamburg: Nannen, 1965.

44. ———. *Society and Democracy in Germany*. New York: Doubleday, 1967.

45. *DDR-Handbuch*. 2nd ed. Wissenschaftliche Leitung: Peter Lutz. Herausgegeben vom Bundesministerium für innerdeutsche Beziehungen. Cologne: Wissenschaft und Politik, 1979.

46. Denkler, Horst. *Die deutsche Literatur im Dritten Reich. Themen, Traditionen, Wirkungen*. Stuttgart: Reclam, 1976.

47. Deuerlein, Ernst. *CDU/CSU 1945–1957*. Cologne: J. P. Bachem, 1957.

48. ———. *Deklamation oder Ersatzfrieden? Die Konferenz von Potsdam 1945*. Stuttgart: Kohlhammer, 1970.

49. Deutsch, H. C. *The Conspiracy Against Hitler in the Twilight War*. Minneapolis: University of Minnesota Press, 1968.

50. *Deutsches Mosaik. Ein Lesebuch für Zeitgenossen. Offizielles Geschenkwerk des Organisationskomitees für die Spiele der XX. Olympiade in München*. Frankfurt: Suhrkamp, 1972.

51. De Zayas, Alfred M. *Nemesis at Potsdam: The Anglo-Americans and the Expulsion of the Germans*. London: Routledge, 1979.

52. Donohoe, James. *Hitler's Conservative Opponent in Bavaria 1930–1945: A Study of Catholic, Monarchist, and Separatist Anti-Nazi Activities*. Leiden: Brill, 1961.

53. Dowling, Colette. *The Cinderella Complex: Women's Hidden Fear of Independence*. New York: Pocket Books, 1981.

54. *Dreißig Jahre Deutsche Demokratische Republik*. Friedrich Ebert Stiftung, ed. Bonn: Verlag neue Gesellschaft, 1979.

55. Drewitz, Ingeborg. *Städte 1945: Berichte und Bekenntnisse*. Düsseldorf: Dieterich Verlag, 1970.

56. Durzak, Manfred. *Die deutsche Exilliteratur 1933–1945*. Stuttgart: Reclam, 1973.

57. ———. *Deutsche Gegenwartsliteratur: Ausgangspositionen und aktuelle Entwicklungen*. Stuttgart: Reclam, 1981.

58. Ehlermann, Claus-Dieter, et al. *Neun für Europa: Die EWG als Motor europäischer Integration*. 2nd ed. Düsseldorf: Dieterich Verlag, 1973.

59. Ehring, Klaus, and Dallwitz, Martin. *"Schwerter zu Pflugscharen"—Friedensbewegung in der DDR*. Reinbek: Rowohlt, 1982.

60. *Ein Land lebt nicht für sich allein*. Bonn: Presse- und Informationsdienst, 1980.

61. Emmerich, Wolfgang. *Kleine Literaturgeschichte der DDR*. Darmstadt: Luchterhand, 1981.

62. Enzensberger, Hans Magnus. *Der Untergang der Titanic*. Frankfurt: Suhrkamp, 1981.

63. Erhard, Ludwig. *The Economics of Success*. London: Thames and Hudson, 1963.
64. Essbach, Wolfgang. *Gegenzüge: Der Materialismus des Selbst und seine Ausgrenzung aus dem Marxismus—eine Studie über die Kontroverse zwischen Max Stirner und Karl Marx*. Frankfurt: Materialis Verlag, 1982.
65. *Facts About Germany*. Karl Römer, ed. 3rd ed. Gütersloh: Lexikon-Institut, Bertelsmann, 1982.
66. Fallon, Daniel. *The German University: A Heroic Ideal in Conflict with the Modern World*. Colorado University Press, 1980.
67. *Federal Republic of Germany. Questions and Answers*. New York: German Information Center, 1980.
68. Feuchtwanger, Leon. *Exil*. Rudolstadt: Greifen, 1940.
69. Flechtheim, Ossip K. *Dokumente zur parteipolitischen Entwicklung in Deutschland seit 1945*. Vols. II, III. Berlin: Dokumentenverlag H. Wendler, 1962.
70. Fleming, Denna F. *The Cold War and Its Origins 1917–1960*. New York: Doubleday, 1961.
71. Flores, John. *Poetry in East Germany. Adjustments, Visions, and Provocations*. New Haven: Yale University Press, 1971.
72. *Frauenfrage in Deutschland, 1865–1915: Texte und Dokumente*. Elke Frederiksen, ed. Stuttgart: Reclam, 1981.
73. Freud, Michael. *25 Jahre Deutschland 1945–1970*. Gütersloh: Bertelsmann, n.d.
74. Fried, Alexander. *Befreiung von der Flucht. Gedichte und Gegengedichte*. Hamburg: Claasen, 1968.
75. Frisch, Max. *Homo Faber*. Frankfurt: Suhrkamp, 1957.
76. ———. *Mein Name sei Gantenbein*. Frankfurt: Suhrkamp, 1964.
77. Führ, Christoph. *Education and Teaching in the Federal Republic of Germany*. Bonn: Inter Nationes, 1979.
78. Fürstenau, Justus. *Entnazifizierung*. Neuwied: Luchterhand, 1969.
79. Gatzke, Hans W. *Germany and the United States: A "Special Relationship?"* American Foreign Policy Library. Cambridge, Mass. and London: Harvard University Press, 1980.
80. Gay, Peter. *Freud, Jews and Other Germans: Masters and Victims in Modernist Culture*. New York: Oxford University Press, 1978.
81. Gehring, Hans Jörg. *Amerikanische Literaturpolitik in Deutschland 1945–1953. Ein Aspekt des Re-Education Programms*. Stuttgart, 1966.
82. "Germany After the War. Round Table 1945." Joint Committee in Post-War Planning, ed. *American Journal of Orthopsychiatry*, vol. XVI: 3.
83. Gilbert, Felix. *The End of the European Era, 1890 to the Present*. New York: Norton, 1979.
84. Gimbel, John. *The American Occupation of Germany*. Palo Alto: Stanford University Press, 1968.
85. Glaser, Hermann. *Die Bundesrepublik zwischen Restauration und Rationalismus. Analysen und Perspektiven*. Freiburg: Rombach, 1965.

86. ———, ed. *Bundesrepublikanisches Lesebuch. Drei Jahrzehnte geistiger Auseinandersetzung.* Munich: Hauser, 1980.

87. Goethe, Wolfgang. *Weltanschauliche Gedichte.* vol. I. Erich Trunz, ed. Hamburg: Bech, 1982.

88. Grebing, Helga. *Die Nachkriegsentwicklung in Westdeutschland.* Studienreihe Politik. Stuttgart: Metzler, 1980.

89. Grimm, Reinhold, and Hermand, Jost. *Exil und Innere Emigration.* 3rd Wisconsin Workshop 1971. Frankfurt: Athenäum, 1973.

90. Grosser, Alfred. *Geschichte Deutschlands seit 1945. Eine Bilanz.* Munich: dtv, 1974.

91. Gruchmann, Lothar, "Der zweite Weltkrieg," in *Deutsche Geschichte seit dem ersten Weltkrieg.* Institut für Zeitgeschichte, ed. Stuttgart: DVA, 1973, pp. 9–383.

92. *Die Grundrechte in beiden deutschen Staaten.* Bonn-Bad Godesberg: Friedrich-Ebert-Stiftung, 1979.

93. Günter, W. *Der Film als politisches Führungsmittel.* Leipzig: Robert Noske, 1934.

94. Habbe, Christian. *Ausländer. Die verfemten Gäste.* Spiegelbuch 33. Reinbek: Rororo, 1983.

95. Habe, Hans. *Im Jahre Null.* Munich: Heyne, 1977.

96. Habermas, Jürgen. *Stichworte zur geistigen Situation der Zeit.* Vol. I: *Nation und Republik;* Vol. II: *Politik und Kultur.* Frankfurt: Suhrkamp, 1979.

97. Haffner, Sebastian. *The Rise and Fall of Prussia.* London: Weidenfeld & Nicolson, 1980.

98. Hamburger, Michael. *East German Poetry.* New York: Dutton, 1973.

99. Handke, Peter. *Kaspar Hauser.* Frankfurt: Suhrkamp, 1969.

100. *Hat sich die Republik verändert? Terrorismus im Spiegel der Presse.* Bonn: Bundesinnenministerium, 1978.

101. Hay, Gerhard. *Rundfunk und Hörspiel als Führungsmittel des Nationalsozialismus.* Stuttgart: Reclam, 1976.

102. Heer, Friedrich. *Challenge of Youth.* University, Ala.: The University of Alabama Press, 1974.

103. Heidenheimer, Arnold J., and Kommers, Donald P. *The Governments of Germany.* 4th ed. Crowell Comparative Government Series. New York: Crowell, 1975.

104. Hildebrand, Klaus. *Das dritte Reich.* Munich: R. Oldenbourg Verlag, 1979.

105. Hitler, Adolf. *Mein Kampf.* Munich: Zentralverlag der NSDAP, 1939.

106. Hohendahl, Herminghouse. *Literatur und Literaturtheorie in der DDR.* Frankfurt: Suhrkamp, 1976.

107. Holborn, Luise. *German Constitutional Documents Since 1871: Selected Texts and Commentary.* New York: Praeger, 1970.

108. Hollstein, Walter. *Die Gegengesellschaft.* Rororo Sachbuch 680. Reinbek: Rowohlt 1981.

109. Hughes, Richard. *The Fox in the Attic.* New York: Harper, 1961.

110. Hull, David S. *Film in the Third Reich.* Berkeley: University of California Press, 1969.

111. Hurwitz, Harold. *Die Stunde Null der deutschen Presse. Die ameri-
      kanische Pressepolitik in Deutschland 1945–1949.* Cologne:
      Verlag Wissenschaft und Politik, 1972.
112. *Die Integration der beiden deutschen Staaten in die Paktsysteme.*
      Bonn-Bad Godesberg: Friedrich-Ebert-Stiftung, 1977.
113. Irving, David. *The Destruction of Dresden.* London: Kimber, 1963.
114. Jacobson, Hans-Adolf, and Jochmann, Werner. *Dokumente zur
      Geschichte des Nationalsozialismus 1933–1945.* Bielefeld, n.d.
115. Joffe, Josef. "All Quiet on the Eastern Front." *Foreign Policy* 37
      (1979–1980): 161–175.
116. Johnson, Uwe. *Mutmaßungen über Jakob.* Frankfurt: Suhrkamp,
      1959.
117. Jünger, Ernst. *Auf den Marmorklippen.* Hamburg: Hanseatische
      Verlagsanstalt, 1939.
118. ———. *In Stahlgewittern. Aus dem Tagebuch eines Stoßtruppfüh-
      rers.* Leisnig: Verlag Robert Meier, 1920.
119. Kinser, Bill, and Kleinmann, Neil. *The Dream That Was No More
      a Dream: Germany 1890–1945.* New York: Harper Colophon
      Books, 1969.
120. Klett, Roderich, ed. *Stationen einer Republik.* Stuttgart: Deutsche
      Verlagsanstalt, 1979.
121. Knapp, Manfred, et al. *Die U.S.A. und Deutschland 1918–1975.*
      Beck'sche Schwarze Reihe 177. Munich: Beck 1978.
122. Kolbenheyer, E. G. *Gesammelte Werke.* Vol. 6: *Dramen und
      Gedichte.* Munich: Albert Langen Verlag, 1928–1940.
123. *Konrad Adenauer 1876/1976.* Stuttgart: Verlag Bonn Aktuell,
      1975.
124. *Konrad Adenauer. Seine Zeit—Sein Werk. Ausstellung aus Anlaß
      des 100. Gerburtstages am 5. Januar 1976.* Historisches Archiv
      der Stadt Köln. Cologne: Kopp, 1976.
125. Kopelev, Lev. *To be Preserved Forever.* Anthony Austin, transl.
      Philadelphia and New York: Lippincott, 1977.
126. Koze, Hildegard von, and Krausnick, Helmut. "Es spricht der
      Führer." *7 exemplarische Hitler-Reden.* Gütersloh: S. Mohn Ver-
      lag, 1966.
127. Kracauer, Siegfried. *From Caligari to Hitler.* Princeton, N.J.,
      Princeton University Press, 1947.
128. Krane, Ronald E. *International Labor Migration in Europe.* New
      York: Praeger, 1979.
129. Krautkrämer, Elmar. *Deutsche Geschichte nach dem Zweiten Welt-
      krieg: Eine Darstellung der Entwicklung von 1946–1949 mit
      Dokumenten.* Hildesheim: Lax, 1962.
130. Kröll, Friedhelm. Die *"Gruppe 47." Soziale Lage und gesellschaft-
      liches Bewußtsein literarischer Intelligenz in der Bundesrepu-
      blik.* Stuttgart: Metzler, 1977.
131. Kühnl, Reinhard. *Deutschland zwischen Demokratie und Fa-
      schismus.* Munich: Carl Hanser Verlag, 1969.
132. Langbein, Hermann. *Nicht wie die Schafe zur Schlachtbank. Wi-
      derstand in den nationalsozialistischen KZ's 1938–45.* Frank-
      furt: Fischer, 1981.

133. Lehmann-Haupt, Hellmut. *Art Under a Dictatorship*. New York: Octagon Books, 1973.
134. Lehnert, Herbert. "Die Gruppe 47. Ihre Anfänge und ihre Gründungsmitglieder." *Deutsche Gegenwartsliteratur* 1981: 32–60. Manfred Durzak, ed. Stuttgart: Reclam.
135. Lettau, Reinhard. *Die Gruppe 47*. Neuwied: Luchterhand, 1967.
136. Levin, Nora. *The Holocaust: The Destruction of European Jewry, 1933–1945*. New York: Crowell, 1968. pbk: Schocken, 1973.
137. Lexikon–Institut Bertelsmann, ed. *Deutschland. Bundesrepublik Deutschland. Deutsche Demokratische Republik. Daten und Fakten zum Nachschlagen*. Gütersloh: Bertelsmann—Lexikon Verlag, 1975.
138. Ley, Ralph. *Böll für Zeitgenossen. Ein kulturgeschichtliches Lesebuch*. New York: Harper & Row, 1970.
139. Ley, Robert. *Wir alle helfen dem Führer*. München: Zentralabteilung der NSDAP, 1937.
140. Littmann, Ulrich. *An Introduction to the Confusion of German Education*. Bonn: DAAD, 1977.
141. Löwenthal, Leo. "Individuum und Terror." *Merkur,* Heft 1, 36. Jahrgang, No. 403. Stuttgart: Klett-Cotta, 1982.
142. ———. "Knut Hamsun. Zur Vorgeschichte der Autoritären Ideologie." *Zeitschrift für Sozialforschung,* 1937, Jahrgang 6, Heft 2.
143. ———. *Prophets of Deceit*. New York: Harper, 1949.
144. Loth, Wilfried. *Die Teilung der Welt, 1941–1955*. Munich: dtv, 1980.
145. Ludz, Peter. *Die DDR zwischen Ost und West von 1961–1976*. Munich: Beck, 1977.
146. Lützeler, Paul M. "Von der Intelligenz zur Arbeiterschaft: zur Darstellung sozialer Wandlungsversuche in den Romanen und Reportagen der Studentenbewegung," in *Deutsche Literatur in der Bundesrepublik seit 1965*. Paul M. Lützeler and Egon Schwarz, eds. Frankfurt: Athenäum, 1980, pp. 115–134.
147. McClelland, Charles E., and Scher, Steven P., eds. *Postwar German Culture. An Anthology*. New York: Dutton, 1974.
148. McCreary, Edward. *The Americanization of Europe*. Garden City, N.Y.: Doubleday, 1964.
149. Maerker, Rudolf. *Mitbestimmung: Industrial Democracy in West Germany*. Bonn: Friedrich-Ebert-Stiftung, 1978.
150. Mahlendorf, Ursula. "Creativity of Women." *Dynamic Psychiatry,* 14 (1981): 116–127.
151. *Mandate for Democracy, A*. Bonn: Presse- und Informationsdienst, 1980.
152. Mann, Golo. *Deutsche Geschichte des 19. und 20. Jahrhunderts*. Frankfurt: Fischer, 1975.
153. Mann, Heinrich. *Gesammelte Werke*. Vol. 24: *Ein Zeitalter wird besichtigt*. Berlin: Aufbau Verlag, 1973.
154. Mann, Michael. *Das Thomas Mann-Buch. Eine innere Biographie in Selbstzeugnissen*. Frankfurt: Fischer Bücherei, 1965.
155. Matz, Elisabeth. *Die Zeitungen der US-Armee für die deutsche

*Bevölkerung (1944–1946).* Studien zur Publizistik, Bremer Reihe Deutsche Presseforschung. Vol. 12. Münster: Fahle, 1969.

156. Meinecke, Friedrich. *Die deutsche Katastrophe.* Wiesbaden: Brockhaus, 1955.

157. Meulenbelt, Anja. *Die Scham ist vorbei. Eine persönliche Geschichte.* Munich: Frauenoffensive, 1978.

158. Miller, Mark J. *Foreign Workers in Western Europe: An Emerging Political Force.* New York: Praeger, 1981.

159. Mitchell, B. P. *European Historical Statistics 1750–1970.* New York: Columbia University Press, 1975.

160. Mitscherlich, Alexander, and Mitscherlich, Margarete. *Die Unfähigkeit zu trauern. Grundlagen kollektiven Verhaltens.* Munich: Piper, 1967 (*The Inability to Mourn: Principles of Collective Behavior.* Trans. New York: Grove, 1975).

161. Moeller van den Bruck, Arthur. *Das dritte Reich.* Hamburg: Hanseatische Verlagsanstalt, 1931.

162. Monnet, Jean. *Memoirs.* Paris: Fayard, 1976.

163. Mosse, George. *The Crisis of German Ideology: Intellectual Origins of the Third Reich.* New York: Grosset & Dunlap, 1964.

164. ———. *Germans and Jews: The Right, the Left, and the Search for a "Third Force" in Pre-Nazi Germany.* New York: Fertig, 1970.

165. ———. *Nazi Culture: Intellectual, Cultural and Social Life in the Third Reich.* London: Allen, 1966.

166. Nadler, Josef. *Literaturgeschichte der deutschen Stämme und Landschaften.* 4 vols. Regensburg: Josef Habbel, 1923–1925.

167. Nietzsche, Friedrich. *The Birth of Tragedy.* New York: Doubleday, 1956.

168. Noack, Paul. *Deutschland von 1945–1960.* Munich: Olzog Verlag, 1960.

169. Noakes, Jeremy, and Pridham, Geoffrey. *Documents on Nazism 1919–1945.* London: Trinity Press, 1974.

170. *North-South: A Program for Survival. The Report of the W. Brandt Commission.* London: Pan Books, 1980.

171. Orlow, Dietrich. *The History of the Nazi Party: 1919–1945.* 2 vols. University of Pittsburgh Press, 1969, 1973.

172. Pachter, Henry M. *Modern Germany: A Social, Cultural, and Political History.* Boulder, Colo.: Westview Press, 1978.

173. Paterson, Thomas G. *Soviet-American Confrontation. Post-War Reconstruction and the Origins of the Cold War.* Baltimore: Johns Hopkins University Press, 1973.

174. Pestalozzi, Hans A., et al., eds. *Frieden in Deutschland—Die Friedensbewegung: wie sie wurde, was sie ist, was sie werden kann.* Munich: Goldmann, 1982.

175. Picht, Georg. *Die deutsche Bildungskatastrophe: Analyse und Dokumentation.* Olten: Walter, 1964.

176. Plessner, Helmuth. *Die verspätete Nation; über die politische Verführbarkeit bürgerlichen Geistes.* Stuttgart: Kohlhammer, 1966.

177. Pleyer, Peter. *Deutscher Nachkriegsfilm 1946–1948.* Münster: Fahle, 1965.

178. Poidevin, R., and Bariéty, J. *Frankreich und Deutschland. Die*

*Geschichte ihrer Beziehungen 1815–1975.* Trans. Munich: Beck, 1982.

179. Power, Jonathan. *Migrant Workers in Western Europe and the United States.* Oxford: Pergamon Press, 1979.

180. *Preussen—Versuch einer Bilanz. Eine Ausstellung der Berliner Festspiele GmbH 1981.* Berlin Katalog, vols. 1–5. Reinbek: Rowohlt 1981.

181. Price, Harry B. *The Marshall Plan and Its Meaning.* New York: Cornell University Press, 1955.

182. Prittie, Terence. *Germans Against Hitler.* London: Hutchinson, 1964.

183. Rabehl, Bernd. "From Antiauthoritarian Movement to Socialist Opposition," in *Postwar German Culture.* Charles E. McClelland and Steven P. Scher, eds. New York: Dutton, 1974, pp. 73–77.

184. Raddatz, Fritz. *Traditionen und Tendenzen. Materialien zur Literatur der D.D.R.* Frankfurt: Suhrkamp, 1971.

185. Reich, Wilhelm. *The Mass Psychology of Fascism.* New York: Albion Press, 1970.

186. Reich-Ranicki, Marcel. *Entgegnungen zur deutschen Literatur der siebziger Jahre.* Stuttgart: Deutsche Verlagsanstalt, 1979.

187. Remak, Joachim. *The Nazi Years. A Documentary History.* Englewood Cliffs, N.J.: Prentice Hall, 1969.

188. ———. *The Origins of the Second World War.* Englewood Cliffs, N.J.: Prentice Hall, 1976.

189. Richter, Werner. *Almanach der Gruppe 47.* Darmstadt: Luchterhand, n.d.

190. Roloff, Gerhard. *Exil und Exilliteratur in der deutschen Presse 1945–1949. Ein Beitrag zur Rezeptionsgeschichte.* Worms: Heinitz, 1976.

191. Rosenberg, Alfred. *Der Mythos des 20. Jahrhunderts.* Munich: Hoheneichen Verlag, 1935.

192. Rothfels, Hans. *The German Opposition to Hitler.* Chicago: Regnery, 1962.

193. Rueff, Jacques, ed. *The Third Reich.* International Council for Philosophy and Humanistic Studies. London: Weidenfeld and Nicolson, 1955.

194. Sandford, John. *The New German Cinema.* London: Wolff, 1980.

195. Schiefbaum, Hansjürgen. *Intra-German Relations, Development, Problems, Facts.* Reihe Politologie/Soziologie, vol. 8. Munich: dtv, 1979.

196. Schlabrendorff, Fabian von. *Offiziere gegen Hitler.* Frankfurt: Fischer Bücherei 305, 1959.

197. Schoenbaum, David. "Dateline Bonn: Uneasy Super-Ally." *Foreign Policy* 37 (1979–1980): 176–191.

198. ———. *Hitler's Social Revolution: Class and Status in Nazi Germany 1933–1939.* Garden City, N.Y.: Doubleday, 1966.

199. Schönberg, Hans. *Germans from the East. A Study of Their Migration, Resettlement and Subsequent Group History.* The Hague: Mouton, 1970.

200. Schröder, Gerhard, *et al.,* eds. *Festschrift für Ludwig Erhard.* 2nd ed. Frankfurt-Berlin-Wien: Ullstein, 1972.
201. Schwarz, Egon. "Austrian Literature," in *Encyclopedia of World Literature in the Twentieth Century.* Vol. I. New York: Ungar, 1981.
202. ———. *Nation im Widerspruch. Deutsche über Deutschland.* Hamburg: Wegner, 1963.
203. Schwarz, Hans Peter. *Geschichte der BRD.* Vol. I: *Vom Reich zur Bundesrepublik: Deutschland im Widerstreit der Außenpolitik in den Jahren der Besatzungsherrschaft 1945–1949.* Darmstadt: Luchterhand, 1966.
204. ———. *Geschichte der BRD.* Vol. II: *Die Ära Adenauer 1949–1957.* Stuttgart and Wiesbaden: DVA and Brockhaus, 1981.
205. Schwarzer, Alice. *Der "kleine Unterschied" und seine großen Folgen. Frauen über sich. Beginn einer Befreiung.* Frankfurt: Fischer, 1975.
206. Schwelien, Joachim H. *Encounter and Encouragement. A Bicentennial Review of German-American Relations.* Bonn: Universitätsdruckerei, 1976.
207. Senger, Alexander von. *Krisis der Architektur.* Zürich: Rascher, 1928.
208. Shaffer, Harry G. *The GDR Economy: Into the 1980's* (Draft). Ninth International Symposium on the German Democratic Republic at Conway, N.H., June 17–24, 1983.
209. ———. *Women in the Two Germanies. A Comparative Study of a Socialist and a Non-Socialist Society.* New York: Pergamon Press, 1981.
210. Shirer, William. *The Rise and Fall of the Third Reich. A History of Nazi Germany.* New York: Simon and Schuster, 1960.
211. Smyser, W. R. *German-American Relations.* The Washington Papers, VIII, 74. Beverly Hills and London: Sage.Publications, 1980.
212. Soergel, Albert. *Dichtung und Dichter der Zeit.* Leipzig: Voigtländer Verlag, 1911.
213. Sontheimer, Kurt. *The Government and Politics of East Germany.* London: Hutchinson University Library, 1975.
214. Sontheimer, Kurt, and Röhring, Hans. *Handbuch des politischen Systems der Bundesrepublik Deutschland.* Munich: Pieper, 1978.
215. Sperling, Walter. *Landeskunde DDR. Eine annotierte Auswahlbibliographie.* Munich: Verlag Dokumentation, 1978.
216. Stefan, Verena. *Häutungen.* Frankfurt: Frauenoffensive, 1975.
217. Stern, Fritz. *The Politics of Cultural Despair. A Study in the Rise of the German's Ideology.* Berkeley: University of California Press, 1961.
218. Stolper, Gustav. *The German Economy 1870 to the Present.* London: Weidenfeld and Nicolson, 1967.
219. Strauss, Botho. "Versuche aesthetische und politische Ereignisse zusammenzudenken, Neues Theater, 1967–1970." *Theater Heute,* October 1970.
220. Struck, Karin. *Klassenliebe.* Frankfurt: Suhrkamp, 1973.
221. Taylor, R. R. *The Word in Stone. The Role of Architecture in the Na-*

*tional Socialist Ideology.* Berkeley: University of California Press, 1974.

222. Tietzel, Manfred, compiler. *North-South, the German View.* Bonn: Friedrich Ebert Stiftung, 1977.

223. Toland, John. *Adolf Hitler.* Garden City, N.Y.: Doubleday, 1976.

224. Trommler, Frank. *Sozialistische Literatur in Deutschland. Ein historischer Überblick.* Stuttgart: Kroener, 1976.

225. *Um die Gleichberechtigung der Frauen in beiden deutschen Staaten.* Bonn: Friedrich Ebert Stiftung, 1979.

226. Venohr, Wolfgang, ed. *Die deutsche Einheit kommt bestimmt.* Bergisch Gladbach: Lübbe, 1982.

227. Vesper, Will. *Rufe in die Zeit.* Munich: Albert Langen, 1937.

228. Vogelsang, Thilo. "Das geteilte Deutschland," in *Deutsche Geschichte seit dem 1. Weltkrieg.* Vol. II. Institut für Zeitgeschichte, ed., Stuttgart: DVA, 1973, pp. 387–664.

229. Voss, Werner. *Die Bundesrepublik Deutschland. Daten und Analysen.* Stuttgart: Kohlhammer, 1980.

230. Wagenbach, Klaus. *Lesebuch.* Vol. I: *Deutsche Literatur zwischen 1945 und 1959.* Vol. II: *Deutsche Literatur der sechziger Jahre.* Berlin: Wagenbach, I, 1980, II, 1968.

231. Wagenbach, Klaus, and Stephan, Winfried. *Vaterland, Muttersprache. Deutsche Schriftsteller und ihr Staat seit 1945. Ein Nachlesebuch für die Oberstufe.* Berlin: Wagenbach, 1979.

232. Wagener, Hans. "Der Fall 'Stalingrad': Zufall, Schuld oder geschichtliche Logik? Zur Interpretation einiger deutscher Kriegsromane," in *Elemente der Literatur, II Festschrift E. Frenzel.* A. Bisanz and R. Trousson, eds. Stuttgart: Kröner, 1980.

233. Wander, Maxie. *"Guten Morgen, du Schöne." Frauen in der DDR. Protokolle mit einem Vorwort von Christa Wolf.* Darmstadt: Sammlung Luchterhand 289, 1979.

234. Weber, Eugen. *Varieties of Fascism.* Princeton, N.J.: Van Nostrand, 1964.

235. Wehdeking, Volker C. *Der Nullpunkt. Über die Konstituierung der deutschen Nachkriegsliteratur in den amerikanischen Kriegsgefangenenlagern.* Stuttgart: Metzler, 1971.

236. Weisenborn, Günther, ed. *Der lautlose Aufstand. Bericht über die Widerstandsbewegung des deutschen Volkes 1933–1945.* Rororo Taschenbuch 507–508. Hamburg: Rowohlt, 1962.

237. Wilkinson, James D. *The Intellectual Resistance in Europe.* Cambridge, Mass.: Harvard University Press, 1981.

238. Winkler, Heinrich August. *Politische Weichenstellung im Nachkriegsdeutschland 1945–1953.* Göttingen: Vandenhoeck & Ruprecht, 1979.

239. Winckler, Lutz. *Studie zur gesellschaftlichen Funktion faschistischer Sprache.* Frankfurt: Suhrkamp, 1970.

240. Wolf, Christa. *Lesen und Schreiben. Neue Sammlung. Essays, Aufsätze, Reden.* Darmstadt: Luchterhand, 1980.

241. Wulf, Josef. *Die bildenden Künste im dritten Reich. Eine Dokumentation.* Gütersloh: Mohn Verlag, 1963.

242. ———. *Literatur und Dichtung im dritten Reich*. Gütersloh: Mohn Verlag, 1963.

243. Wulff, Lutz. *Frauen in der DDR. 20 Erzählungen*. Munich: dtv, 1976.

244. Zahlenbild-Sonderhefte. *Drei Jahrzehnte deutsche Geschichte. Die Bundesrepublik Deutschland*. Berlin: E. Schmidt, 1976.

245. Zeman, A. B. *Nazi Propaganda*. London: Oxford University Press, 1973.

245. Zimmerman, Karl. *Deutsche Geschichte als Rassenschicksal*. Leipzig: Quelle & Meyer, 1936.

247. Zweig, Stefan. *Die Welt von Gestern. Erinnerungen eines Europäers*. Stockholm: Bermann-Fischer Verlag, 1941.

# Index